Fear in Contempo

FEAR IN CONTEMPORARY SOCIETY

Its Negative and Positive Effects

Vladimir Shlapentokh

First published in 2006 by
PALGRAVE MACMILLAN™
175 Fifth Avenue, New York, N.Y. 10010 and
Houndmills, Basingstoke, Hampshire, England RG21 6XS
Companies and representatives throughout the world.

PALGRAVE MACMILLAN is the global academic imprint of the Palgrave Macmillan division of St. Martin's Press, LLC and of Palgrave Macmillan Ltd. Macmillan® is a registered trademark in the United States, United Kingdom and other countries. Palgrave is a registered trademark in the European Union and other countries.

ISBN-13: 978–1–4039–7389–4 hardback
ISBN-10: 1–4039–7389–X hardback

Library of Congress Cataloging-in-Publication Data

Shlapentokh, Vladimir
    Fear in contemporary society : its negative and positive effects / by Vladimir Shlapentokh.
        p. cm.
    Includes bibliographical references and index.
    ISBN 1–4039–7389–X (alk. paper)
        1. Social structure. 2. Fear. 3. Social values. I. Title.

HM706.S498 2006
303.3′72—dc22   2006044764

A catalogue record for this book is available from the British Library.

Design by Newgen Imaging Systems (P) Ltd., Chennai, India.

First edition: September 2006

10 9 8 7 6 5 4 3 2 1

Printed in the United States of America.

I dedicate this book to my wife Luba, with whom I have tried to overcome all sorts of fears in our Soviet and American life

Contents

List of Tables   ix

Acknowledgments   xi

Introduction   1

Chapter 1   Social Order in the Contemporary Sociological
            Literature: The Evolution of a Concept   9

Chapter 2   The Major Theories about the Nature and
            Origin of Values and Order   21

Chapter 3   The Limited Role of Positive
            Internalized Values   39

Chapter 4   Aggressive Negative Values   65

Chapter 5   National Common Values: Partially a Myth   87

Chapter 6   Changes and Stability of
            Social Values and Norms   105

Chapter 7   Fear as a Neglected Variable   125

Chapter 8   The Leading Role of Formal
            Control as the Basis of Order   153

Concluding Remarks   175

Notes   177

Bibliography   187

Name Index   227

Subject Index   231

LIST OF TABLES

4.1	Institutions with a high level of trust	83
4.2	Institutions with a middle level of trust	83
4.3	Institutions with a low level of trust	84
5.1	Developed countries	96
5 2	Post-communist countries	96
5.3	Developing countries	97

Acknowledgments

First of all, I wish to express my deep gratitude to Joshua Woods for his editing of this book and for his many valuable comments. I also want to convey my thanks to Larry Busch for his support of this book and at least some of its ideas. I am also thankful to Andrzej Korbonski and Peter Stavrakis for their enthusiastic backing of the main tenor of this book and for their important comments.

Introduction

When I am asked what, for me, is the most salient characteristic of Soviet society, I always answer "fear." By fear, I mean a feeling of anxiety caused by the presence of danger, real or imagined. When I reached the age of 12 (Piaget's "operational stage") and became a competent, adult-style thinker, I realized fully what it meant to fear the state and its secret police (the NKVD, ministry of internal affairs, the heir to the notorious CheKa and future KGB). I understood how vitally important it was to make a distinction between private and public life, and how necessary it was to control each word you utter.

When I reached the age of 17, beyond the Piaget scheme, I already felt the fear of the political police. The reason I suffered from fear to a greater extent than some of my peers can be explained by my intellectual evolution in 1946–1949, which brought my best friend and me—we were both students of history at Kiev University—to an understanding of the savage nature of the totalitarian state in which we lived. We began to understand that there was a relatively high probability that a system that destroyed its loyal citizens would be even less merciful to those who hated it. The fact that we were both Jews, in a deeply anti-Semitic state, could only enhance our chances of ending up on one of the islands of the archipelago. I was always terrified when I heard the noise of a car approaching my home at dawn, the time when most arrests took place. In summarizing her feelings over four decades, and having named a chapter in her memoir "Fear," Nadezhda Mandel'shtam, the wife of a famous poet who died in the Gulag, wrote, "Akhmatova (a leading Russian poet) and I once confessed to each other that the strongest feelings . . . stronger than love and jealousy, stronger than anything which is human . . . were fear and its derivations: the heinous awareness of shame, restrictions, and full helplessness" (Mandel'shtam, 1990). The sentiments of Akhmatova and Mandel'shtam were echoed by Evgeni Gabrilovich, an experienced filmmaker. Speaking rather philosophically about his life across the last five decades, Gabrilovich commented, "As a close witness of those years, I can contend that the Academies of Sciences, Art, and Marxism, in establishing the moving forces of history, have neglected a crucial, and perhaps even the most important, main-spring: fear. In order to understand so many of the puzzles, secrets, and absurdities of our complicated life, it is necessary to comprehend, most of all, the real significance of fear" (Gabrilovich, 1989).

My fear declined significantly after Stalin's death in 1953, but it remained an essential part of my mind. This fear did not leave me, of course, when a few of my colleagues and I began conducting socio-logical studies in the early 1960s. All of our decisions—the choice and wording of questions in surveys, the sampling, and the selection of interviewers—had to be endorsed by the party apparatus. At each turn, the sociologist faced the risk of being accused of working against the Soviet order, which came with various consequences. As I was not an open dissident, I was always afraid to reveal my real thoughts and feelings at public meetings or in one of my classes, where at least one of my students was an informer. As all other Soviet people, I was very careful about inviting people to my home and was almost sure that our domestic gatherings were followed by the KGB, which used informers and technical listening devices. In 1979, as the plane taking my family and me from Moscow to our first visit to a Western airport touched down in Vienna, my initial feeling was that of elation. Now I was out of reach of my Soviet fears.

My experiences in the USSR familiarized me with the complex nature of social fear. First, I saw how fear can demoralize people, how it can degrade even the finest human beings and the closest human relations.

My Soviet experiences also helped me discover fear in American society, which is hidden from the surface and often denied by the people who experience it. Whatever objective and justifiable reasons there may be for fear, this feeling still remains one of the most humiliating of human emotions. An ability to hide it, control it, or even ignore it makes some people very different from others. Fear is probably not as shameful as envy, but it is quite difficult to admit to it when your life or even your job or reputation is at stake. With a well-trained eye, I have discovered, for instance, colleagues, particularly those on the tenure track, who were afraid to reveal their views, if it meant a confrontation of opinions with someone who makes decisions about their future.

The difficulties of detecting fear lies in the ability of people to rationalize it with various specious arguments and pretend that they fully agree with their superiors. It was my Soviet experience that helped me appreciate to the fullest extent one of Orwell's greatest ideas—that is, the love of Big Brother as applicable not only to a totalitarian society of the Soviet type, but to any society, including democratic ones, and even to any social unit. Orwell described the transformation of omnipresent and humiliating fear into a love of the source of fear (i.e., the supreme leader of a state or the head of a department at Wall Mart). The devotion of the Soviet people to the regime reached its highest level in the times of the cult of Stalin. Established in the early 1930s, this cult was evidently supported by the majority of active Russians in the cities, much like the cases of Hitler in Nazi Germany, or Mao in Communist China. The cult of Stalin penetrated the heart and soul of many Russians, from apparatchiks to ordinary people. Stalin was glorified by ordinary people, even in their private communications. The intensity with which people mourned Stalin's death on March 5, 1953, was indeed amazing. Stalin's funeral was witnessed by a stampede of thousands of people yearning to deliver their last respects. The funeral stands among the most memorable events in Soviet history. With Stalin's death and the softening of the totalitarian regime, the love of Big Brother did not disappear, but was concentrated on the devotion to the system and to its ideology.

Orwell was the first to understand that fear can generate love and both emotions are perfectly compatible. Further it is the fear of sanctions (or simply disapproval) that pushes many people to support the dominant ideology in their environment. This blend of fear and love, along with the ideology that serves this alliance, is the basis for accepting Big Brother, the regime and the dominant ideology as key explanations of public opinion in any society. The Western authors who wrote about Orwell almost totally ignored this great discovery. Even Erich Fromm—whose book *Escape from Freedom* treated this part of Orwell's vision, and who wrote the famous foreword to *1984* in 1961—failed to mention the role of one's love of Big Brother in this society (Fromm, 1961, 257–267).

It is remarkable that contemporary social psychologists almost totally avoided the role of the fear–love complex in hierarchical organizations. Among the 93 different types of love cited in a study by Beverley Fehr and James Russel, the love of one's superior in an organization was absent, though they did mention the love of animals and food (Fehr and Russel, 1991).

The Soviet experience also demonstrates how fear can turn decent people into informers, who work either for the political police in the USSR, or the head of any office in contemporary America. Memoirs discussing the 1949 anti-cosmopolitan campaign, which were not published until the period of Glasnost, graphically depicted the fear that plagued the intellectuals, and the numerous cases of betrayal between friends and colleagues. Sergei Iutkevich, a prominent film director, recounted how his friend Mark Donskoi, the famous film figure, ardently attacked him at a public meeting devoted to the denunciation of cosmopolites (Iutkevich, 1988, 106). Similarly, Simonov joined in the persecution of those he had previously protected (Borshchagovsky, 1988, 161; Rudnitsky, 1988, 151). Much later, during Perestroika, Yurii Arbatov, the director of the Institute of the USA and Canada, who himself was a typical conformist in the 1970s, wrote: "I thought several times about why even people who bravely fought during the war later behaved as cowards. They were more afraid of the negative opinions of their bosses than bullets" (Arbatov, 1992, 4). Although, in the 1970s, the fear of those in power had diminished significantly relative to the past, it remained sufficiently strong. Many intellectuals severed their relations with friends and colleagues who became targets of official critiques. Alexei German, a famous film director, described how his circle of friends became smaller and smaller when his movies started to be shelved, and ultimately he had no one to invite to his birthday party (see Kornilov, 1988). For this reason, my Russian colleagues and I saw the developments during the McCarthy era as déjà vu. It looked to us like the "normal" behavior of frightened people. In Russia, we were confident that we had more compassion for the victims of McCarthyism and a better understanding of how easy it was to turn decent people into snitches and traitors than the average educated American. Our understanding of the role of fear in a totalitarian society also allowed us a better understanding of China, the essence of the Cultural Revolution in the 1960s–1970s, and the crucial impact of fear on the behavior of millions of Chinese people, whom many experts in the United States described as sincere devotees to Mao's ideas.

Life in the Soviet system taught us also to recognize how the authorities and the opposition (or the leaders of any social movement), however noble their ideologies, tend to exploit real fears or create imaginary ones to achieve their goals. Soviet leaders fueled people's fear of foreign intervention, class enemies, foreign spies, non-Russian nationalists, Jews and Zionism. The Soviet experience sensitized me to any references to dangers in U.S. political life and suggested that I analyze the real and fictitious basis of fear.

My memories of the USSR are also useful for understanding the influence of fear on human relations. Friendship is a good example. This institution played a much bigger role in Soviet society than it does in Western society. Indeed, it was only with friends that one could psychologically stand up against the monster; only among friends could one ease the tension from the constant self-control in communicating in the office or with unfamiliar people. Only with friends was it possible to discuss the "danger indicators" emanating from various centers of power (such as the party committee, the director, or the "special department," i.e., the branch of the KGB in a Soviet institution) and determine the degree of their menace. Friends were completely irreplaceable when you were summoned to the KGB, and the conversation turned to the subject of enrolling you as secret informer.

My Soviet experience, while sensitizing me to the role of fear in society, was, at the same time, an initial obstacle to understanding the role of fear in democratic societies and even in post-Soviet Russia. My hatred of the Soviet system engendered deeply rooted illusions about American society. The idea that Americans do not suffer from fear was nurtured by my friends and me in the Soviet Union. It took time to overcome this wrong perception of the United States and understand the significance of fear in this society.

Of no less importance was my almost blind belief in mainstream American sociology as a perfect reflection of American society. As almost all my Soviet colleagues, I was under the strong influence of Talcott Parsons and believed that order in American society is based on internalized values and that Hobbes has nothing to do with life in America.

First, I did not understand how the state, in even a democratic society, could be a source of fear. For my friends in Moscow and for me, the idea that Orwell's *1984* could be linked to American society seemed absurd. Still a "fresh immigrant," I organized a conference on *1984* at Michigan State University, which I joined as a faculty member almost immediately after my arrival to this country. As chairman I had to contain my anger as one American speaker after another presented this book as a description of American society. I realized later that the monitoring of the private life of ordinary people by state agencies, as well as by various private companies, is a serious problem and deserves special attention.

My Soviet experience and hatred of the Soviet state were behind another one of my mistakes: the underestimation of the role of the state as the guarantor of order in society. In fact, even in the Gulag, about 80 percent were ordinary criminals: their imprisonment was not due to political reasons. Only later, when I was writing the book *A Normal Totalitarian Society* (2001), I realized that the Bolsheviks headed by Lenin gained the support of the population during the civil war and after, because they represented a force that promised order in society and instilled fear not only in their political opponents but also in the anarchic and destructive elements in the country. This circumstance is now being disregarded by anti-Communists of all sorts in the West as well as in Russia.

The role of the state in maintaining order in society was ignored also by Orwell. With his tendency to share the liberal, almost anarchistic vision—he hated inequality, but also hated the state as an institution—he did not take into account the fact that Big Brother is a guarantor of order. In part, this circumstance accounts for the love of Big Brother. Living in such a nice country as England, where the police did not have to fire weapons, and with the world of Hobbes lost to the distant past, Orwell could not grasp the importance of order for the Russians after the civil war, or for the Germans after the chaos of the Weimar republic, or for the Chinese after the conflict between warlords in the 1920s and 1930s.

In this respect, Orwell neglected the importance of order just as most Western social scientists did in the second half of the twentieth century (I examine this topic in depth later). Part of the love of Big Brother should be attributed to the yearning of the masses for order and stability. For the same reason, many post-totalitarian societies have experienced nostalgia for the old leaders and the old systems.

I can be partially exculpated for my underestimation of the state as an agent of order and the positive role of the fear of sanctions due to the fact that most American sociologists also believed that social order in society can be sustained only with moral norms, which are internalized by people during childhood. They too ignored the fear of sanctions as a powerful instrument of society.

I had to overcome yet another view also shaped by my hatred of the Soviet system and my romanticizing of America. Under the impact of my Soviet experience, I was confident that ordinary people suffer mostly from "centralized fears," that is, the fears generated by the highly centralized state. Whereas, people in America as well as in post-Soviet societies suffer from numerous "decentralized" fears: the fear of unemployment, the fear of discrimination of various sorts (racial, ethnic, religious, gender and other), the fear of bankruptcy, and the fear of being unable to pay for hospital bills, education, or bank credits. And, of course, there is the fear of crime in the streets, in homes and in schools. Again, I may be exonerated for my underestimation of these fears, because many American sociologists in their textbooks and general analysis of society did the same. Seemingly, despite their concern about ordinary people and with their critical assessments of many aspects of American society, most sociologists did not dwell at length on the fears that are always present in the minds of Americans. Indeed, I found that professors of sociology discuss criminal behavior at length, focusing only on the origin of crime and the responsibility of society for the emergence of criminals; however, they do not discuss the victims of crime and the dangers of crime to the fabric of society.

Setting out to study order, I operate with two major concepts—fear and values—as variables that explain, among other things, the basis of social order, which is a major social asset and a precondition for the functioning of any society. I try to prove that there has been a tendency in mainstream social science, since the second half of the twentieth century, to underestimate the role of fear in maintaining social order and determining the quality of life.

I suggest that in connection with this tendency the mainstream tends to:

(1) disregard the crucial role of social order and the danger of crime and corruption to society;
(2) overestimate the role of internationalized values in the maintenance of order;
(3) confound values with rules;
(4) overestimate the role of common values in society;
(5) ignore the destructive character of many values;
(6) focus excessively on the spontaneous origin of values and rules from "below";
(7) underestimate the origin of many values and rules from "above" as a result of the activity of elites;
(8) overestimate the role of informal control and underestimate formal control, particularly the positive role of the state in the maintenance of order.

In this book, which intends to analyze the tendencies in American sociology, I use as an empirical basis the textbooks from sociology and political science in the last 20 years, as well as scholarly works that claim to discuss society in general. These textbooks reflect the state of mainstream social science: its central concepts and theories and recent achievements. Only these textbooks offer a general picture of society as it is held by current science, as is the case in all other sciences, including mathematics and physics. Thomas Kuhn considered textbooks in his book *Structure of Scientific Revolution* in the same light. I try to show that fear, as an important phenomena in society, is absent in most sociology textbooks. There are many publications on various issues related to fear that I use in this text. However, the textbooks and general works on society tend mostly to ignore fear as a crucial social phenomenon. Another example includes the role of negative, destructive values and the way they are learned by young people. Again, we can easily find studies on "negative socialization" in which sociologists talk about immigration and gangs. However, this issue has not been elevated to the level of macro social theory.

As another important methodological consideration, I try to make this study as comparable as possible. Although I use data from various countries, I focus on the data from three societies with respect to which my expertise is highest: the United States since World War I (WWI), the Soviet Union, and post-Soviet Russia. These societies are very different from each other. I use the comparative approach in an effort to identify universal trends, as well as explain the differences in the role of fear in various societies.

Social Order in the Contemporary Sociological Literature: The Evolution of a Concept

ORDER IN CONTEMPORARY SOCIAL SCIENCE

The problem of fear is intertwined with two important issues: social order and the quality of life. I concentrate primarily on the role of fear in the maintenance of order. The disregard of fear in contemporary sociology is determined directly by the status of social order in the literature and how it is explained.

Social order is an essential condition for people who live in the same territory or act in the same social unit. The maintenance of social order in a nation requires an effective observance of law, traditional norms and the commands of supreme institutions (state or religious) by central and local bureaucracy, business people, members of various units of civil society and citizens. The observance of law guarantees stability in society, the stability of social relations in all spheres of life, and the normal functioning of the given economic and political system (democratic or not), as well as the physical safety of the population.

Social order is a transcendent, universal value that underlies the functioning of every society in the world. In biblical times, the people lived in deeply troubled environments. When order emerged, it was seen as a sort of miracle. It was Augustine, a famous Christian philosopher, who, in the fourth century, in his book *The City of God*, praised peace and order more than anybody before Hobbes as the supreme value. Yet, the same desire for order is still being felt in many corners of the world. The eagerness of the people to support a celestial monarch in the Middle Ages (particularly during the transition period from one ruler to the next) stemmed from their perennial yearning for order. As history progressed, monarchy eventually lost its magical glance and social scientists looked to more terrestrial explanations for the creation of order.

Order is not a dichotomous variable (either present or absent). In fact, order is a continuous variable that can take various forms ranging from complete chaos (as seen, for instance, in Somalia in the 1980s and 1990s, or in post-Soviet society in the 1990s, or in New Orleans in September 2005 following Hurricane Katrina, or in French cities during the riots in October 2005) to almost ideal order, as is supposed to exist in Norway or Sweden. For this reason, all territories in the world can be classified, with some approximation, into those with high, middle and low levels of social order. The level of order is indeed the first piece of information on his destination sought by a traveler. An American journalist noted that when Iraqis were asked about their priorities in the aftermath of the American invasion, besides being liberated from Saddam Hussein, they invariably answered, "order, order, order" (Burns, 2003).

Social Order in the Social Sciences

In the nineteenth century, with the emergence of contemporary social science, social order was not a leading issue per se. It was economists who discussed the role of social order as a condition for the development of a market economy and the state as the guarantor of order and the observation of law in society. Even Durkheim rarely talked about social order directly. As David Lockwood aptly noted, he was preoccupied more with the problem of disorder and anomie than directly with order, even if one can argue that it does not make a big theoretical difference (Lockwood, 1992, 17). However, it should be noted that Anthony Giddens (1972, 39–41) rejected Parsons's statement that "the problem of order" was central in Durkheim's social theory. In the collection of Durkheim's writings, *On Politics and the State*, edited by Giddens, this term is practically absent (Giddens, 1986).

In the early twentieth century, the issue of crime and corruption emerged when the power of organized crime grew significantly and the question of social order was on the agenda of leading American social scientists, primarily those from the Chicago School (e.g., Burgess, Wirth, Park, Thomas, Znaniecki, McKenzie and others). Between the two wars, they studied the influence of urbanization on order and social disorganization. They tried to understand criminal behavior with a more "scientific" approach and help society fight it.

Order, "the Hobbesian problem," was definitely the major theme of Parsons's work and his grand theory, but he de-dramatized this issue and depicted order as an almost automatic product of his "social system," which easily restored the equilibrium and eliminated any "strain" when it emerged, often with the help of "the insulation mechanism." Parsons was right that Hobbes tended to ignore the ability of society to create its own regulation of behavior through culture. But Parsons made an even greater mistake than Hobbes when he ignored completely the role of the state in maintaining order and, particularly, the role of the state and law in inculcating values in people's minds.[1]

Parsons's attitude toward order reflected the general mood in American society. By the end of the 1940s, Americans could claim that they lived in an orderly society and tended to ignore order as a vital social problem. As Francis Fukuyama noted, "many wrote in the early 1970s that 'the American people by and large are law abiding' " (1999, 446). The author of a textbook, talking about some evidently heinous crimes ("killing another person, taking sexual liberties with one's daughter or son, destroying another's property or physically assaulting an individual"), commented quite complacently, "as a general rule . . . acts that violate rules . . . are noticed and punished," as if the law enforcement system in the United States or other countries worked perfectly (Turner, 1985). As Robert Meier (1982, 43) stated, "In the 1950s, the problem of order that Hobbes agonized over was assumed to be solved."

Notwithstanding some chaotic incidents, such as the race riots in the 1960s, this feeling was supported by empirical facts. It is typical that the term order was absent in most introductory textbooks on sociology and social psychology published between 1970 and 2000, and the term "law" was used only rarely.[2]

Seymour Lipset, in his famous book *Political Man*, discussing the conditions for sustaining stable democracy, talked about economic developments and social change, but paid very little attention to the observance of law (Lipset, 1960). Even those who, like Lipset, approached the subject of order in new nations did it with the assumption that order depends only on "political instability" and the function of democratic institutions. In the noted book *The Good Society*, Robert Bellah and his illustrious coauthors (1991) tried to describe the model of American society, but made no mention of the term order or even "crime," and only perfunctorily mentioned "corruption." No less remarkable is how "social order" is treated in the works of Ronald Inglehart (1997). He included "maintenance of order" in his list of "materialist values," suggesting that with the movement toward post-materialist values, the importance of order has declined. This view is substantiated by the inclusion in the list of post-materialist values of such concepts as "more say in government" and "less impersonal society." In any case, in Inglehart's publications, including the book he wrote with Paul Abramson (1998), social order as a special subject (besides mentioning it in the list of materialist values) is totally ignored; even the book's index does not contain this term. Among the 41 items in their questionnaire on values, order, crime, and corruption are absent. The term order was included as a value of second rank in the aggregate "post-materialist values."

There was no room for the terms order or crime in the long index of another 500-page book on life in Western Europe in the 1990s, which was based on the same methodology as the World Values Surveys (see Arts et al., 2003, 28, 50–58). It is also remarkable that Garry Triandis, whose book cries for a discussion of order (1994), totally ignored the concept. The same is true of the works of Stephen Sanderson, whose book *The Evolution of Human Social Life* (2001) requires at least a brief debate on the place of order in the process of social evolution.

There are some American authors who have shown interest in order as a major social problem. They belong to two ideologically loaded groups. In the first group, sociologists with leftist tendencies who follow Foucault see social order and the "regimentation of society," with its "confinement institutions," as a way to guarantee control over the working class by the dominant classes (Davis and Stasz, 1990, 13–14).

The second group of conservative authors paid great attention to social order as a precondition of progress. One of them, Samuel Huntington, with his *Political Order in Changing Societies*, published in the late 1960s, focused on order and stability in new nations. This book (along with a few other publications) was a glaring exception, though he looked mostly at the factors influencing political structures in society (Huntington, 1968; see also Zollberg, 1966). However, in his latest book, *Challenges to America's National Identity* (2004), in which he discussed the function of American society, he said nothing about order or how much the Anglo-protestant culture and religion (the central institutions in America according to the author) influence social order.

Another prominent author who focused much attention on order was Dennis Wrong. The title of his book—*The Problem of Order: What Unites and Divides Society* (1994)—looked rather unique in the American social science literature by the end of the previous century.

Moreover, with its focus on the changes and conflicts typical for American social science since the late 1960s, order was treated as an obstacle to progress, identifying (and not without reason) the advocates of order with conservatism. For them, order in society is much less important than the values included in the liberal and Left agenda. Several American authors directly accused those who saw order as an important issue, such as Huntington, as helping conservatives in "the preservation of their position of power" (Hopkins, 1972). As another critic of order suggested, "order is imposed from above on the masses who remain the manipulable objects of government policy"; "the absolute priority accorded to the achievement of political order led to a reconsideration (and denigration) of some other objectives emphasized in the past such as economic development, social reforms and also (if more ambiguously) political democratization" (Smith, 1986, 532–561). In this respect, Isaiah Berlin was considered an outstanding political philosopher in postwar Europe, particularly in England. In his numerous publications, he praised liberty, positive and negative, but he almost completely avoided the topic of order and demonstrated an almost blind belief in the magical properties of individual freedom. Only toward the end of his life (1996) did he begin to say that "both freedoms . . . were necessarily limited and both concepts can be perverted" (Berlin, 2002a,b; Ringen, 2002, 26).

THE OVER-SOCIALIZATION OF DEVIANCE AND THE DISREGARD FOR ITS CONSEQUENCES

A natural consequence of downgrading the importance of social order and the role of fears in society is the downgrading of the importance of crime in society, particularly the impact of crime on social order and the well-being of society. Another consequence is the focus placed on society as being solely responsible for crime, which implies that society (e.g., American society) deserves the crimes that it generates.

There is a strong tendency in the literature to discuss deviant behavior only in terms of "structures" (economic and political), and almost totally ignore the role of "agents" as well as cultural traditions. While focusing on the current structural factors, many scholars do not regard the formal institutions of social control, such as law enforcement agencies, as powerful factors in the fight against crime and the maintenance of social order. They argue that the level of crime in society cannot be diminished by an efficient penitentiary system. With a clear and strong tendency to hold the state and society responsible for disorder, and turning criminal organizations and individual criminals into victims, many authors suggest that society has the power to eliminate deviant behavior if it can overcome the egotism of the ruling elites, as if it is possible to imagine society without crime and corruption.

Indeed, the studies on deviant behavior in the 1950s–1990s were abundant. Although most of them invented interesting theories explaining the origin of crimes they tended to focus only on the responsibility of society for crimes, particularly in the 1960s and 1970s (Henslin, 1989, 17). In 1955, Albert Cohen proposed the idea of perceiving criminals as seekers of a decent status in society, which forces them to rebel against middle-class values (Cohen, 1955). Many years later, Messner and Rosenfeld added an analysis of the influence of the dominant American political and social institutions on crimes, and continued to insist that crime is only a product of the specific social environment (Messner and Rosenfeld, 1997).

There is no doubt that various structures that cause unemployment, social inequality, a low standard of living, various sorts of discrimination and broken families represent, a long with cultural traditions, the leading causes of crime. Of no less importance is the role of "agents." People belonging to the same socio-demographic group show very different propensities to commit crimes. This is true not only for common crimes, but even more for corruption.[3]

THE RELATIVIZATION OF CRIME

At the same time, in the second half of the twentieth century, many sociologists tended to describe deviant behavior as "normal" (to use Durkheim's term) and even as positive behavior for society, as adaptation to the conditions of life (a sort of functionalist approach) or as a result of social or relative deprivation (the lack of proper education, family socialization or job opportunities). It is amusing that Nietzsche, with his individualistic challenge to society, and his refusal to operate with "traditional norms" in the evaluation of supermensch, became almost surreptitiously a sort of radical and liberal critic of traditional attitudes toward crime (Garland, 1990).

Moreover, this behavior was considered as useful to society. Robert Merton regarded it as "innovative behavior." He followed Durkheim's perception of crimes as "the signs of tomorrow society" (1964). In some cases, this is indeed true. It is enough to refer to the totalitarian societies where freedom fighters were treated as criminals along with underground entrepreneurs who would become innovators during Perestroika, and particularly after the collapse of the Soviet regime. But treating most criminals as innovators and as leading elements in describing deviant behavior, as Merton and the legion of his followers did, is wrong.

Those who took the next steps in the relativization of crime and the downgrading of the effects of crime on society advanced "labeling theory," according to which behavior is considered "deviant" only because society labeled it as such or because "labeled" persons begin to act as they are labeled, setting off a cycle in which a labeled person behaves worse and worse (so-called secondary deviance) (Lemert, 1972; Turner, 1985, 133). Donald Black (1983, 39) labeled many crimes, including "physical attacks," as "self-help" or "moralistic crimes"; he thought that "the capacity of criminal law to discourage them—the so-called deterrent effect—must be weakened."

In the same spirit, a major emphasis was placed on the policy toward criminals, as if this policy was the single, or the most powerful, factor that increased the level of crime in society. Garland describes the change in the attitudes toward order and crime as "profoundly politicized and populist" (Garland, 2001, 13). He offers data on the gigantic increase in the number of inmates in American prisons (an increase of 500 percent from 1973 to 1997) as a result of a change in the public mood, which now "demands public safety and harsh retribution," and a sudden appearance of the conviction that "prison works" (Garland, 2001, 14).

The immersion of the crime issue in the postmodern and cultural discourse on the interaction among the police, media and the social construction of crime is another example of "sociological escapism," which allows scholars to flee the harsh reality that crime influences the life of most people in almost every country in the world. This escapism seems to be an organic feature of the methodologically brilliant book *Making Trouble* (1999), whatever were the explicit intentions of the authors. In light of its content, the title suggests that "troubles" are products not so much of criminal or dangerous behavior, but of labeling and "demonizing" acts. It is media with its language and metaphors and "associated culture industries" that produces the "cultural and social constructions" related to crimes (Ferrell and Websdale, 1999, 6–12). None of the authors, with their refined "epistemic analysis," mentioned the "material processes" in society, the objective factors (economic, political and social), the psychological or even biological factors, which influence self-control and determine the level and dynamics of deviant behavior in society.[4] All of them tend to ignore crimes. An American doctor mocked the overstretching of the term "social construction," explaining that "disease is a social construction until you happened to find yourself in bed with one" (Markel, 2004, 16).

As Irving Horowitz put it, "by mystifying the relationship between those who commit crime (violate norms and laws), and those who are victimized by criminals, crime is liquidated as readily as deviance" (Horowitz, 1989, 65–67). What is more, as Horowitz states, some sociologists went even further and "abolished crime by fiat" (Horowitz, 1989, 65–67).

The relativization of deviant behavior and crimes was combined in the 1970s–1990s with the relativization of law. This development reached its peak in the so-called social school of law, which proclaimed that the interpretation of law is completely dependent on the social context of the act committed. The relativization of deviance and even heinous crimes, and the tendency to blur the border between law-abiding and non–law-abiding behavior were typical for the absolute majority of sociological textbooks (Babbie, 1983, 332–334). None of them cited the famous Roman dictums that reveal the Romans' high respect for law: "Dura lex sed lex" and "Pereat munduis fiat justicia." In the extreme cases, when it was impossible to deny the ugly character of behavior such as rape and murder, the responsibility was shifted from the individual to the group to which the individual belonged or to society in general.

The Disregard of Corruption and Crime as a Vital Social Issue

Another typical feature of Western and particularly American introductory sociological and political science textbooks is their almost complete disregard of corruption and white-collar crime as serious social issues. Corruption and the participation of governmental officials in bribes are often not even mentioned in the sections devoted to social control and deviant behavior; at most they are mentioned perfunctorily.[5] It is not difficult to explain such indifference toward this sort of crime. Whereas street crime, or even murder, can be attributed to the flaws of society, bribes and related crimes are difficult to "justify" in this way. In the cases when the authors mention white-collar crime, they do not mention corruption and the involvement of state officials in criminal activity in the list of these crimes. Although in recent textbooks white-collar crime drew some attention, "rent seeking activity" and the collusion of corporations and the authorities is totally ignored (Henslin, 2004, 149–151; Macionis, 2004, 142–144; see also Doob, 1994, 178).

Even Leftist sociologists avoid corrupt activities in government as a major social issue. Anthony Giddens, unlike many other sociologists, paid a lot of attention to white-collar crime, but he focused only on embezzlers in the business community. He said nothing about government officials and their participation in bribery and not one word about the connection between organized crime and officials (1989, 144–147).

Only a few Leftist sociologists who belong to the so-called conflict school, which was visible in the 1970s and 1980s and clearly declined in the 1990s, paid some attention to corruption and bribes in the framework of their anti-capitalist critique and description of "street crimes" as a result of class inequality (Quinney, 1979). The same interest in corruption can be found among conservative social scientists, who have libertarian orientations and never miss an opportunity to castigate the government.

Order in Social Science in the 1990s and Early 2000s: The Aftermath of the Collapse of Communism

By the late 1990s and particularly in the beginning of the new century, a serious shift occurred in Western social science. A growing number of scholars (not so much sociologists but criminologists) began to acknowledge that order in society has been deteriorating and instead of focusing the responsibility on society for crimes, they concentrated their attention on the shortcomings of the fight against crime, and saw the victims, not the criminals, as the ones who deserve compassion (Garland, 2001, 11).

This process was particularly strong in Europe. At the end of the 1990s, and particularly in 2000–2002, Europe faced a big rise in crime as well as ethnic riots, mostly in England. Many Europeans linked these developments to the immigrant population, mostly from Arab countries in Africa and also from Turkey and Pakistan. These developments gave rise to the growth of a "law and order" movement headed by the Right, and openly xenophobic parties and movements emerged in almost all countries of Western Europe, particularly in Austria (Jorg Heider was the leader of the anti-immigrant movement), France (Jean-Marie La Pen),[6] Belgium (Filip Dewinter), Holland (Pin Fortuyn),[7] and others. The rise of radical Right extremism in Europe in 2000–2005 was reminiscent of the Nazi success in Germany in the late 1920s and early 1930s, which was based on the growing chaos and disorder in that country. All of these movements challenged the democratic systems in the given country as unable to maintain law and order.

However, the major factor that roused an interest in the subject of order in Western social science was the collapse of the Communist regimes and the transformation of international terrorism into a major social and political issue for many countries in the world. In the 1990s, media and social scientists found that order was the most deficit resource for many countries in the world. Order as a value was much more important to people than such values as democracy.

Post-Soviet Russia is a good example. After being asked in the mid-1990s by pollsters, "What is more important to you, order or democracy?" the absolute majority of Russians (about 70–80 percent) in the last ten years chose "order." The popularity of this response discouraged the Western promoters of democracy in Russia, and became a source of schadenfreude for those Russian elites who were hostile toward democratization. Indeed, the high level of lawlessness in Russia is an admitted fact by the Russians themselves, as well as foreign visitors and businesspeople. The same priority of order as a value orientation can be found in many countries in the world including those with strong democratic traditions.

The developments in the post-Communist world rekindled the interest in order in former colonial countries and developing countries in general. Until the 1990s, the publications on these countries, under the pressure of political correctness (i.e., you should not criticize those who liberated themselves only recently from the yoke of imperialism), mostly ignored the issue of order in these countries or ascribed its absence to the Western imperialism of the past (this was the strategy of Left-leaning and nationalist authors). The post-imperial guilt felt by the former colonial empires, along with America's hatred of colonialism and the growing trend of political correctness, with its special sensitivity to black issues, made it almost impossible for African experts to write about disorder and mass suffering in many former colonial states.[8]

Most authors who described the evolution of postcolonial countries ignored the issue of order as a preliminary condition for their functioning.[9] Rampant corruption and crime were seen as separate phenomena in new nations. The prominent political scientist Lucien Pye, when he talked about the "development syndrome" (equality, political capacity and secular orientation), did not deem it necessary to include the issue of order.[10] At best, some authors such as Mancur Olson mention order and law at the bottom of their lists of desirable values for new nations (Almond and Powell, 1966, 39; Olson, 1963, 529–552).

Joel Migdal (2001, 89–93) can be credited for describing the weakness of most postcolonial states, even if he did not pay much attention to corruption and disorder in these regions. Whatever is the merit of the grand theory advanced by Jeffrey Herbst (2003; see Chege, 2003), he ascribed the high level of political instability in Africa to the lack of interstate wars on this continent and the ensuing inability to build up a strong state as Europeans managed to do. Herbst at least discussed the issue of order and the role of the state in maintaining order; in fact, he made it a central part of his analysis of the African processes in our time.

The advocates of dependence theory contributed to the distortion of the postcolonial analysis with its focus on the dominant classes in strong states who exploit weaker, dependent nations, ignoring the corruption and crime of domestic origin (Frank, 1969; Wallerstein, 1974). Other scholars with liberal and radical leanings also ignored the lawlessness in many African countries after their decolonization, accusing as race biased the authors who demand that Africa should be viewed through the same rigorous analytical lens as other parts of the world (Kaplan, 2000, 55). Talking about the weakness of African states, they do not cite as evidence the high level of disorder. The closest these authors come to the issue of order in these countries is when they talk about "the looseness of the public–private distinction" (Bates, 1981).

For similar reasons, Western scholars, on the Right and Left, failed to test their social theories in countries such as Mexico or Colombia, where criminal organizations and corrupt institutions greatly impact the country's political and economic structures. The textbooks on comparative politics marginalize the role of crime in Latin America, implying that lawlessness does not have a major impact on political systems.

Robert Kaplan, a prominent investigative journalist, was one of the few authors who tried to draw the attention of the American public to the destructive processes in various countries, particularly in Asia. The reviewers of his books characterized his work as "alarmist," and "not scientifically founded." Kaplan's ideas were widely rejected by liberal critics with a seemingly unlimited propensity for seeing the world through rosy glasses (Kaplan, 1993; 1996; 1997; 2000).

In the 1990s, American scholars gradually began to deal with this issue more often. Neil Smelser and Bolivar Lamounier noted in 1994 that "the literature on democracy has ignored the situations which lack basic order" (Smelser, 1994, 80). Juan Linz and Alfred Stepan also put emphasis on the observance of law as one of the preconditions for the building of democracy; however, they looked at this issue in a rather narrow way, only having in mind the direct conditions for the functioning of democratic institutions. They ignored corruption and criminality, which make genuine democracy weak or even impossible.[11] Several books that came out in the 1990s and 2000s described the crucial role of crimes in the life of various societies, for instance, in Brazil.[12]

CONCLUSION

Social order is an essential condition for people who live in the same territory or act within the same social unit. In the early twentieth century, the issues of crime and corruption emerged as the power of organized crime grew significantly and the question of social order featured on the agenda of leading American social scientists. By the end of the 1940s, Americans could claim that they lived in an orderly society and tended to ignore social order as a major social problem. This position explains why there has been a strong tendency in the literature to downgrade, in one way or another, the role of deviant behavior. However, whatever the causes of disorder, the impact of crime on social order and the quality of life is enormous, though it varies from one society to the next.

By the late 1990s and particularly in the beginning of the new century, a serious shift occurred in Western social science. This process was particularly strong in Europe. At the end of the 1990s, and particularly in 2000–2002, Europe faced a big rise in crime as well as ethnic riots. However, the major factor that roused an interest in the subject of order in Western social science was the collapse of the Communist regimes and the transformation of international terrorism into a major social and political issue for many countries in the world. Media and social scientists found in the 1990s that order is one of the most needed resources in several countries.

CHAPTER 2

The Major Theories about the Nature and Origin of Values and Order

The tendency to disregard the crucial role of social order in society—in the West as well as in other countries—should be ascribed to the dominant notion that this issue has been solved, that the maintenance of order is evident and that order is maintained almost automatically by self-regulated mechanisms. The sociological mainstream tends to ignore or underestimate the role of fear as an important regulator of human behavior, and it focuses on social values and culture in general as the main regulators of social life.

VALUES AS A CONCEPT

For most sociologists, "values" represent a leading concept and the key factor that shapes social order. I understand values not so much as objects or entities but, following Milton Rokeach, as "the criteria" that are used for evaluating various developments in the world (Rokeach, 1973, 4–5). It is possible to accept Garry Triandis's definition of values as "the principles that guide our lives"; values tell us what is "desirable" for the individual and society (Triandis, 1994, 111). Values make up "the core or axial elements of a culture" (Barry, 1998, 1). This concept belongs to a cluster of similar concepts, including norms, schemata, rules, beliefs and attitudes—terms that have many interpretations.[1]

There are two types of values, terminal and instrumental, to use Rokeach's definition. Terminal values can be defined as the goals of human activities, or "ultimate ends," using Parsons's terminology. Instrumental values can be defined as social standards, which are used by people to assess the means by which people achieve their goals from a moral point of view (Fine, 2001, 139; Rokeach, 1973, 5–10).

In some ways, the terms values and attitudes are interchangeable.[2] The concept of beliefs (or images), the cognitive part of attitudes, is also used as a substitute for values (Eagly and Chaiken, 1998, 274–275; Fishbein and Aizen, 1974, 59–74).

Finally, another concept that is used as an equivalent to values is "social norm." There is a tendency to look at values as broader social imperatives and social norms as narrower ones.[3] Norms are often described as psychological constructs that "prescribe and proscribe behavior in specific circumstances."[4] Making only a slight distinction between these concepts (or equating them), Coleman and Hechter talk about "internalized norms" in the same way that they talk about "internalized values."[5]

It is only natural that authors such as Robert Ellickson, who gravitate toward behaviorist perceptions of the world, are inclined to almost abandon the term values in favor of norms or "laws," depriving these concepts of any moral connotation.[6] A few authors, especially in recent years, operate with the term schemata, which, even if it focuses on the cognitive dimension, clearly includes the concept of values as a leading element (DiMaggio, 1997, 269–270). And finally, several authors, such as Friedrich Hayek in *Rules and Order*, prefer to operate only with the term rules, totally ignoring values and attitudes (Hayek, 1973, 43).

I place special focus on internalized values (or norms), that is, those values that are supposed to dictate human behavior directly. In no way am I inclined to underestimate the role of non-internalized or weakly internalized values, which make up the basis of law and in this way influence social life immensely.

At the same time, fear cannot be treated as a social value without stretching this concept. In some ways, fear and social values are in confrontation with each other in human life. A human being cannot accept fear, a pure negative emotion, as desirable for the individual or society. People and nations always try to get rid of their fear and only pathological or masochistic individuals enjoy being immersed in the state of permanent fear and troubles.

Three concepts that explain the maintenance of order have been circulated in the social sciences in the last two decades.[7] The first—let us associate it with Parsons and name it "culture from above"—sees socialization as the main process of transmitting culture to new generations. It holds that the dominant culture, whatever its definition, broad or narrow (Kluckhohn counted almost 200 different definitions), includes as its essential parts values that define people's attitudes toward social issues and the goals of human activity, along with the norms that specify value orientations. All other ways of coordinating human behavior are precarious or infeasible.[8]

Second, Locke's concept of "culture from below," suggests that social values, norms and order is shaped from below through the interaction of rational individuals who pursue their long-term interests and observe the norms that emerge in the process of interaction.

The third concept, which can be labeled "Hobbesian," interlaces with the first and suggests that social norms, which regulate order, are created not so much through the interaction of individuals, but mostly from above, by the various institutions (political ones in the first place, but also religious, educational and others). In this chapter, I discuss only the first two concepts, which are dominant in the contemporary sociological literature, leaving the debate over the third concept to other chapters.

To use the elementary relations of the market as an example it is possible to say that order (i.e., the honest interaction between buyers and sellers) can be explained in three ways: from Parsons's perspective, actors internalize the Ten Commandments and feel badly if they deceive each other; from Locke's view, people's long-term interests force them to be honest with each other; and from the Hobbessian perspective, the state severely punishes those who violate the law.

The first and the second schools of thought, which are dominant in the American social sciences, tend to disregard the crucial role of the fear of sanctions (or the loss of reward) and correspondingly the role of the state and law as the basis of social order. This tendency is clearly seen, as mentioned earlier, in the works of authors such as Parsons, Rokeach and Inglehart, for whom values are the major objects of study.[9] Even those scholars who deal directly with social control and who gravitate more toward the "classic culture school" tend to avoid the issue of sanctions and the fear of them.[10]

It is remarkable that among popular social scientists it was only Michel Foucault who talked about, "the machinery," "power," "power relations and domination" and "political technology," particularly in his *Discipline and Punishment* (1995, 21, 23, 25–27). For Foucault, "the power of the dominant class" plays a crucial role in society in practically the same way as it does for Hobbes. The only important difference is that Foucault, unlike Hobbes, places a special focus on knowledge and ideology as a major instrument of the state (102). For Foucault, the purpose of the whole penitentiary system is not so much to punish criminals or prevent his or her dangerous behavior in the future, but to demonstrate the power of the political machine (48–50, 53).

As David Garland aptly noted in his description of the role of political power (2001, 157–175), Foucault totally ignored all other variables, among them culture, that influence the major developments in society, among them the penal system. However, the big difference between Hobbes and the French author lies in their different appraisals of the role of the state: for the former, it plays a positive role in society, for the latter only a negative one.

The Cultural Model: Order as Given by the Past

The dominant view in contemporary American sociology that internalized values (common for the whole nation) are the basis of social order in society has been shaped over many decades, inspired by several great European sociologists, such as Weber, especially with his theory of religion, and Durkheim, who participated in building the view that people's behavior is mostly determined by social, collective values and cultural traditions.

Essentially, the Durkhemian tradition supposes the superiority of collective values over individual ones. It also supposes a quest for solidarity and the attachment of the individual to a group as the major drive of such social animals as human beings. This belief in the almost supernatural role of the "collective conscience" bears a direct similarity to religion (in fact, one author talks about Durkheim's society as "a religious entity"; see Lockwood, 1992).[11]

Basically, the same logic moved most sociologists of the nineteenth and twentieth centuries who insisted that social order is determined by the culture given to him or her from above, by the circumstances of his or her birth or by some other factor that forced him or her to change environments, such as in the case of immigration.

To some degree, with its focus on objective, cultural conditions, this approach is close to any structural theory, whatever the character of its main structure (economic in the case of Orthodox Marxists, mental structures for Levy Strauss, or some paradigm such as those proposed by Foucault or other structuralists). But the Parsonian model of society is still the clearest explanation of the dominant role of culture in shaping "normative" order from above. Parsons himself directly speaks about "a symbolic system of meanings which is an element of order 'imposed' " (Parsons, 1951, 11). It is also interesting that the advocates of the cultural approach to order, much more than their opponents, refer to the evolutionary theories, trying to bolster their image of the world as shaped by evolution itself.

According to Parsons, internalized social values entail "a sense of responsibility for the fulfillment of obligations" and "constitute, within the area of relevance of these values, a collectivity" (Parsons, 1951, 12; see also Smelser, 1994, 86). The coordination of the activity of various actors, after Parsons, is possible because of "common culture" (Parsons, 1977, 168; Parsons and Shils, 1951, 105). For Parsons, with his "over-socialized" concept of human beings, to use Dennis Wrong's famous locution (1961), people live under the permanent influence of the norms accepted in society and internalized by them. Each action is "normatively oriented" and people choose between different alternatives under the impact of internalized values (Parsons, 1960, 732).

Parsons's vision of society supposes the possibility of the achievement of "a perfect integrated social system" based on common internalized values (Parsons also used the term "generalized universalistic norms"), and first of all a "collectivity orientation" with some additional help from "prohibitive role expectations" (e.g., law) (Parsons and Shils, 1951, 126; see also Farraro, 2001, 149, 158). Although being critical of both Hobbes and Locke as utilitarianists and deniers of social values as the major determinants of human behavior, Parsons was still closer to Locke. He supported Locke's rejection of the use of "force" as the main regulator of society (Parsons, 1951, 15).

It is interesting and even amusing that the greatest allies of Parsons in the second half of the twentieth century were the neo-Marxists who believed in the power of social values from above as much if not more than Parsons did. Drawing on Gramchi, they started to make the cultural component the crucial factor in their revised Marxist constructions. Georg Lucacz, then member of the Frankfurt School, Hochheimer, Adorno and Marcuse advanced Marx's concept of "false consciousness" to the forefront of their vision of society. This school added to their Marxist repertoire the idea of "domination," which explains how the capitalist society is able to inculcate the bourgeois values in the minds of the masses by using repressions, in order to divert people from a realistic assessment of their society and persuade them to be absorbed with redundant consumption (Marcuse, 1955, 32–34; 1964, 4–6). Habermas wrote about "the goals and values of the social system" and the "normative structures" as the main elements of the social system (1973, 8, 12). For Bourdieu, a cultural capital that contains values is the major instrument used by the dominant class to run society (1993). Whatever the reasons, Parsons was seen as the epitome of bourgeois society and his anti-bourgeois critics and haters converged on the belief in the resolute role of internalized values in society (see Agger, 1991).

Socialization in Macrocultural Theory

Of course, the Parsonian model of society supposes the crucial role of socialization as a process that provides each generation with traditional values and patterns of behavior. For Parsons and those who accepted his explanation of social order, socialization is the process of learning what is good and what is bad (or, to use a different formulation, as "teaching the individual to *want* to follow norms"; see Cohen and Scull, 1983, 6), disregarding the fact that the lion's share of socialization is devoted to teaching children the rules, whatever their ethical connotation, such as learning how to drive or how to behave in public places.[12]

Along with Parsons, all the advocates of the "cultural model of social order" (and to a lesser extent the "norms creation school," which is discussed later) place a special focus on socialization and the belief that internalized values control human behavior. The followers of the cultural model talk about "self-control" and "self-discipline" as the basis of social order, often without making a distinction between the conduct inspired by internalized values or by the fear of violating rules (see Wilson and Hernnstein, 1985, 514–525). In Inglehart's grand theory of the postmodern shift of values, socialization is treated as always a positive mechanism ("cultural norms are usually internalized very firmly at an early age and play a crucial role in explaining why the old generation in developed countries does not accept post-materialist values with the same intensity as young generations"; Inglehart, 1997, 41).

This view on the crucial role of socialization as the basis for order became part of the official ideology taught in American schools: from community colleges to Harvard. In the courses of various disciplines— sociology, political science, anthropology and history—order is described as a natural product of self-regulation from below based on common internalized values: a result of the activity of all members of society. The same thing happens in a market when the spontaneous interaction between producers and consumers generates its own rules, as suggested by the most consistent apologists of the neoclassical model.

Parsons's vision of socialization, which is accepted by the majority of sociologists and social psychologists, is almost incompatible with the adaptation of the behaviorist approach, which supposes that individuals are moved by their interests, and despite their cultural traditions can easily move from one social environment to another, using Goffman's technique of impression management to look at each of them as "their own," and claiming to share the values and norms in the given social milieu.

Belief in the System

Parsons's belief in the crucial role of culture as the basis of social order is closely connected with his grand *theory of society* as a big system, which has been described by one of the authorities on system analysis as "a whole that cannot be divided into independent parts without loss of its essential properties or functions" (Ackoff, 1999, 8).[13] Parsons himself insisted that he operated with "a completely patterned consistent cultural system" (Parsons, 1951, 16, 27).

In some ways, Parsons's claim to describe a society as one system apparently did not differ from Marx's ambition. Although Parsons had several predecessors in his understanding of society, such as Durkheim and Weber, as well as several anthropologists, he was the only one to propose the idea of a system that embraces all parts of society as regulated by the same principles. Probably only Spencer, among the social scientists before Parsons, tried to describe society on the basis of one concept that equated society to a living organism.

Parsons and his predecessor held a holistic vision of society and believed strongly in universalism as a major trend of contemporary society, whereas particularism was considered a conservative, archaic tendency. In Parsons's works, the axis of universalism versus particularism was used as one of the most important dimensions or pattern variables of any society. Parsons was confident that progress would unswervingly diminish the role of particularism in the modern world. "Generalization of common values" and the generalization of "legal order" based on "formal rationality" would be the dominant trend in modern society, a trend he did not consider contradictory to the increasing differentiation of society, with its growing numbers of institutions, associations and various functions.

The holistic vision of society and culture was typical for many scholars in Parsons's time and after it. Almost all textbooks on sociology in the last three decades assume that the concept of the system is the best cognitive instrument to describe America. Several authors, including Bellah and his coauthors in *Habits of the Heart* (1986) and *Good Society* (1991), describe American society from a positive or critical perspective as a whole integrated system. Both Marxist and neo-Marxist scholars accept the concept of a social integrative system as the key methodological instrument in their analysis (Habermas, 1973, 4–9).

The Parsonian grand system was very close to "the neoclassical model" in American economics. The advocates of the neoclassical model share, to use Robert Solo's expression, the same "singular approach," describing the Western economy as a system based on perfect competition with prices as the single regulator of the economy. Mainstream economists support the neoclassical model as a good approximation for the description of the market economy, in the same way that sociologists believe in the cultural model with social values generated like prices by the spontaneous activity of the masses. Using perfect competition as the point of reference, economists describe the object of study in a rather elegant and seemingly consistent way, using complicated mathematical models.

The Actuality of Parsons's Vision of Society

Parsons's vision of order in society, as based on internalized values, outlived many of his other concepts and theories. Despite the harsh radical critique of many of his works and the decline of functionalism as a leading grand social theory, his ideas about the role of internalized values are almost folklore. They represent a part of most writing on human behavior, attitudes and social order. The statement that "values are the foundation for a whole way of life" was an undisputed thesis for American sociological textbooks in the last four to five decades. Parsons has legions of followers in contemporary social science, who talk about culture as "the property of individuals" (Fine, 2001, 139; Wrong, 1994, 103–105).

The same view was supported with some modifications by Geertz (1973) and several other authors who insist, without reservation, that "cultural ideas and practices" play the dominant role in human life (Fiske et al., 1998).

As Javier Trevino, the author of the introduction to *Talcott Parson Today* stated, "We are on safe ground arguing that all of Parsons' work from his earliest writing to his last work constituted an attempt to account satisfactorily for social order." Contrary to Hobbes, Trevino continues, for Parsons, the basis of social order "is not in the coercive but the normative." "That is to say that for Parsons social order does not lie with the external forces of the state, keeping people in line; rather it lies with society's common values that obligate people to voluntarily constrain their behavior, to cooperate with one another" (Trevino, 2001, XXXII). Joel Migdal (2001, 4), another contemporary researcher, describes the same Parsonian approach, saying that it "subsumed both the state and society in a broad conception of the so called social system, whose various parts are bound together by an overarching and unified set of values." It is wrong, as Christine Horne suggested, to revise Parsons words and use his comments on sanctions to deprive his vision of the world of its originality and consistency (Horne, 2001, 5). John Hall and Charles Lindholm hold the same view (1999). As one author stated in 2000, "that social order emanates from, and is supported by common values is intuitive. The notion has a distinguished scholarly pedigree: it pervades much social and political theory."[14] Essentially Parsons's vision of society is shared by Samuel Huntington, who described American society as run exclusively by culture and the dominant values (*Challenges to America's National Identity*, 2004). It is amazing that as a political scientist he almost totally ignored all political institutions in his book, which evidently was intended to show how America functions.

An interesting attempt to save the Parsonian vision of society was made by those scholars who try to argue against the conflict between the concept of common values and diversity. Presenting diversity as a rather superficial phenomenon, authors such as David Pearson and Viviana Zelizer argue that mass culture creates the ultimate cultural homogeneity. The victory of the national holiday traditions won over "ethnic particularity, eclecticism and localism" (see Pearson, 1993, 22; Zelizer, 1999, 206–207).

Textbooks

A popular textbook by Le et al. (1995), which has stood the test of several editions, stated that "the members of a society are united by a shared culture." Authors of a legion of textbooks have repeated this dogma. Robertson, in his textbook *Sociology*, stated that "In the process of growing up in society we unconsciously internalize the norms of our culture, making the conformity to them a part of our personality and following social expectations without question" (1981, 61).

MICROCULTURAL APPROACH: SOCIAL ORDER FROM THE BOTTOM-UP

As a matter of fact, the concept about the origin of norms from below is rooted in the belief that it is the individual and his happiness and not the wealth and security of society that is the supreme value, and it is the individual who creates social order. Many thinkers in the history of mankind shared this view. In ancient times, it was Socrates and Aristotle, with their belief in happiness as "the ultimate good."

A special role in the history of the concept belongs to John Locke, who had a major influence on political philosophy and whose impact we see clearly in rational choice and other theories, which suggest that society is built from below, and that "Government, even in its best state, is but a necessary evil." Only two other thinkers of the eighteenth century (Rousseau and Kant) can claim to be influential advocates of the contract as the basis of society. The interpretation of feudalism as a set of relations between a vassal and his lord, as if based on equality, was one of many examples demonstrating the influence of the Lockean view on society (Bloch, 1961).

In the eighteenth and nineteenth centuries, it was utilitarianists such as Jeremy Bentham and John Stuart Mills. In the twentieth century, this vision of human beings and society was represented by Hayek and John Rawls in political theory, Milton Friedman in economics, Skinner in psychology and Homans in sociology. All these thinkers are the allies of the bottom up perspective.

By the end of the twentieth century, the Lockean ideas inspired the so-called microcultural approach to explaining the origin of norms. Michael Hechter and Karl-Dieter Opp noted that "the principal disagreement separates the authors who view the norms as clear constraints on action from those for whom norms are more plastic social constructions." They added, "This amounts to a distinction between a conception of norms as 'given and obeyed,' on one hand, and norms as 'negotiated and performed' on the other" (Hechter and Opp, 2001a, 394). As Francis Fukuyama emphatically stressed, "The systematic study of how order, and thus social capital, can emerge spontaneously and in a decentralized fashion is one of the major tasks of social science" (Fukuyama, 1995).

In his book *Foundation of Social Theory* (1990), James Coleman followed this vision of society from below. Instead of values, he used norms as the elementary particle of society. Coleman tends to suggest that norms emerge primarily as a product of "social consensus" among social actors. He differs from Parsons in that he gravitates toward the rational choice approach, with its focus on the interaction of people as the sources of norms, even if he does not accept it formally. In his opinion, "norms are macro-level constructs, based on purposive actions at the micro level." It is also characteristic that Coleman makes no distinction between norms that regulate the most important elements of social life, such as property relations or the safety of human life, and the norms that affect the behavior of small children or a game of cricket (Coleman, 1990, 241–246).

In many respects, the bottom-up concept, which places the focus on the interaction of individuals, is a modification of the old contractual theory, which assumes that "human agreement is of central importance for the understanding, explanation and justification of society or government" (Dunn, 1996, 42). This concept can be linked to the theories of various intellectual trends of the past. The most powerful trends were those that advanced the concept of natural rights, which supposed that people could concede some of their rights or liberties only on a voluntary basis. There are four schools that support the bottom-up approach to the origin and maintenance of order.

Symbolic Interactionists

Symbolic interactionism is dear to the advocates of the bottom-up approach, because they present society as existing only in "action" and in "elementary collective processes," which are interpreted specifically in each particular case by the individuals involved in them (Swanson, 1970, 124–125). This idea has something in common with Parsons's views. Symbolic interactionists reject the antisocial and pure individualistic (and, in fact, in many respects, biological) approach that ignores social interaction in the explanation of social behavior. This approach was quite prevalent in the first half of the twentieth century due to the popularity of Freud. It strongly underestimated the role of cultural and social institutions, which Freud tended to explain (e.g., in the case of religion) mostly as the peculiarities of human biology and psychology. Blumer is explicitly against the Freudian "ego" as the major variable explaining human behavior (Blumer, 1969, 81).

At the same time, there is a radical difference between the understanding of human behavior of the symbolic interactionists and that of Parsons. Blumer does not agree with those who describe human beings as being influenced by forces outside the self (the social systems, social structures, culture, institutions, collective representation, social norms and values). He does not want "to lodge social action in the action of society or in some units of society," but "in acting individuals" (Blumer, 1969, 83–84). For him, order in society was gradually built up through the processes of interaction, as in Defoe's *Robinson Crusoe*, or in Golding's *Lord of the Flies.*

Of course, symbolic interactionists cannot agree with the Parsonian vision of the origin of values and norms (Blumer, 1969, 14).

The interactionist approach to the emergence of new norms relates explicitly to "local expectations of behavior," "local interpretation of social life," or "local norms."[15] Indeed, trying to explain the meaning that people attribute to the things around them, mostly through "self-indication" and the exchange of indications, they talk not about the broad social milieu in which individuals find themselves but about "the situation in which he is placed" and "the direction of his action." Without denying the role of some elements outside the specific interaction between individuals (mostly groups, not societal factors), a typical symbolic interactionist, such as Blumer, will insist that "individual interaction is vitally important in its own right," and claim that "by the virtue of symbolic interactionism, human group life is necessarily a formative process and not a mere arena for the expressions of preexisting factors," "a process in which objects are being created, affirmed, transformed, and cast aside" (Blumer, 1969, 1–12). Even Blumer's allies rebuked him for ignoring "preestablished understandings and or traditions" (Swanson, 1970, 139).

Blumer's disregard of the macro world was inherited by prominent scholars such as Erving Goffman, who discussed the interaction of people, for instance, in developing impressions of each other or in elaborating rules in micro worlds, as if the macro world, with its institutions, laws and ideology, does not exist (Goffman, 1959, 73, 251).

A more complex position is held by Berger and Luckmann (1966), who also belong, though perhaps to a lesser degree, to the same school and pay serious attention to interacting individuals and the experiences of "others" (17, 33). Some scholars such as Kenneth Gergen suggest that both authors effectively "removed objectivity as a foundation of science and replaced it with a conception of socially informed and institutionalized subjectivity" (Gergen, 1973, 43). In fact, both authors, although characterizing social reality as defined by the mind of the individual, equate "knowledge" and "reality." They both recognize that an already existing "symbolic universe" is imposed on new generations. In this way, they show affinity toward Parsons's approach from above, even if they are very critical of Parsons; this is contrary (17) to classic symbolic interactionism with its theory about the formation of culture from below.

Postmodernism: The Focus on Individual Activity and Free Will

Postmodernism strengthened the view that everyone, on the same basis, is engaged in the social-construction process. Postmodernists saddled the intellectual trends in American sociology, particularly symbolic interactionism—which in fact developed from "bottom to top"—and focused on the role of individuals in the formation of order. Postmodernists, in some ways, are close to French existentialists, who focus on the freedom of choice of human beings. Sartre's famous phrase, "man makes himself" sounds very much in the spirit of the postmodernist belief in the potential of the human being. Describing the formation of cultural models, postmodernists contend that "each person interprets, reproduces and transforms cultural realities" (Fiske et al., 1998, 917), or to use other terms, each individual is his own "self-legislator" (Robin, 1999, 18).

Under the evident influence of postmodernism, constructivist sociologists go so far as to declare that people do not "obey" norms, people do them; that is, "norms are generated entirely in situ." One of their major arguments is that norms from outside are ambiguous and only in situ is it possible to determine the conditions for their implementation (Hechter and Opp, 2001a, 395). This thesis, however, does not pass empirical scrutiny. It is true that many norms from above could be "contingent" under specific conditions but these conditions do not usually change the essence of the norms. It is possible to say, with only a little stretching, that it was Nietzsche who, with his total denial of values from above (Christian values in the first place), proclaimed that "there are no general and universal rules for finding oneself . . . everyone creates his own truth and morals for himself: what is good and bad, useful or harmful for one man is not necessarily so far for another" (Nietzsche, 1955).

Rational Choice Theories

The vision of the world of this group is based not only on the theory of symbolic interactionism, but also on rational choice and game theory, which became popular in the 1970s and 1980s. They have a special interest in Nash's theory of equilibrium and the Prisoners' Dilemma, which describes the basis of coordination (Tullock, 1985). Among the advocates of the bottom-up origin of social norms, economists who focus on the emergence of nongovernmental institutions stand out. They talk about the importance of economic processes from below and discuss "the demands on norms" (Cooter, 1996). A few authors, such as Robert Ellickson, recommended the game theory as the best theoretical concept for understanding the origin of norms (Ellickson, 1991, 8–9, 156–166).

The concept of social capital can be seen as a version of the rational choice theory, which also tries to explain the origin of the cooperation that emerges between individuals in their search for jobs, the creation of car pools (a beloved example of Fukuyama) and even the creation of some informal savings institutions. Fukuyama is so enthusiastic about social capital that he proclaimed it as "critical for healthy civil society" (Fukuyama, 1999, 18,144–145).

The New Norms Theories

In the last years, the theories that focus on the interaction of people in shaping norms and conventions became in some ways a cottage industry in economics,[16] as well as in other social sciences (Fukuyama, 1995; 1999). These authors tend to describe these nonformal conventional relations in a limpid and serene way as if they are based on the best traits of human nature, or on its inclination toward cooperation, reciprocity and mutual help and altruism. This tendency found a major predecessor in Herbert Spencer, who, following the tradition of Anglo-Saxon utilitarianism started by Locke, saw the world as a network of intelligent and goodnatured people who like to cooperate with each other without being bound by the formalities of law. Utilitarianism found a new breath in the second half of the twentieth century (Ellickson, 1991, 38–39). The utilitarian ideology influenced the theory of games and rational choice, as well as the authors who operate with the concept of conventions, which supposes that social norms are invented by the participants of specific social relations. Kenneth Arrow talked in the 1970s about "the invisible institutions" that regulate social relations using ethical norms and trust (Arrow, 1974, 26).

The authors who began to study the origin of "new norms" in the 1990s clearly belong to this group (McAdams, 1997). They focus on "the dynamic interaction of purposive actors" in specific social relations as the creators of new values, or norms. They also emphasized the theory of "the market" origin of new norms, which supposes the participation in norm making of all members of the group, dealing usually with relations of minor importance, such as the behavior at a dinner party (Ellickson, 1991, 36–52; Hechter and Opp, 2001b, XII; Voss, 2001, 105–136). Further, most advocates of the origin of new norms from below disregard the social and cultural differentiation inside any society and do not make any distinction between the ruling elites and the masses. They even tend to disregard the role of such "aggregations as cultures and social classes as operative agents in the generation of norms." It is curious that some authors who belong to this group, in terms of their determination to focus on the origin of norms from below, revised Hobbes, suggesting that he described the installation of law by Leviathan as a result of the interaction between the covenant among citizens and the monarch (Ullmann-Margalit, 1977, 66).

In fact, there is no doubt that the emergence of some norms can indeed be described as a sort of spontaneous process in which its participants, coordinate their views, make contracts and gradually create stable patterns of behavior that will be observed by the next generation; however, it is hardly relevant to the formation of key values, without speaking of the fact that any contract supposes the preexistence of the norms that make it possible.

The advocates of the from below approach tend to ignore the difference between major and minor values, and between initial and derivative norms. This flaw was typical for social interactionists such as Mead and Blumer, as well as for the advocates of ethnomethodology (Garfinkel, 1967). Later, several authors such as James Coleman and Francis Fukuyama (2000, 103–104) followed this line of reasoning.

These authors tend to equate the character of norms of secondary importance at the micro level with the values and laws at the macro level, which direct the absolute majority of significant human decisions.[17] Fukuyama recognizes, rather reluctantly, that the authors of modernization theories (Henry Maine, Weber, Durkheim, Tönnies) suggest the possibility to "hypothesize, as many have done, that as society modernizes, norms tend to be created less from 'below' than 'above' by the state which becomes the chief source of order in modern societies." But as an argument against this hypothesis, Fukuyama cites "the thicket of unwritten rules concerning gender relations in a modern American workplace or school," as an example of the sphere where norms and rules emerge spontaneously. It is amusing that he refers to the sphere of human relations that is now evidently regulated by harsh law and rules from above (Fukuyama, 2000, 107).

Thomas Voss builds up his concept of the emergence of norms, operating with such cases as how people applaud in a concert house after each piece, or at the end of the program, how athletes regulate their use of drugs during competitions, how people in some Catholic countries celebrate carnival and so on (Voss, 2001, 106). Gary Fine uses the activity of mushroom collectors in his analysis of social norms (Fine, 2001, 139–164).

It is remarkable that the greatest enthusiasts of the norms from below do not cite any examples of crucial values and norms that emerge according to their vision. Even a scholar such as Eggertsson, who gravitates toward this concept with a more balanced view than his colleagues, when discussing the origin of secure property rights, the fundamental condition for economic growth, recognizes the role of "the elites, the public and the state" in this process (Eggertsson, 1991, 84, 86). Criticizing those institutionalists who believe in the ability of "small, homogeneous groups and competitive business environments . . . to develop efficient private rules and norms to organize their affairs," he notes that "the state should provide communities with secure property rights . . . and should solidify such private institutions by enacting them into law." Further, describing the ideological struggle in Iceland among the advocates of capitalist, socialist and traditionalist models, he clearly points to the leading role of the elites in the shaping of the new system of values in the new nation (Eggertsson, 1991, 84, 86, 94–95).

The advocates of values and norms from below should take note that even the traffic in cities, a relatively simple social problem, cannot be regulated by the conventions among drivers. Watching the traffic in Baghdad after the collapse of the old regime, Daniel Klein, an expert on modern traffic problems and the evolution of cooperation, suggests that there is only one solution: the "Hobessian one." Klein points out that the chances for the creation of rules from below are better if people are personally engaged in repeated interactions, but this is not the case with "road people" (Tierney, 2003).

Ellickson's Case

Robert Ellickson aggressively defends the "conventional" version of the bottom-up theory in his book *Order without Law*, which mocks "law-and-society scholarship" (Ellickson, 1991, 6–8). He came to the general conclusion that "law is not central to the maintenance of order" based on his observance of how ranchers in Shasta County in California, who make up "a close-knit group," managed to regulate their relations in raising cattle without law or law enforcement agencies. He focused on how the lack of fences (i.e., cattle were not contained) influences the relations between neighbors. His main conclusion is that the ranchers, in view of the relatively high cost of the intervention of law enforcement agencies, managed to find equilibrium and "the maximum welfare function" for their community without "the supervision of the state," even ignoring the state ordinance on "closed-ranges." They had no idea about the relevance of "judges, attorneys and insurance adjusters" to their lives. The author openly calls upon American society to follow the example of the cattle ranchers, praising their informal control in Shasta County.

Ellickson fervently defends the high potential of self-organization of a community without the intervention of law and the state. He claims that there are no grounds to doubt the results of his empirical study and he is probably right in his confrontation with those who believe that formal law is all-pervasive. The first major problem with Ellickson is that he does not see that many federal and state laws hover over Shasta County, even if the ranchers do not resort to using them. These laws are always in the background and immensely influence the life of ranchers. Even within families, all parties resort to the law in the case of serious conflicts. The life and property of his ranchers are protected by federal law not by their mutual agreement. He ignores also the fact that many other elements of their life are regulated from above.

It is interesting to compare Ellickson's approach with that of Durkheim. Both see the contract as the major instrument for the coordination of human activity and both, particularly Ellickson, tend to downgrade the role of law. However, for Durkheim, "solidarity" based on "the general consensus" precedes contracts (he talks about "contractual solidarity"), and order is determined not only by "the individual's attachment to the group," but also by "regulation" (see Durkheim, 1960, 316; see also Lockwood, 1992, 6). For Ellickson, social relations start and end with a contract.

The second problem with Ellickson's book is the contention, based on a confusion of micro and macro issues, that his study of the life of ranchers can shed light on the function of society as a whole. With all due respect to informal norms in a civilized society (definitely not in Somalia or even in contemporary Russia), they determine only a tiny part of human behavior.

Conclusion

The negligible interest in social order in the sociological literature in the last decades of the twentieth century should be ascribed to the belief that the maintenance of order is almost automatically ensured by the dominant culture and more specifically by social values. The dominant concept about the origin of social order belongs to Talcott Parsons. His theory supposes that culture, with values as a macro-societal phenomenon, is a stable entity and is transferred from one generation to another. Culture influences the mind and behavior of the members of society from above, mostly through the mechanism of socialization, which has social values at its core. The Parsonian concept, with some modifications, is used as the basis for educating students about order in high schools as well as in colleges.

The second concept related to the origin of values supposes that they are shaped from below, that is, at the micro level with the active participation of all members of society. This concept is nurtured by several trends in contemporary sociology, such as symbolic interactionism with its focus on the interaction of individuals, postmodernism with its focus on individual activity and free will, rational choice theories with their focus on rational behavior of people, "social capital" theories and "the new norms theories," with their focus on the ability of people to develop conventions or norms from below.

I am inclined to support the Parsonian idea about culture, which influences the human mind and behavior from above. I think that those who focus on the formation of values and rules from below greatly overestimate the importance of this process. At the same time, I am critical of the Parsonian concept as it ignores the crucial role of the state and elites in shaping values and sustaining their observance by the public. Parsons and his followers tend to disregard the close connection between values and laws, as well as the role of fear of sanctions as an important factor in the maintenance of order in society.

CHAPTER 3

The Limited Role of Positive
Internalized Values

In chapters 4 and 5, I try to show why a social mechanism based on internalized social values cannot, in many cases, guarantee order in society.

INTERNALIZED POSITIVE VALUES:
THEIR IMPACT ON BEHAVIOR

Culture and values play a very important role in sustaining social order in society. To deny the role of values in human behavior would be to deny the role of people's previous experiences. In human society, values, with their hierarchy of priorities, define desirable behavior for individuals and society. Values would be a redundant concept if human beings and social units of various types started their relations from scratch each time, as suggested by behaviorists and new behaviorists, utilitarianists, the advocates of the rational choice theory and some neoclassical economists who suppose that individuals or units reinvent the rules of behavior each day or even more often.[1] Meanwhile, as aptly noted by Marx, Robinson Crusoe, when he found himself on an uninhabited island, totally cutoff from civilization, continued to look at the world, through the lens of the bourgeois values that were inculcated in him in England.

Indeed, a considerable part of the population in democratic societies has digested several positive values and respects human life, freedom and property. They also respect the leading role of the church and major sacred texts, such as the Bible or Koran in deeply religious societies, or the leader of the nation and the glorification of the state in totalitarian societies. People internalize these values in the process of socialization in the family, church and school, and under the impact of media and arts. People observe the leading values of their society without being concerned about being punished in this or another world, even if the fear of sanctions (religious or secular) was at the origin of this loyalty to values.

There is no doubt that in the process of socialization many young people learn and internalize a number of values to which they remain loyal until the end of their lives. It is particularly true about those values hallowed in religious education in the family and schools. These values force the individual to follow their prescriptions, using compunctions and feelings of guilt. Gallup data, for instance, show that the difference in the behavior of youth who attend church and those who do not attend is indeed quite significant. Among church-goers, 8 percent "tried marijuana," but among non-churchgoers 18 percent tried it. The data about alcohol consumption and "smoking cigarettes in the past week" have the same pattern: 12 and 22 percent, 3 and 7 percent, respectively (Gallup, 2005b).

These internalized values continue to be active as young people grow up if the mechanism of reinforcement works and they stay in an environment in which they are supported by schools, media and arts and if they maintain a close relationship with their family and church. The moral core of the population—if it exists in society—plays an important role in the maintenance of the existing order. However, the culturological approach to social order strongly exaggerates the weight of the moral core of society, as Durkheim (1965) did in his interpretation of social values as sacred and as the content of a secular religion. Several contemporary authors do the same when they try to apply Durkheim's concepts to explain life in contemporary society, American society included (Hall and Lindholm, 1999, 92). But even more important is the fact that even the members of the moral core of society, the most respected citizens in the given society, do not always behave according to the dominant values. In this case, when they are not afraid of sanctions they violate several values for different reasons, rationalizing their behavior with various arguments and demanding that others do what they cannot or do not want to do. Still, with all these caveats, the moral core of the nation plays a very important role in maintaining social order, serving among other things as the model for others and as the voluntary supervisors over those who ignore positive values.

A considerable number of Americans not only share verbally, but also behave in accordance with key values of the dominant culture. They respect law, property, other's rights, privacy and many other values. The behavior of Americans in times of crisis, such as during the terrorist attacks on September 11, is one of the most eloquent evidences that many people in this country indeed conduct themselves according to the dominant values.

The American participation in self-government and various voluntary programs, such as the Peace Corps are telling indicators of the materialization of American moral values in social life. The contribution to various welfare programs with money and physical activities represent other examples of American behavior that is inspired mostly by internalized values. For instance, according to a Gallup poll, 82 percent of Americans gave money to a charitable cause. Almost half of all Americans sent money for relief efforts to help Tsunami victims in December 2004 (Gallup, 2004a; 2005b).

Even in a totalitarian state such as the Soviet Union, there was a considerable number of people who could be regarded as sincere believers in the dominant values and who behaved accordingly, even if they were not supervised by the authorities or any other member of society (Shlapentokh, 2001; 2004a,b).

However, it is impossible to build up social order based only on internalized values. Before moving directly to this issue, it is necessary to discuss the literature's tendency to ascribe the maintenance of order to "false values"—rules that are deprived of the moral dimension, an essential part of values.

VALUES AS THE COVER OF RULES AND THE RATIONALIZATION OF FEAR

Quite often the devotion to values hides the rules that are necessary to observe in order to survive or make progress and avoid losing a reward or incurring a punishment. It was Dennis Wrong who described human beings first of all as "acceptance seekers." Fifty years ago, in an unforgettable article, he wrote, "Modern sociology, after all, originated as a protest against the partial views of man contained in such doctrines as utilitarianism, classical economics, social Darwinism, and vulgar Marxism. All of the great nineteenth and early twentieth century sociologists saw it as one of their major tasks to expose the unreality of such abstractions as economic man (the gain-seeker of the classical economists), political man (the power-seeker of the Machiavellian tradition in political science), self-preserving man (the security seeker of Hobbes and Darwin), sexual, libidinal man (the pleasure-seeker of doctrinaire Freudianism), and even religious man (the God-seeker of the theologians). It would be ironic if it should turn out that they have merely contributed to the creation of yet another reified abstraction in socialized man, the status-seeker of our contemporary sociologists" (Wrong, 1961, 190).

Lawrence Kohlberg, following Piaget's famous theory of the six-stage evolution of the moral conscience, described the first and second stages as the periods when the learning of social norms was strongly influenced by the threat of punishment. However, even in the next stages (the third and fourth), the "good behavior" of teenagers is also influenced by "the necessity to obey law and respect authorities" (Kohlberg, 1969; see also Crain, 1985, 118–136).

A good example is the case of labor ethics in the United States, an extremely complex phenomenon. Some authors tend to take at face value the verbal statements of respondents. Samuel Huntington considers the high respect for work given by Americans as the most important element of American Anglo-Protestant culture, not only in the past but also in the beginning of the twentieth century (Huntington, 2004, 31). He ascribes this respect to the core of the Anglo-Protestant ethic.

Insisting that Americans, as devotees of Protestant culture, are the most laborious workers in the world, Huntington (2004, 31) is only partially right. He tends to embellish American labor ethics in the last 50 years. In fact, a great part of the U.S. labor force is alienated from their work. At best, they tolerate it, waiting for retirement, and at worst, they hate it. The World Values Survey shows that whereas 84 percent of Americans verbally acknowledge their high respect for work (evidently a desirable value in the dominant American ideology), only 16 percent of Americans (this figure is not cited by Huntington) declared work as "the most important thing in my life."

Collecting various data, a prominent American sociologist, Herbert Gans, wrote in the late 1980s, when labor ethics were higher than now, that working people (the working class or lower middle class) saw work as fundamentally unpleasant (Gans, 1988). Various studies create a much less pleasant picture of American attitudes toward their work than Huntington's. I can refer to the sociological data collected by Melvin Kohn (1977). I can also refer to such authors as David Shipler (2004) who wrote about "the working poor," a big chunk of the American population. I can also refer to the respected writers who describe American work in their novels, including Arthur Hailey's *Wheel* (1971), or Tom Wolfe's *A Man in Full* (1998).

However, even more important for this analysis is the explanation of why most Americans indeed work well regardless of their attitudes toward their jobs. Huntington (2004, 31) and Neil Ferguson (2003) argue that the high productivity of Americans when compared to those in Western Europe (using as an indicator the number of hours spent working during a year) should be ascribed to the religiosity of American citizens as against the more secular Europeans. Ferguson had in mind religion in general whereas Huntington only thought about the Protestant culture (2004, 71).

This factor may have played an important role in the past in defining labor ethics (high or low depending on the intensity of religiosity), but it does not explain the very different levels of productivity for Asian workers, various minorities and millions of whites. Both authors compare America to Western European countries, completely ignoring social factors. Americans work more hours than Europeans not because the former are more religious, as both of these authors contend, and not because Americans like a longer work week, but because the American economic and social system demands hard work and does not have a welfare system that makes the life of the unemployed almost attractive, as in France or Germany. Huntington (2004, 74) treats the work ethic as the independent variable with respect to American and European employment and welfare, yet it is possible to say the inverse: Europeans work less than Americans because their welfare system is much more generous than the American one.

In search of another factor that accounts for Americans' extremely high labor ethics, Huntington subscribes to the myth about the "absence" of a rigid social hierarchy in America (2004, 71). He also points to a typical exaggeration of an important feature of American society, following Judith Shklar, that "throughout American history social standing has depended on working and earned money by working" (Shklar, 1991).

The Learning of Rules, not Values

Another powerful argument against the overestimation of the role of values in society was given by Peter Berger and Thomas Luckmann in *The Social Construction of Reality* (1966). Ignoring almost completely the term values, along with its moral dimension, they reasonably show that the continuity in human behavior should be ascribed not so much to human values, as to the process of the cognition of rules, that is, to "habituation" and typification (32–33, 53). As the authors convincingly show, "any action that is repeated frequently becomes cast into a pattern, which can then be reproduced with an economy of effort and which, *ipso facto*, is apprehended by its performer as that pattern." They continue, "Habituation further implies that the action in question may be performed again in the future in the same manner and with the same economical effort. This is true of non-social as well as of social activity." Like Parsons, they talk about socialization, but unlike him they focus on the learning of the rules. For them, socialization is first of all the process of acquiring knowledge about the world. For this reason, these authors perceived the sociology of knowledge as the best road for understanding society (2,128). To some degree, all scholars who focus on explaining socialization with learning, including Lawrence Kohlberg (1969) and Albert Bandura (1969), accepted Berger and Luckmann's perspective.

The Case of War: Rules and Values

Since the *Iliad*, war has been considered a crucial episode in human life that tests the virtues of people: primarily their courage and devotion. Plato saw courage as the distinctive virtue of the warrior class. Aristotle considered courage to be an essential part of "the virtues of character," which are all acquired through education and habituation (see Hardie, 1980). It is supposed that people show courage and devotion to the goal of the war especially when they defend their country from foreign adversaries or during civil wars when people defend their views. However, even in such wars, the role of internalized values should not be overestimated; coercion and the fear of sanctions have a great deal of influence on the behavior of soldiers during war. The external factors include the authority of ideology (positive and negative), the image of enemies and their goals in war, the behavior of the enemy, particularly the degree of its cruelty in handling prisoners and the civilian population, the belief in victory and of course the fear of sanctions of commanders and the disapproval of peers. All of these exert more influence on the conduct of warriors than the values internalized during childhood.

The Soviet war against Nazi Germany is a good example, particularly because anti-Soviet sentiments were quite strong among soldiers and officers from the countryside (and they made up the majority of the army) where cruel collectivization and the terrible famine offered a good excuse for less than valiant conduct. Some authors indeed saw the courageous behavior of Russian soldiers simply as a byproduct of the people's fear of the KGB and other institutions.[2]

In my opinion, the war was decidedly a people's war. The people were given a kind of freedom of choice in that they could perform feats of heroism, or refrain from such actions. There were, in fact, numberless acts of heroism. However, it would be wrong to underplay the role of the fear of the Soviet authorities and officers during the war; this subject has been hotly discussed in Russia since 1991.

Indeed, the fear of the KGB, its notorious branch Smersh (the death to spies), the arrests and absurd accusations of anti-Soviet activity, along with the heavy recruitment of informers, were ever-present in the army during the war. A special government decree issued in July 1941 assured punishment for individuals who "spread false rumors." More importantly, there was the role of special police units in the war. These units were positioned behind the frontline, where they mercilessly shot any soldier who fled before the over-whelming might of the adversary, or who wanted to evade participating in the hopeless or extremely costly attacks ordered by the Soviet commanders, who were almost indifferent to the human losses. According to some sources, the number of deserters amounted to two million people. More than five million people in Ukraine and Belorussia evaded the draft in the first days of the war (see Radzikhovsky, 2005). The situation changed radically after the Stalingrad battle and the resurgence of spirit in the army and country. The number of deserters declined drastically and the number of heroic feats increased. However, in this period the external sanctions continued to play a key role in forcing people to join the army (the draft) and to fight according to the rules.

Internalized values probably played a modest role in the conduct of American soldiers during war. As the famous study *The American Soldier* (United States Department of the Army, 1975) showed, only a minority among the military was motivated by the American value system and had a strong ideological motivation for war. Referring to empirical data about the attitudes of soldiers to war, the study said, "there was little support of attempts to give the war meaning in terms of the principles and causes involved" (433). About two-thirds of the soldiers said that in a time of combat they felt that "the battle was not worth the cost" (154, see 430–438). Studying combat motivation, the authors of the book concluded that "officers and enlisted men alike attached little importance to idealistic motives—patriotism and concern about war aims" (111).

Thirty-nine percent of enlisted men named "ending the task" as their combat incentive; 14 percent said, "solidarity with the group"; and 6 percent, "self-preservation." Only 9 percent said, "sense of duty and self respect" and 5 percent, "idealistic motives" (108). In discussing the discipline in the army, the authors did not deny the role of "internalized patterns of conformity," but they did underscore the high importance of rewards and the fear of punishment, along with "the coercive institutional authorities" (both formal and informal sanctions) (112–118).

The Case of Immigrants

Immigrants present an important argument against the assumption that internalized values mostly or even completely sustain order in society. The role of immigrants in many countries is significant. In the United States, 20 percent of the population is composed of immigrants: first and second generations.

Indeed, socialization is a process in which young people or immigrants learn the rules and the punishments that come from violating the rules. This process is very different from the adaptation of dominant positive social values. At the same time, following the rules, which are not internalized as guides of behavior, people often try to appear as if they adopted these values by using impression management techniques, to use the terminology of Goffman. These techniques allow them to hide their hostility toward the social values that are dominant in society (Goffman, 1959, 73, 251).

The behavior of many new immigrants, which is discussed later, is a good example that illustrates how millions of people observe laws in a new country without being committed to its dominant culture and values. One of the central ideas of Huntington's recent book (2004) was that in the past, before the 1960s, when the assimilation of immigrants was undisputed by American ideology, all immigrants (66 million between 1820 and 2000) almost instantly accepted and digested the Anglo-Protestant values. As Huntington writes, though without understanding the irony behind his description of the socialization of immigrants, "during the nineteenth century and until the late twentieth century, immigrants were in various ways compelled, induced, and persuaded to adhere to the central elements of the Anglo-Protestant culture" (2004, 61). It is amazing how Huntington ignores the conventional wisdom that the first generation and to some degree even the second were able to learn only rules of behavior without elaborating positive emotional attitudes toward the values behind these rules. Even demonstrating loyalty to American culture was necessary for survival.

In addition to immigrants, many native people demonstrate the same denial of values while observing the rules that are based on them. Millions of Americans preach tolerance toward people of different races, but have prejudices against several ethnic and religious groups. It is well known that many white and black Americans continue to share racist views against each other. During elections, the racial factor has a major influence on many groups in American society. However, in everyday life, people are controlled by their environment and therefore behave quite decently, even claiming publicly to be race blind. The complexity of white–black relations has been well described in all three novels of Tom Wolfe as well as in Spike Lee's movies such as Jungle Fever. Attitudes toward Jews can also serve as an illustration of this thesis. Data show that no less than one-third of Americans harbor various prejudices against Jews. However, in everyday life this is not readily apparent.

There is no doubt that the full assimilation of immigrants, that is, their acceptance of a new culture, contributes to the sustenance of social order in any society (Gordon, 1964, 127, 244–245). The American experience of the "melting pot" was indeed very successful and I do not share the view of those who, as previously mentioned, deny it. Did American immigrants adapt to Anglo-Saxon cultural patterns, the culture of the founding fathers, as contended by Milton Gordon (1964, 89), and Michael Novak (1977, 59), or did immigrants adapt to this culture only partially, the concept of "tomato soup," which unlike "the melting pot" consists of ingredients that the immigrants brought from their old culture (Huntington, 2004, 129–131). In any case, new immigrants digest some elements of the new culture.

However, the concept of assimilation in it various forms is not sufficient, as suggested by Huntington (2004), for understanding how social order is sustained in a country with a big influx of immigrants. Most immigrants, particularly the first generation who are far from being assimilated, observe social order based on law enforcement agencies. They quickly realize the rules of a new country and honor most of them, when the authorities demand it, not so much because some of these rules overlap with the values of their own culture (as has occurred with Asian cultures with their high respect for education and family) or that the rules have a universal character (such as the laws against murder or stealing), but mostly because they fear the violation of law and rules. Even the immigrants who came to the United States with an inbred hatred of America and who do not wish to stay in this country over many years are mostly law abiding people who do not express their true attitudes toward America or violate its laws. Indeed, an immigrant's behavior from "9 to 5" in his or her place of work, in educational institutions, in public transportation or in the entertainment sphere does not differ significantly from that of the rest of the population, even if the former has been in the country only for a year or less. It is remarkable that new immigrants quickly realize the character of the political process in a new country and often actively join those parties and movements that supposedly are on their side. As the history of immigration to America shows, even the illiterate peasants from authoritarian countries were extremely quick to grasp the meaning of voting, even if the immigrants' votes were controlled by their bosses (Traverso, 1964, 66). For instance, half the members of the Socialist party in the United States in 1919 were non-English-speaking people (Rosenblum, 1973, 153).

The author of a lengthy article (a full page in *New York Times*) gave a detailed description of the successful adaptation to life in Las Vegas of Graciela Diaz, a new female immigrant from Mexico with admittedly imperfect English. It is interesting that the author did not deem it necessary, in describing her adjustments to American life, to mention even once the issue of American values. He depicted in detail how fast Diaz and her husband learned the best way to survive and even prosper in the new country. Coming to the United States illegally, after only ten years, they had joined the middle class, purchasing a house for $125,000 (Greenhouse, 2004). Of no less interest was a comparison made by an investigative journalist of the fate of two immigrants in New York—one successful, one not. Even if they came from different countries (Greece and Mexico) several years ago, their initial conditions were very similar (they were the same age, lived in the same city and could not speak English). The author of the article did not even mention the issue of culture as a factor that explained these two different life stories. A major explanation was that one was able to get legal status, and the other was not (DePalma, 2005).

The general education and professional education received in the old country is much more important for the survival in a new country than the cultural assimilation and even the discrimination against them. As suggested by Alejandro Portos and Ruben Rumbault, the authors of an influential book on immigration in America, the most important thing for an immigrant's success is not to forget their cultural past, but what "they bring with them in motivation, knowledge and resources" (Lee, 2003, 30). The success of Indian, Taiwanese or Iranian immigrants in the United States was due to their high level of education in comparison to the much lesser success of the immigrants from such countries as Mexico, Guatemala and Columbia. In 1989, the median household income of immigrants from the first three countries (the median household income in the United States was then 30.1 thousand) was 48.3, 39 and 35.8 thousand; for the second group, 21.9, 24.3 and 29.1 thousand. Meanwhile, among the immigrants from the first three countries, in 1990, the percentage of people with professions was 35, 29 and 24 percent in comparison to 3, 3 and 9 percent (Portes and Rumbaut, 1996, 68, 78).

The data compiled by George Borjas are even more supportive of the high level of adaptation of immigrants to the economy in a new country. By the beginning of the 1990s, the immigrants who had lived in the United States for more than 20 years had wages higher than the natives and those who lived in the United States for 10–20 years had wages lesser than the natives by no more than 18 percent. The number of college graduates among immigrants who entered the United States between 1960 and 2000 was much higher than among natives (Borjas, 1999, 24). As Borjas shows, it is the professional skills of immigrants, their human capital, and not the gap between cultures, which mostly determines their success and explains the differences in the assimilation of various cohorts of immigrants (Borjas, 1999, 31). The new culture was not a serious impediment to the initiation of businesses. Koreans, Iranians and Russians surpassed the U.S. average in the number of self-employed people (Borjas, 1999, 72).

It is also remarkable that the rate of naturalization in the United States—an action that demands from immigrants the demonstration of familiarity with English and American law—of ethnic groups from countries with radically different cultures from that of the United States was even higher than for people from countries with more similar cultures. Indeed, whereas by 1979, 48 percent of the Asians who came to the United States in 1970 got citizenship, the same indicator for the people who came from countries with the Christian religion was much lower (from Europe only 19 percent, and South and Central America, 20 percent) (Portes and Rumbault, 1996, 118).

Several negative factors that hinder immigrants' adaptation are more important to the lives of immigrants than their ties or even their inability to internalize a new culture. Discrimination often occurred not because the majority of immigrants do not know the rules and values of a new country, or do not want to know them, but because of the hostility of native residents who see immigrant peoples as a drain on public coffers and as competition for their jobs (Tienda, 1999, 136).

People see immigrants as unfair competition for jobs and as leading to an increase in criminality and other dangers related to the demographic composition of the country and its culture, particularly if the ethnic enclaves expand significantly.[3] The hostility of a new country on the part of the population can be combined with the active encouragement of immigration by the government and businesses. This combination of positive and negative attitudes toward immigrants generates, as Portes and Rumbault contend, dissonant acculturation, which increases the gap between immigrants and the dominant culture, and leads to downward socialization (Portes and Rumbault, 1996, 251). In 1979, 36 percent of Mexican immigrants and 26 percent of Cuban immigrants declared that they felt discriminated against (Portes and Bach, 1985; see also Lee, 2003, 12).

It is particularly important that the second generation of immigrants, which evidently made progress in assimilation and in learning the language (86 percent compared to 34 percent for Mexicans; 99 percent against 42 percent for Cubans), values and rules of the new country, suffer from discrimination no less or even more (Cubans 29 percent, and Mexicans 65 percent) (Portes and Rumbault, 1996, 258–259).

Immigration and Crime: Nothing to Do with Cultural Assimilation

There is a well-accepted opinion that immigrants are more inclined to commit crimes because they come from another culture and have not internalized the values of the host country (Escobar, 1999; Lamm and Imhoff, 1985, 53; Lee, 2003, 15; Thomas et al., 1966, 197–198). Huntington (2004, 181) stated that now "the greatest threats to the societal security of nations come from immigration" (see also Albrecht, 1993; Hebberecht, 1997; Solivetti, 2005; Tournier, 1997). In 2003, 46 percent of Americans believed that the growing number of newcomers from other countries threatened national American customs and values.

The idea that the level of crime among immigrants should be ascribed to the degree of assimilation is very vulnerable.

In the United States, at the beginning of the twentieth century, the level of crime among all foreign-born people was 2 percent lower than among all native-born people, whereas the degree of criminality varied enormously among immigrants of different stock. Take 100 percent as an indicator of the number of criminals per 100,000 people born in America, the same indicator for immigrants from Switzerland would be 28 percent, from Ireland, 31 percent, from Spain, 660 percent, and from Serbia, 1,400 percent (see Traverso, 1964, 55; see also National Commission on Law Observance and Enforcement, 1931).

The developments in Western Europe in the last decades, particularly in relation to young immigrants and the second generation of immigrants, apparently worked in favor of "the assimilation concept of crime." Until the 1980s, the level of crime among immigrants and residents was almost the same, but in the 1980s–1990s the situation changed drastically and the crime rate for "non-nationals" rose to a level that surpassed nationals by 3–4 times. However, the immigration-begets-crime thesis was called into question by several researchers (Hagan and Palloni, 1999; Martinez, 2002; Martinez and Lee, 1998). Some of them even tried to prove the opposite view, that is, in some cases immigration stabilizes the region, as it happened in Miami after the mass Cuban immigration (Millman, 1997, 52–53; Portes and Stepick, 1993). Even if in some countries the rate of crime among certain groups of immigrants is higher than in the general population, the cause of this phenomenon should be ascribed to other factors not to the low level of assimilation. The city riots of the second and third generations of immigrants in France in October–November 2005 emerged not because the young people did not know the rules of order—the failure of assimilation—but because they were deeply discontented with their lives and their status in French society.

I suppose, as various data show, the correlation between the level of crime and immigration is not a universal law and the character of the correlation, its sign and intensity, depend on contextual factors. However, I object to the thesis that the differences in culture cause the high crime rate.

No culture or religion praises the violation of major crimes, such as murder, theft and rape, within its own community. The cases in which a culture praises cannibalism or damaging members of their own ethnic or cultural groups are extremely rare. As explained by several American progressive intellectuals in the beginning of the twentieth century, the values brought by immigrants to the new country were often complementary to traditional American values (Alexander and Smelser, 1999a, 4).

The role of religion in the explanation of crime is even more dubious than the famous attempts to resort to these factors for the explanation of labor ethics. There are no signs that the differences between Catholicism and Orthodox culture, or between Christian and Asian cultures, could be cited as a variable that explains the differences in the crime rate. Data from Laughlin's study in the beginning of the twentieth century, while supporting the thesis of the special role of Protestantism, dismisses the differences between other cultures and religions.

Indeed, immigrants from a Catholic and an Orthodox country—Spain (660) and Serbia (1,400)—had the highest crime rates, as shown earlier. The Christian Portugal was close to Shinto and Buddhist Japan (186 and 153), and Christian Bulgaria was close to Buddhist China (367 and 337) (for more about Laughlin's study, see Traverso, 1964, 55).

Without denying the role of the cultural factor in determining the level of crimes among immigrants, I suppose that the major explanation for order lies in the social situation in the new country. First, a major factor is the state of the labor market, which, when it expands for immigrants, helps diminish crime among young immigrants. It has been well established that most violators of law among immigrants are unemployed people. As Lane's study of homicide involvement of Italians and blacks in the first two decades of the twentieth century in Philadelphia showed, as soon as Italians were incorporated in the labor market their involvement in crime declined substantially; however, the blacks remained the same, which Lane explained as an effect of the discriminating labor market (Lane, 1989). Another powerful factor is the efficiency of law enforcement agencies.

There is probably only one factor of cultural character that can be cited as influencing the behavior of immigrants in a new country: that is, the respect for law and self-control, which, however, depends not only on culture or religion, but on the ability of the state in the old country to enforce law and in this way to make the observation of law a sort of internalized rule. If immigrants come from a society in which the fear of sanctions for the violation of law was low, they are indeed more prone to commit crimes in the new society, at least until they learn the rules of the new society.

THE WEAKNESS OF POSITIVE VALUES AS THE BASIS FOR ORDER

Moving from rules to "true" positive values, we see that even these values often cannot fully perform the role ascribed to them.

The Low Correlation of Values and Behavior

The support of positive values does not always imply the correspondent behavior. Stouffer (1955) was one of the first who cautioned against taking "the answers to any specific question as explicit predictions of action" (48). Reviewing their own results with this puzzle in mind, Prothro and Grigg (1960) suggested that the disjuncture between what people say and what they do should, in this instance, be regarded as a blessing, concluding that democracy may depend more on habits of behavior than agreement on principle. Since then many researchers continued to point to the loose relations between values and attitudes, on one hand, and behavior on the other (see the survey of the studies on this issue in Petty and Wegener, 1998, 368–369; see also Rokeach, 1973; Williams, 1979).

The Conflict between the Ideological and Pragmatic Functions of Values

Another limitation of social values as the regulator of behavior lies in the fact that values perform two functions: one ideological, the other pragmatic. In performing its first function, social values are used by people only to demonstrate their loyalty to the dominant social order. In its second function, values also influence people's material behavior.

People tend to accept values in the abstract form when they perform an ideological function but reject them in a more specific, pragmatic form. The low predictability of abstract values (though they are exactly the major subject of most studies about the role of values in maintaining social order) has been noted, though reluctantly, by strong advocates of the values approach to the analysis of society (see Inglehart, 1997, 51).

The case of the Soviet society is quite instructive. Many studies show that until the end of the Soviet system, the Russians believed in the superiority of public property over private property. More than half of them preserved this belief even ten years later. However, when the Russians moved from supporting abstract values as public property to specific conditions their attitudes changed radically. The Soviet people easily combined this respect for public property at the abstract level with the regular pilfering of goods from factories and offices when they felt they could escape punishment (Shipler, 1983; Shlapentokh, 1989, 90). Moscow sociologist Alexander Grechin explored the attitudes of Moscow workers to various work violations. Asked about pilfering at work, only 17 percent (despite the highly loaded character of the questions) felt violators should be punished. The vast majority (79 percent) openly refused to condemn this act, and 3 percent even approved of the theft (Grechin, 1983, 124).

The Mutual Conflicts of Values

One of the reasons why social order cannot rely on the inside feelings of people and internalized values lies in the deep conflict between these values. The most fundamental values, even those in the Ten Commandments, are often in conflict. This is true of terminal values (or goal values) as well as instrumental values. Such terminal values in American society, such as material success and independence, family and career, individualism and patriotism, are in fierce conflict with each other. The same is true about many instrumental values.

Honesty and compassion, courage and rationality, along with many others are in permanent conflict. Deviant behavior is often the result of the victory of one value over the other. Only those scholars with such unconditional beliefs in reason, such as Amartya Sen (2002), can believe that "values and priorities" are exposed to "reasonable scrutiny" by the average human being. As Alan Ryan, Sen's critic, notes, "even the much diluted principle that a person's 'values' or 'ultimate preferences' must be consistent over time may be wrong." He continues, "Should we not learn from experience and revise our values and preferences in the light of that experience?" (Ryan, 2003). Leon Festinger's concept of cognitive dissonance has a very limited area of application. The eclectic mind of most people and their tendencies to compartmentalize mutually exclusive emotions, beliefs and values is confirmed by many studies (Converse, 1964). John Barth vividly described this in his brilliant novel *The End of the Road.*

The conflict of values rages in environments where pressure from above is strong and many social values imposed from above are incompatible with individual terminal values. Only those who believe unconditionally in the rational behavior of human beings (as Sen does) could dare to ignore the conflict of values.

Values for Me and Values for Others: Conformity in Values but not in Behavior

A special case that shows the weakness of values as a basis for social order lies in the distinction between "values for me" and "values for others." To use Kiesler and Kiesler's terminology (1969), it is possible to single out four combinations of compliance in behavior and acceptance of the dominant values: (1) compliance in behavior and private acceptance of values; (2) compliance in behavior and private rejection of values; (3) refusal to comply in behavior and private acceptance of values; (4) refusal to comply and private rejection of values. Until now, sociologists have devoted most of their attention to the first (i.e., studies of conformity) and the fourth (i.e., studies of social deviance) combinations. Type two has attracted little interest. The third type has not been considered viable and has been practically ignored by sociologists (Shlapentokh, 1982).

The third type, however, plays an extremely important role in social life. In some ways, this type can also be described as the case when people make a distinction between two types of values: "values for me" and "values for others." The ideological function of values is exactly related to values for others, which influences human behavior often in a very restrained way. Many people in various societies with seemingly strong beliefs in the dominant values expect others, but not themselves, to behave according to them. It can be contended that official values are regarded by many people as "gala values," as values that are not for them personally, but as values for others. People also expect others, not themselves, to be coherent in their views. In many societies, people profess their devotion to their country without being ready to make any sacrifices for the country

As a matter of fact, it was young Montesquieu, in *The Persian Letters*, who described in detail this sort of phenomenon. The hero of this piece, Uzbek, a highly educated person, is a great admirer of Western moral principles, culture, science and pluralism. At the same time, in his own country he maintains a harem of women, which he has violently punished if they trespass his draconian rules. In no way does the author suggest that Uzbek is a hypocritical person; he simply divided his mind into two different sections, each controlling its own sphere of thinking and behavior.

In Soviet society, I discovered that many citizens were sincerely supportive of the various official values and expected that their countrymen would behave accordingly. Patriotism, along with the duty to choose work that is socially useful, was among those Soviet values that were seemingly internalized by most Russians Yet, they did not link these values to their own behavior. Several sociological data substantiate this thesis.

Many empirical sociological studies in the USSR since the late 1950s found that in practice Soviet people often expected other people to choose a job that was important for society, but for themselves preferred a job that was more satisfying to their individual values.

Another example is related to labor ethics. There is little doubt that the majority of Soviet workers sincerely shared in the official glorification of labor. A study conducted by sociologists at the Institute of Sociological Research in 1975–76 showed that no less than 95 percent of all workers in four large cities in the Soviet Union (Ivanovo, Moscow, Perm, Rostov) supported such statements as "labor is one of the most important human needs and a basis for man's self-esteem," or "labor is the major source of well-being of the Motherland and of each citizen" (Changli, 1978).

However, the studies of labor turnover were the first to find a discrepancy. They showed clearly that workers left their jobs mainly for highly personal motives and in absolute disregard of official values, which treated turnover as an antisocial phenomenon. In one study, 12 percent of the job-leavers declared that they had quit because they were simply dissatisfied with their wages; 10 percent claimed inadequate housing conditions; 9 percent complained about their profession; and 7 percent referred to an absence of facilities for their children (Bliakhman et al., 1965). The results of these studies on the causes of turnover were received with amazement both by the intelligentsia (including specialists in the social sciences) and by the elite. Here was empirical evidence that a number of Soviet workers put their own personal interests above the common good, and above the ultimate goals of society.

In a study conducted in the mid-1970s on the role of the mass media in the life of rural residents in the USSR, I obtained convincing evidence to support this hypothesis. It was established that people ranked reading books—an activity highly touted by official culture—first among all leisure-time activities; 51 percent of respondents named it as their preferred activity; 27 percent of the respondents preferred television. At the same time, their actual behavior was quite different: 75 percent of the respondents watched television every day, whereas only 25 percent of them read books with the same regularity. The hypothesis that respondents were insincere with sociologists was rejected because a considerable number (72 percent) acknowledged that, in the last 5–10 years, they were reading less than before. They were willing to recognize that their behavior was not in compliance with the dominant view that reading is a more valuable activity than watching television, a view that they seemingly shared. What is more, answering a question about the importance of reading for their children's future, 77 percent of all respondents declared their allegiance to the dominant value.

The phenomenon, "values for me and values for others," can be found in America as well. Indeed, most Americans evidently enjoy the idea that others will observe core American values, but not necessarily them personally. Americans see tolerance as one of the most important human virtues. It takes a leading place in the list of qualities that children should be encouraged to learn at home, according to the prestigious World Values Survey, carried out by the University of Michigan in the late 1990s. Three-quarters of Americans consider teaching tolerance as a main goal in the education of their children (compared to 49 percent who point to hard work and 29 percent to thrift; Inglehart, 1997).

However, it would be wrong to exaggerate the level of tolerance in various segments of American society. As Ronald Kinder wrote, the American public seems more intolerant in its opinions than in its activities. Americans believe that objectionable groups should be silenced, but very often they do not seem to act on this belief (Kinder, 1983).

Although almost all Americans praise the idea of being tolerant of differing opinions, many of them demand it from others but not from themselves. Several cases from American life seemingly support the thesis advanced by McClosky and Brill (1983), who argued that tolerance cuts deeply against the human grain. Intolerance, they say, is natural, since people "distrust what they do not understand and cannot control" and need to "feel safe against the terrors of the unknown" (McClosky and Brill, 1983, 13–14).

Take, for instance, the American academy in the early 2000s. Sociological data seemingly bolster the dogma that was born in the times of Plato and Aristotle and strengthened by the age of Enlightenment that with the increase of knowledge people become more and more tolerant. Indeed, in each study, including the World Values Survey, with the rise of education, people value tolerance more and more. Several researchers support this view. Hyman and Wright concluded that education produces "large, lasting and diverse good effects on values" (1979, 61; see McClosky and Brill, 1983; Nunn et al., 1978; Stouffer, 1955). This view is supported without reservation by Donald Kinder who argued that general education enhances tolerance. Public opinion on matters of free speech and due process provides another case for the benefits of education, which supports the work of Hyman and Wright (1979; see Kinder, 1983). Several scholars, to take only the works of the 1960s–1980s, have supported this view, including Greely and Sheatsley (1971; 1974), Lipset (1981) and many others (see Condran, 1979; Converse, 1964; Hyman and Sheatsley, 1964; Jackman and Muha, 1984; Martire and Clark, 1982; Nunn et al., 1978; Prothro and Grigg, 1960; Quinley and Glock, 1979; Selznick and Steinberg, 1969; Stouffer, 1955).

However, as Jackman and Muha showed, using convincing empirical materials, this thesis is more wrong than right. Of 43 items in the survey administered by the Survey Research Center of the University of Michigan in 1975, which measured intergroup relations, only three of the items bear clear and positive relations to education (Jackman and Muha, 1984, 751–769). Jackman (1978) also argued that education exposes people to a diversity of ideas, but it does not always rank their significance. Hence, the well educated are more familiar with democratic principles, but their priorities have not been sufficiently reshaped to place those principles systematically ahead of other principles that they have learned. Merelman (1980) has argued that "high schools make poor nurseries for the propagation of democratic values." The conflict between egalitarian norms in American society and the school's need for order, coupled with the confusion of values and facts in social classes limits the transmission of democratic values in American schools. As a result, "democratic values rarely become deeply rooted within students' minds" (Merelman, 1980, 317–332). Alan Abramovitz joined this debate from another angle, even if his conclusion was the same. The higher people's education, the higher is their involvement in ideological debates, which has all types of consequences (see Abramovitz and Segal, 1992; see also Brooks, 2004b).

There is no doubt that the ideological function of values, when they do not influence people's behavior, still perform an important role. Even the superficial allegiance to patriotism, a low cost for those who do not go further than praising himself or herself as a committed patriot, is much better for society than a proclamation of hostility toward it.

VALUES WITH AMBIVALENT EFFECTS ON ORDER

Social order is threatened not only by the obvious negative social values, such as intolerance or even support of violence, corruption, racism, reckless driving and drunkenness (I discuss these values later), but also by values that have a good reputation. There are several values that can affect order in different ways. They can cement order, but they can also beget tension and conflicts, which sometimes destroy order.

Status Values

Among such values are status values. These values reflect the desire of the individual to enhance his or her status in the family, in the groups to which he or she belongs, to his or her society and also in the world. The status value that is strongly connected with the social, national and religious self-identity of human beings influences human behavior.[4] This variable is also close to another value that describes the eagerness of people to be "respected" in their environment (as well as outside it) and particularly by the bureaucracy (see Sennett, 2004). The importance of this value in society was described by several authors (see Oakeshott, 1975; Wrong, 1994, 77–79).

The status variable is deeply intertwined with competition and human striving for achievement and success, and for maintaining one's "honor"—the factors that Hobbes saw as a powerful source of conflict. In Leviathan, he exclaimed that "obscurity is dishonorable" (1996, 59–62). Recognizing both the constructive and destructive character of striving for high status in society, James Henslin refers to Merton's "the strain theory," which describes the conflict between cultural goals and institutionalized means that "may," as Henslin cautiously warns, "motivate people to take a deviant path" (Henslin, 2004, 148).

The status value connected to the self-identity of human beings is so strong and so widespread that it seems to have at least some biological roots. The deeply rooted desire to be higher or at least not lower than others is an extremely powerful value whose role can be discovered in many different milieus. For the first time in history, vanity was described with clarity by such French writers as La Rochefoucauld and Jean de la Bruyere in the seventeenth century. It was Rousseau who, as nobody else in history, considered vanity and seeking prestige ("amour proper") a major source of calamities in the world (see *Discourse on Inequality*, 1992, 38; see also Shklar, 1988, 264–265; Wrong, 1994, 95–97).

The same phenomenon occurred in such miserable milieu as the Gulag or Nazi concentration camps, as can be seen from the numerous memoirs of its inmates who almost unanimously insist that those inmates who lost the feeling of self-respect and dignity were the first to perish (Shalamov, 1981; Solzhenitsyn, 1975).

Describing the obsession with social status and the anxiety of being below or behind in status, Alain de Botton, a famous British author, thinks that "the predominant impulse behind our desire to rise in the social hierarchy may be rooted not so much in the material goods that can accrue or the power which we can wield as in the amount of love we stand to receive as a consequence of high status" (2004). With some empirical data, another British author, epidemiologist Michael Marmot (2004), insists that the failed expectations of status have a serious deleterious impact on people's longevity. Another author, Peter Whybrow, a psychiatrist (see his *American Mania*, 2005), contended that Americans' drive for success leads to a decline in social constraints.

As a matter of fact, the status variable, or rather the cluster of various types of statuses (in the family, in intragroups, in intergroups, in society and in the world) determines to a great degree the attitudes of people, especially the most active, energetic and ambitious people, toward several instrumental values that can maximize the status variable. Education, marriage, wealth, political and ideological affiliations are only a few of the values that can enhance or diminish the level of status variables.

The various types of patriotism, local or national, as well as the pride in the school from which the individual graduated, the pride of belonging to a company, to a sports team or to a criminal gang are all manifestations of the individual's desire to heighten his or her place in society. The literature across nations describes the role of prestige seeking and vanity in the most vivid way. Thackeray's *Vanity Fair* is only one of numerous examples.

The status value can be a powerful unifying factor of a nation or a group. The feelings of superiority as well as of inferiority can help mobilize people to defend their own country or bring order in society. At the same time, the impact of the status value can play a very negative role that undermines order in society. Without the restraint of law, the passion for high or the same status can shatter the fundamentals of society, as it has happened several times in history: for instance, in the case of ethnic, religious or civil wars, which have claimed millions of victims. Indeed, the cluster of status values is at the root of xenophobia, rabid nationalism, class hatred and several other feelings that all have social envy as a component. Most ethnic conflicts occurred inside national states. In the postwar period (until 1989), they led to 80 percent of all deaths (Russett and Starr, 1989, 171). Many internal ethnic conflicts are fueled not so much by the struggle for material resources, but by the ability of ethnic elites to use national pride and the desire for prestige and revenge (Williams, 1994).

Furthermore, the fealty of people to their national traditions, religion, style of life, even clothes and food to a great extent has to be attributed to the willingness of people to preserve their national and religious identity as a challenge to others, and as a demonstration of their uniqueness and their superiority over others (the "barbarians" or "infidels").

Social Envy

Envy has different objects: neighbors, friends and colleagues, people belonging to the same group or other social, ethnic groups and people and institutions in other societies. In most cases, envy is a destructive force that pushes people toward antisocial behavior. The public, particularly in societies influenced by political correctness and high respect for everybody, skirts the issue as something "mean," and as a source of denigration not only of the individual, but also of big groups of the population. Social scientists tend to avoid the concept of envy in their analysis of social problems. You will not find this value in the sociological textbooks that presumably describe the major impetuses in social life or in the political science textbooks that help us understand the motivation of politicians and voters. Only social psychologists are less afraid to talk about envy; they talk about "affective faculties." However, the two volumes of the *Handbook of Social Psychology* (1998) almost totally ignored this issue.[5] For many years, social psychologists shied away from negative interpersonal emotions.

The role of envy as a source of negative values in social life is difficult to overestimate. The predisposition of envy is deeply ingrained in the human mind. The behavior of people, groups and even nations is often influenced by envy. Privately, most people recognize its important role in their lives, but they generally avoid debates on this "mean" feeling. However, people have elaborated several rules in order to avoid making the individual an object of envy or forestall as much as possible the emergence of this feeling in the same individual. Take, for instance, the iron rule in colleges that prohibits the access of students to the grades of their peers: on billboards you can find grades linked only to a student number, not a name. The American custom of not revealing one's income even to good friends has the same origin.

Meanwhile, all religions talk about the impact of envy on human behavior. The ancient Greeks ascribed envy even to their gods. Envy as one of the seven deadly sins (it holds the fourth place) was discussed in detail by religious philosophers such as Thomas Aquinas from the thirteenth century in his *Summa Theologica*. Many great minds in the past from Homer and Roman Virgules to Dante, Shakespeare in *Othello* and *Julius Caesar* and Pushkin in *Mozart and Salieri* talked about envy as one of the most powerful motives for people.[6] The famous British philosopher Bertrand Russell talked about the tendency of envious people to direct their frustration and hatred against the more powerful or prosperous (Russell, 1930, 82). Other authors who are famous for their works on envy include Herman Melville (*Billy Budd*, 1948), Soviet writer Yuri Olesha (*Envy*, 1975) and more recently, the shrewd observer of American life Tom Wolfe (*The Bonfire of the Vanities*, 1987; *A Man in Full*, 1998; and *I Am Charlotte Simmons*, 2004).[7]

Envy has a universally negative meaning and is almost never acknowledged by those who bear it.[8] Because of the extremely bad reputation of envy in all cultures, the bearers of envy never acknowledge its existence and always try to substitute it with decent motives such as injustice or unfairness, the "bad" behavior of the object of envy, the individual or the nation.[9] Foreigners who brim with envy of American achievements have never confessed to having these mean feelings, constructing instead various explanations for their anti-Americanism, among which envy is certainly absent.

It would be wrong to consider envy as a purely negative phenomenon. In some cases, envy plays a constructive role: it pushes people to greater achievements. In this case, social comparison strengthens the stimulus for achievement. This was understood by the ancient Greeks who ascribed to Themistocles, a famous Athenian commander, the envy of Miltiades, the victor of Marathon (490 B.C.), as the major stimuli for his greatest exploits, and first of all the naval victory of Salamis over the Persian fleet ten years later.

However, in general, envy creates permanent discontent with respect to the object of envy and diminishes the quality of life of individuals and groups. Feelings of inferiority make up an important component of envy, which is usually combined with such key elements of envy as ill will, or hatred of the object of envy. This hatred generated by envy is particularly intense if people, groups or even nations are unable for various reasons to stay on par with the object of envy, even if it is the result not so much of so-called objective conditions but simply of the refusal of the subject of envy to change his or her life and work hard. In this case, the subject of envy wishes mishaps on the object of envy. Whereas constructive envy pushes people to imitate the objects of their envy (people or nations), destructive envy is usually based on feelings of hopelessness and can even push people to destroy the object of their envy. Another important implication of deconstructive envy is its ability to undermine perceptions of reality and to foster irrational behavior, that is, behavior that goes against the long-term interests of individuals, groups or even nations.

CONCLUSION

The tendency to exaggerate the role of the values mechanism as the basis of social order is based on the disregard of several of its weaknesses. First, what researchers consider internalized values are in fact often the rules that people follow because of the fear of being punished for violating them. People often rationalize their behavior, as though it is dictated by their values. In the process of socialization, people learn formal rules not values, which have a moral dimension. The dominance of rules over values is evident in the first generation of immigrants' adaptation to their new countries.

The role of values, as a basis of order, is limited also because quite often the correlation between values and behavior is quite low. The next obstacle to the high influence of values on behavior is the strong conflict between values. Many values are considered by people as obliging "others" but not themselves—the phenomenon of "values for me and values for others." Some values, even if they have been internalized, have an ambivalent impact on social order. This is true about the cluster of status values. The obsession with social status can have a very destructive effect on the social fabric. Social envy often also exerts a negative impact on social relations.

CHAPTER 4

Aggressive Negative Values

THE ROLE OF NEGATIVE VALUES IN SOCIAL LIFE

The analysis of society would be deeply flawed if we assumed that only "good," positive values influenced human behavior. This is indeed a major problem in values studies that assume all values play a positive role in society. Parsons, Rokeach, Williams and many other scholars who use the term values, mean explicitly or implicitly that values are only positive, normative or desirable standards (Parsons, 1951; Rokeach, 1973; Williams, 1968; 1979). Merton, in his theory of anomy, makes a distinction between two types of values: those accepted and those not accepted by society. But for him negative values, which are shared by his innovators, rebels and retreatists, emerge only in the process of the breakdown in the cultural structure, but not as a normal part of social life (Merton, 1949, 162).

I suppose that values play the role as not only positive standards that are useful for society (Parsons's main theme), but also as negative standards. Only a few social scientists, such as Collingwood in his *New Leviathan* (1942, 183), wrote about "negative elements" in value systems, which impact social life and obstruct order in society. It was Freud who insisted that love and hatred for the same object is an essential feature of emotional life, as in the coexistence of Eros and Thanatos, as reflected in unfettered sexual desire and the urge toward violence. Culture can only partially repress the destructive tendencies of human beings, and without the fear of sanctions society can hardly function, even when the positive values are deeply embedded in the mind of the majority of the population.

Additional support for the importance of negative values in human life comes from the liberal theologian Reinhold Niebuhr. In his famous books, including *Moral Man and Immoral Society* (1932) and *The Children of Light and the Children of Darkness* (1944), Niebuhr, in the words of Arthur Schlesinger Jr., "emphasized the mixed and ambivalent character of human nature—creative impulses matched by destructive impulses, regard for others overruled by excessive self-regard, the will to power, the individual under constant temptation to play God to history." Schlesinger points out how Niebuhr's perception of human beings was deeply hostile to his generation, which was inclined "to believe in human innocence and even in human perfectibility." Schlesinger, not without irony, cited Andrew Carnegie, the famous industrialist and philanthropist of the early twentieth century, who declared: "Nor is there any conceivable end to his march to perfection." Schlesinger also cited another believer in the perfection of human nature, Charles E. Merriam of the University of Chicago, the dean of American political scientists, who wrote in *The New Democracy and the New Despotism*: "There is a constant trend in human affairs toward the perfectibility of mankind. This was plainly stated at the time of the French Revolution and has been reasserted ever since that time, and with increasing plausibility" (Schlesinger, 2005, 12–13).

Whatever the judgment of Niebuhr's religion—the idea of original sin—as Schlesinger suggests, he was much more realistic in his understanding of society than his opponents. It is quite evident that negative values, such as hatred of foreigners or even some groups of the population inside the country, can be helpful for the maintenance of the regime and the social order connected to the regime. In this case, we are talking about a "negative ideology" that is directed against the "enemy of the nation." This ideology has played an enormous role in human history. It was used to maintain the regime and social order, as in the case of the Soviet ideology, with its focus on class hatred and antagonism toward capitalist countries.

However, in this book, I concentrate only on those negative values that undermine social order, not support it.[1] Indeed, the values that justify and even commend drunkenness, drug addiction, violence, promiscuity, rudeness and anti-intellectualism are only a small part of a long list of values that play key roles in the value systems of a big part of the population in any society. Behavior based on negative values prospers in America. Sixty five percent of American adults were concerned about drug use in the country, according to a Gallup Poll conducted on April 5, 2005. A Gallup Youth Survey reports that 17 percent of teenagers (age 13 to 17) were willing to admit that "they have on occasion used alcohol"; 13 percent say that they "tried marijuana," and 5 percent "smoked cigarettes in the past week" (Gallup, 2005c).

Let us discuss a few examples of the mass violations of law that were publicized in 2005. A special case that illustrates the role of negative values in American society is the mass fraud in the Medicaid and Medicare programs. In New York, the Medicaid program pays more than a million claims a day and feeds, as a *New York Times* author pointed out, a $44.5 billion river of checks (July 20, 2005). Meanwhile this program, according to an editorial in the same newspaper, became "a honey pot for unscrupulous practitioners." The stealing of taxpayers' money in these systems is overwhelming with the participation of doctors, social workers and, of course, patients who have very little compunctions about the defrauding of the federal and state administrations. The level of control over fraud is quite low, particularly in New York. However, even with the understaffed offices responsible for controlling fraud, the fraud unit in this city was able to recover from overpayment $62.5 million in 2004 and $40 million in 2003. The single way to diminish fraud in the Medicaid and Medicare systems is, according to all experts, to increase the level of control and inculcate fear of sanctions in the minds of all those who can abuse the rules (Luo and Levy, 2005; *New York Times*, July 20, 2005b).

Among other developments in 2005, it is possible to mention the investigation of corruption in Chicago, which indeed embraced all levels of local authorities, from the office of Mayor Richard Daley and down. Eight members of Daley's Cabinet resigned or have been fired since May. Federal authorities investigated City Hall for months, first examining bribes traded for jobs in a contract-hauling program and most recently looking into allegations of fraud in the city's hiring practices (*New York Times*, March 9, 2005a).

Almost at the same time, federal investigators were studying the criminal corruption of George Ryan, the former governor of Illinois. Mr. Ryan faced 22 counts of racketeering, mail and tax fraud and lying to federal agents. Federal prosecutors contend that Mr. Ryan and his relatives received cash, luxury vacations and other gifts worth at least $167,000 in exchange for state contracts and political favors in the dozen years in which he was governor or secretary of state (Wilgoren, 2005).

There is not much information about the attitudes of people toward negative values in Russia as well as in other countries. However, even with what is available, it can be shown that there has been an acceptance of negative values in Russian society. More than half of the respondents in various surveys supported the idea that "Russia is only for Russians" (VTSIOM-A, 2002a). One half of the Russians did not hesitate to tell interviewers in December 2003 that it is not necessary for citizens to pay taxes, and endorse "the use of any opportunity to evade them." One-quarter of the Russians endorsed the evasion of taxes by businesses (VTSIOM-A, 2003b); 91 percent of the Russians are for the sale of beer to teenagers aged 14 to 15 (VTSIOM-A, 2004; 2002b; see VTSIOM-A, 2003a). One quarter of the Russians, in October 2004, were against the freedom of speech (Levada-zentr, 2004).

There are also many data showing how Russians espouse negative values with their behavior. Drunkenness is considered one of the Russian plagues. According to a recent study, no less than one-third of all deaths in the country, three-quarters of all murders and almost one-half of all external causes of death can be ascribed to alcohol (Nemtsov, 2001; 2003). In the last ten years, the role of alcohol as the cause of death increased from 320 per 100,000 people in 1990 to 478 in 2001 (Nemtsov, 2003). It is also noticeable that the number of Russians who died from alcohol poisoning increased from 1999 to 2003 by almost one-third (from 30 thousand to 40.6 thousand) (see Shestoperova, 2005). In Russia alcoholism accounts for one-half of all divorces (Dolgova, 2003; Oleinik, 2003).

XENOPHOBIC VALUES

One of the most popular negative values in almost every society is the hostility to other nations and ethnic or religious minorities. Mutual ethnic and racial animosity is a source of major disturbances in most societies. Let us take examples from only the last four decades.

Even in America, one of the most tolerant nations in the world, a considerable number of people cherish the values that suppose their superiority over various racial and ethnic groups. Only 17 percent of American teens said that they are friends with people from other racial or ethnic groups (Gallup, 2004b). Almost one-quarter of Americans said in 2004 that when "they come into contact with different races" they "always, frequently or occasionally experience unpleasant thoughts or emotions because of their race" (Gallup, 2004c). In 2003, only 34 percent of blacks said that they had been discriminated against either "never" or "less than once in a year" (Gallup, 2003a). Fifty seven percent of Americans said that "anti-Semitism" is "a very serious" or "somewhat serious" problem in the country (Gallup, 2003b).

The degree of xenophobia in Russia is higher than in the United States. Thirty two percent of the Russians in 2004 reported that they "experience irritation" when in the presence of national minorities in their region; 63 percent would approve bans on the arrival to their regions of "some ethnic groups"; 44 percent would approve deportation from their region (Fund of Public Opinion, 2004c). According to another source, only 48 percent of the Russians condemned those who called the Russians to fight non-Russians (Levada-zentr, 2004b).

The adherence to xenophobic values not only influences individual behavior in a "peaceful way" with open hostility, hate speeches and discrimination of "others," but quite often stimulates violence on a greater scale.

The race riots in the United States in 1968 and 1973 caused chaos and disorder. The ethnic conflicts in Russia and in the former Soviet republics after 1991, which were accompanied by collective violence, took hundreds of thousands of lives. It is even truer about the former Yugoslavia, India and, of course, Africa in the 1990s when the number of victims of ethnic conflict numbered in the hundreds of thousands (see Brubaker and Laiten, 1968; Horowitz, 1985; Montville, 1990; Olzak, 1992).

The high level of ethnic and racial animosity definitely influenced the genuine adherence to various social values that were seemingly shared by the people. Is it possible to believe a committed racist is an admirer of justice, tolerance, respect for law and other values that are considered the basis for social order?

It is not surprising that in any civilized society the state tends to adopt laws that make various racial and ethnic prejudices punishable. Even more active is a civil society that condemns and reprimands bigotry in one or another ways. The majority of people in such countries favors the fears of chauvinists and racists to vent their hatred against minorities.

Asocial and Pro-Social Groups in Heterogeneous and Homogeneous Societies

One of the most powerful arguments in favor of the major role of "negative," or "antisocial" values is the intensity of antisocial behavior and the disregard of social norms and rules, without speaking about serious crimes. Even in countries with the most effective law enforcement agencies, the number of officially registered crimes is much lower than the number of crimes committed. This is particularly true in the case of white-collar crime and corruption.

In fact, antisocial behavior has attracted the attention of social psychologists and criminologists (see, for instance, Lykken, 1995; Shiraev and Levy, 2004).

Shiraev and Levy offer the following description of "anti-social personality disorder," which is typical for people who are dangerous to social order:

> Failure to conform to social norms with respect to lawful behaviors as indicated by repeatedly performing acts that are grounds for arrest, deceitfulness, as indicated by repeated lying, use of aliases, or conning others for personal profit or pleasure, impulsivity or failure to plan ahead, irritability and aggressiveness, as indicated by repeated physical fights or assaults, reckless disregard for safety of self or others, consistent irresponsibility, as indicated by repeated failure to sustain consistent work behavior or honor financial obligations, lack of remorse, as indicated by being indifferent to or rationalizing having hurt, mistreated, or stolen from another. (Shiraev and Levy, 2004, 120)

However, Lykken, Shiraev and Levy approach antisocial behavior in a dychotomic way, as if people who suffer from the antisocial syndrome and people who do not suffer from it are separated by an iron curtain. In fact, most people indeed are not inclined to behave in antisocial ways in all cases. They look absolutely "normal" and formally have nothing to do with the "syndrome." However, they share several negative values and have the tendency to commit some antisocial acts quite often.

American society contains a big chunk of the population that, at each given moment, is deeply at odds with the law. In 1998, about 31 million crimes were performed in the country. Each year, 11 million Americans are arrested, including 400 thousand juveniles. Each fifth American has contact with the police each year as a victim or as an offender. In the beginning of the twenty-first century, 2.1 million Americans were in jail (Garland, 2001; Shiraev and Levy, 209, 211, 214). At the same time, many Americans are engaged systematically in relatively minor violations of the law, without speaking of the consumption of drugs and tax evasion, or the theft of high-value portable goods (Garland, 2001).

A separate group of people who systematically challenge values and laws is composed first of all by de-socialized lumpen elements. It consists of people who have lost their jobs (or never had one), families and housing for various reasons a long time ago. This class includes people who are accustomed to violence (in the family, on the streets or in war) and who live in a subculture of violence, the level of which varies from country to country (Archer, 1994; Archer and Gartner, 1984). The asocial class also includes people with psychological disorders and criminal orientations, some of them genetically inherited and of course all others with weak self-control. There are people who refuse to live by the norms of society and in some ways conscientiously choose criminal careers (DeBlois and Stewart, 1980). The activity of many members of the first two groups and all members of the third and fourth groups make almost ridiculous the dogma about internalized social values as the basis of social order.[2]

In other words, the issue here is about the degree of sociability, or in inverse terms, "unsociability," "dysfunctionalism", "antisocial behavior," or even "antisocial society," a term often used in England in the last few years.[3] Meanwhile, antisocial behavior, the violation of simple rules of decent behavior, along with pure criminal behavior, became a leading problem in many countries, including those that were considered as "the most civilized," such as Great Britain. Britons even gave a special term to people with "pathological criminality," naming them "chav." According to an American journalist, they, "whether rich or poor, tend to favor gaudy jewelry and expensive-but-tacky clothes with big logos and to behave in a way that others find coarse or obnoxious," such as "outrageous spending sprees, drunken brawls, inappropriate public displays of affection, screaming matches with loved ones in bars, destruction of property, late-night stumbling and/or vomiting" (Lyall, 2005).

The antisocial behavior in England, as suggested by Frank Field, a member of parliament, in his book *The Politics of Behavior* (2003), is so important that the differences in the behavior of people are now more significant than class distinction. Tony Blair, the British prime minister, wrote in *The Observer* in 2002, "Many neighborhoods became marked by vandalism, violent crimes and the loss of civility. The basic recognition of the mutuality of duty and reciprocity of respect on which civil society depends appeared lost" (Lyall, 2004).

THE BEHAVIOR OF PEOPLE OUTSIDE THEIR COMMUNITY OR TEMPORARILY OUTSIDE OF CONTROL

Along with the asocial behavior of many people inside their country, the case of the behavior of people outside their community demonstrates a good example that goes against the belief in the magic role of internalized values. People often change their behavior radically when they leave their families, their communities and jobs.

Inside the Country

A special case can be seen in the behavior of college students when they feel free from the supervision of their parents, neighbors and school teachers. Tom Wolfe vividly describes this phenomenon in *I Am Charlotte Simmons* (2004, 157). The hero of this novel was stupefied by what she, as a freshman, saw in her prestigious Dupont University—heavy drinking and promiscuous behavior in the first place. As a girl from a lower-class religious family in a small settlement in North Caroline, Charlotte called her old school friend. Laurie, a very tactful girl, immediately understood the problem. She answered her friend cautiously, suggesting that she exploit this opportunity: "I guess what I really mean is college is like this four-year period you have when you can try anything and *everything* and if it goes wrong, there are no consequences. You know what I mean? Nobody's keeping score. You can do things that if you tried them before you got to college, your family would be crying and pulling their hair out and giving you these now-see-what-you've-gone-and-done looks? And everybody in Sparta would be clucking and fuming and having a ball talking behind your back about it? And if you tried these things after you left college and you're working, everybody's gonna fucking blow a fuse . . ."

Many Americans radically change their behavior if they feel that their illicit behavior will go unpunished. The boisterous behavior of American students in Florida during their spring breaks is quite notorious, as well as the miraculous change in the conduct of many respectable scholars when they travel far from their universities and families. Students who go abroad often behave even nastier. As the chief operating officer with the Institute for Shipboard Education noted, students "assume that they are immune to law abroad." A few other examples from 2000–04 include the following: in Amsterdam, students used their dorm-room windows to dispose of their trash, raining it down on those who passed by. In Vietnam, a group of American students was hauled off to jail after getting drunk and jumping off a bridge into the river (see Winter, 2004).

In an analysis of the 1977 blackout in New York City, researchers at the York State Research Psychiatric Institute concluded that small-time criminals began the looting, but that "within two hours," the researchers wrote, "it became apparent that the situation was not going to end quickly, and thousands of otherwise law-abiding citizens joined in what was to become the largest collective theft in history" (see Carey, 2005b). The developments in September 2005 in the aftermath of hurricane Katrina also brought up the issue of how a sudden change in behavior can take place for a tiny but dangerous part of the population, which went berserk in looting and raping during the few days when police did not sustain order in New Orleans and particularly in shelters (see Rich, Frank, 2005).

Outside Their Country

People change their behavior even more radically when they leave their countries. British writers, from Kipling to Orwell, described how British gentlemen radically changed their behavior in the colonies.

The behavior of tourists outside their countries is another interesting example. In 2003, the behavior of British tourists in Greek resorts became international events and created complications in Greek–British relations. Having arrived for their vacations, the tourists went berserk and began to organize on the public beaches for sexual orgies, including public competitions in sexual prowess. The thin fortitude of seemingly internalized values is revealed when people temporarily leave the places where they live under informal and formal control.

However, the developments in Iraq in 2003–04 provide the most convincing case in favor of the abovementioned thesis. Several American and British soldiers and officers indulged in the torturing of Iraqis in the cruelest ways. Many of them were brought to court as defendants. The soldiers' obedience to the commanders who expected to get useful information from the prisons probably played a role, and the lawyers of the defendants at the military courts referred to obedience as the major exculpating argument. However, the character of the torturing was so heinous that each person implicated in the process had plenty of opportunities to take part in such actions, which were in jarring contrast to the dozens of values that supposedly made up the conscience of these people. As Defense Secretary Donald Rumsfeld said at the Senate hearings in May 2004, these few soldiers have betrayed our values (Schmitt, 2004). General Ricardo Sanches, a leading military commander in Iraq, noted in connection with these nasty developments that about 10 percent of his soldiers could be criminals and that "the only reason they manage to stay in line is because of the training and the discipline and the leadership that is provided by our institution." He continued, "And if you don't provide them with that, they'll walk away, and revert to that instinct of being criminals" (see Burns, 2004). The media published detailed information about the people prosecuted for crimes. Several of them look like "typical" American men and women. As pictures and other materials showed, the defendants really got satisfaction, almost sadistic pleasure, in resorting to the ugliest forms of sexual torment of the prisoners.

THE CRIMINAL AND THE CORPORATIVE SECTORS: THE SUPPORTERS OF NEGATIVE VALUES

The role of negative values is linked to the segmented character of societies. Indeed, in each society there are segments that in one or another way confront social order as the majority of the population understands it. On one side, the contemporary corporative (or oligarchic) ideology in the United States, Russia and Italy recognizes several elements of the liberal ideology, such as the role of the market, private property and political freedoms. On the other side, the corporative ideology contains many values that justify directly or indirectly the violation of social order by oligarchs.

Let us mention first the values that justify the so-called rent-seeking activities of big businesses.[4] Rent-seeking activity supposes the blending of political power and big money as a normal phenomenon of contemporary society. This activity directly challenges the essential element of any orderly society. The core of rent seeking is an exchange of money for various governmental privileges at all levels, from the township and county to the nation. Rent seeking is usually defined as the political activity of individuals or groups who devote scarce resources to the pursuit of monopoly rights granted by governments. The actual methods and instruments of rent seeking and giving are designed to be concealed. They contain favorable legislation, the endorsement of contracts without bidding, governmental subsidies in the case of bankruptcy on research and development, semi-legal tax evasion or tax privileges, price supports, tariffs, farm or import quotas, licenses and, of course, getting a position in government—from ambassadors to the members of the cabinet (Hart, 2001; McChesney, 1991). The highest form of rent-seeking activity is the privatization of offices by people from corporation, a case that was particularly clear in post-Soviet Russia in the 1990s when the country was ruled by oligarchs (Shlapentokh, 1995; 1996; 1998).

The benefits that go to officials are usually in the form of open or hidden bribes with cash or stocks, the payment of travel and vacation expenditures and high-paid jobs for relatives, friends and lovers (see Domhoff, 1998; Ferguson, 2001; Lewis, 2000). John Boies (1989) showed that, in the 1976 and 1980 election cycles, companies involved in defense contracting and mergers were the most politically active. Hart (2001) shows that this trend continued with high-tech firms engaged in rent-seeking activities in the form of political contributions during the 1980s–90s.

The important part of corporate behavior that is not directly included in rent-seeking activity, but is deeply against social order, is the selection of cadres on the basis of personal relations. As Sorenson wrote, "What is essential is the idea of an advantage obtained by getting access to a position in the social structure irrespective of the behavior of the occupant of this position. In other words, it is an advantage the individual has not earned" (Sorenson, 1996).

The corporative (or oligarchic) ideology contains various values and simple ideological tricks that justify rude violations of law by rich people and preach tolerance toward corruption, the manipulation of elections and the media and the nonobservance of federal laws. The manipulation of elections by power and money was considered, for instance, the only way to get reasonable people into the legislature who could work with oligarchs. This ideology does not hide, in fact, its contempt for the masses, democratic procedures and their manipulation by money.[5]

The contempt of corporate America toward many dominant values is not ostensible. It does not permit even the most outspoken ideologues of corporations to flaunt their views. But it would be impossible to have the epidemic of corruption in corporate America without the adequate ideological underpinning of CEO (Chief Executive Officer) behavior. Frank Rich, with full grounds, talks about the existence of CEO culture, or ethos, which "rules in Washington: uninhibited cronyism, cooked books, special-favors networks, the banishment of whistle-blowers and accountability"; he talks about the Enron case as being a typical product of this culture (Rich, Frank, 2005; see also Lowenstein, 2004; Partnoy, 2003; Stiglitz, 2003).

One of the best sources for understanding the minds of the American corporate class is, in fact, high-quality novels and movies. Sociological studies can hardly understand the minds of people on Wall Street. Marx noted once that people can learn more about French society from *Human Comedy* than from various scholarly writings, placing a special focus on Balzac's classification of human types. Probably yielding to the quality of the French literary giant's social analysis, several American novels, from Theodor Draiser's *American Tragedy, The Financier* and *The Genius*, Upton Sinclair's *The Flivver King, King Coal* and *The Jungle*, and contemporary novels, such as Tom Wolfe's *Bonfire of the Vanities* and *Man in Full* give us a relatively plausible picture of the morals of the American moguls of high and middle rank.

In this respect, Russian oligarchs are more open in promulgating their negative values. Anatolii Chubais, a leading Russian oligarch, along with other corporate ideologues advanced the theory that corruption in Russia has a "cultural origin," which exonerates bureaucrats and oligarchs.[6] Some contend that corruption is invaluable as "grease" for the proper functioning of the state machine, or as an antidote against "the inefficient organization of society and bad state policy." It was Gavril Popov, then Moscow's mayor and a prominent liberal, who was a pioneer in proclaiming this theory in the early 1990s (see Kagarlitsky, 2002; see also Polterovich, 1998). But still Russian novels, such as Iulii Dubov's *Big Ration* (2003) or Iulia Latynina's *Steel King* (2002), or *The Hunting Manchurian Deer* (2003), are best at penetrating the mentality of the oligarchs.

THE VALUES OF CRIMINAL STRUCTURES

The hostility toward official social values is much stronger in the ideology that serves organized crime than that of corporations. There is a criminal segment found in any country. The active members, along with a considerable part of the population that is thought to be law-abiding, are hostile toward positive values. It is enough to mention drugs, the production, transportation and selling of which involves millions of people in various countries, without speaking of their consumers. The underground economy in the United States consists of $650 billion in products and services (Schlosser, 2003). Organized crime has its own ideology, which contains values that are deeply inimical to social order: the cult of violence and the contempt for law (its omerta), the disdain for hard work, a belief in the possibility to corrupt officials and the indifference toward the national interests of the country.[7] In his book *Cosa Nostra* (2004) John Dickie describes the major rituals used by mafia in order to instill in its members their own system of values (see Liddick, 1999; Reppetto, 2004). Such a famous book as the *Godfather*, or the serial *Sopranos*, along with many other novels and movies, such as *Scarface* with Al Pacino, a gangster "who trusts only himself," illustrate the value orientations of gangsters.

The ideology of the criminal sector, including its specific language, exerts a tremendous impact on law-abiding segments of society up to the highest level of the social hierarchy. The criminalization of mentality, particularly in terms of language, became a very important factor in post-Soviet Russia. The criminal sector of Russia has provided all classes of the population with models of behavior and with slang that is used not only by the average Russian but also by the intellectuals and officials, starting with President Putin who became notorious for using bandit locutions (see Dolgova, 2003; Pridemore, 2005).

Negative Socialization

At the center of the Parsonian vision of society lies the idea that people grow up through a process of socialization, and that this process provides them with the values necessary for the maintenance of social order. In fact, Parsons and all other sociologists who share this view followed Thomas Aquinas's conviction about the existence of "the natural law" that forces people to accept the norms of decent behavior. With great belief in the intellect, Aquinas was confident that it plays a crucial role in the acceptance of divine and earthly laws of behavior. In fact, there are no grounds to believe in the divine project or in the "good culture" that provides such nice ways of maintaining order.

In fact, the mainstream of sociology has operated with this over-simplified view, as can be seen from American textbooks, for several decades. This view of socialization conspicuously ignores the complicated and dramatic character of the process. The Freudian struggle between the id and the superego conveys in some ways a better picture of this process, an observation made by Dennis Wrong (1961).

The mainstream in sociology not only neglects negative values, but also has a tendency to avoid such an issue as negative socialization.[8] It is treated only as a process that is positive for society. Very few sociological textbooks discuss failed socialization when families and schools are unable to infuse positive values in the mind of children and teenagers. Even less attention is paid to negative socialization, or the acquisition of negative values and negative skills, including the use of guns in school, alcohol, smoking and drugs as well as the hatred of other gangs, or people of different races, ethnicities and religions. Most textbooks ignore the negative socialization that occurs on the streets and in schools (see, for instance, Andersen and Taylor, 2002, 92).

Meanwhile, the concept of negative socialization was raised in the works of Clifford Show (Show, 1929; 1931) and particularly Edwin Sutherland in the late 1930s. Sutherland, in the spirit of interactionism and also under the impact Gabriel Tard's theory of imitation, elaborated the concept of Differential Association Theory (TAD; finalized in 1947), or culture-learning theory in the terms of Messner and Rosenfeld (1997, 46–47), which showed how criminals transmit their patterns of behavior to others and in this way are responsible for the growth of crime (Sutherland, 1939).

Sutherland's studies inspired a certain number of works that are considered as versions of learning theory. Among them was the theory of Daniel Glaser (1956), who used the concept of roles for explaining crime (see also, Goode and Ben-Yehuda, 1994, 83–84).

However, until the 1990s, Sutherland's works were in general ignored or rejected by sociologists, probably because they challenged the idea of criminals being victims of society (a major premise of most social scientists at the end of the twentieth century) and focused on the behavior of the individual under the impact of reinforcement (positive or negative). For instance, John Macionis (2004, 142) dismissed both Sutherland's differential association theory and Hirshi's control theory as providing "little insight into why society's norms and laws define certain kinds of activities as deviant in the first place."[9] Among others, Sutherland's critics were Gibbons (1992) and several other authors.

Sutherland's approach found support from those who studied the downward assimilation and oppositional subcultures in the 1990s (see O'Kane, 1992). Of special interest are the studies of "downward assimilation" in the United States as described by Portes and Rumbaut (2001), which is discussed later.

Another development in social science that can be considered an offshoot of Southerland's approach is "social norm theory." It suggests that the behavior of people is influenced by perceptions of how other members of a social group think and act. A teenager may overestimate the permissiveness of peer attitudes or behavior with respect to alcohol. The theory predicts that overestimations of problem behavior will increase these problem behaviors. The perception of social norms have been found to be more influential in shaping individual behavior than biological, personality, familial, religious, cultural and other influences (see Berkowitz, 2004; Perkins, 1986a; 2004).

Meanwhile, the failed socialization ignored by sociologists has drawn the close attention of developmental psychologists and criminologists (Bohm and Haley, 1999, 86–88). In 1950 itself, Sheldon and Eleanor Glueck from Harvard published *Unraveling Juvenile Delinquency*), based on a longitudinal study, which brought them to the conclusion that failed socialization during childhood is a powerful predicator of delinquency in adult years. Many criminologists stuck to their thesis about the continuity of "maladaptive behavior." Among them were prominent scholars such as Michael Gottfredson and Travis Hirschi (1990), as well as a large number of other criminologists and psychologists (see Brim and Kagan, 1980, 1–25; Caspi and Bem, 1990, 549–575). As Caspi and Moffit (1992) showed, strong continuity in social behavior was found in different nations, including Canada, the United States, Sweden and others.

In subsequent years, studies by a host of criminologists, although confirming partially this conclusion, focused on "the child factor" (temperament and self-control), and on such agents of socialization as family and school, which often failed in their efforts to implement "positive socialization." Authors such as Hirschi (2002) and Hagan (1989, 210–212) emphasize the attachment to parents, while Loeber and Stouthamer-Loeber (1986) and Patterson (1982) focused on coercion. Sampson and Laub formulated a sort of consensus among several researchers in terms of the obligation of the family to guarantee "discipline, supervision and attachment" (68), supposing that the Gluecks (1950, 96, 261) would have accepted this formulation, too.

A special area of "negative" re-socialization is the prison system in all countries, where inmates teach each other, particularly young prisoners, how to challenge order (Macionis, 2001, 133–134). The penitentiary system, although it punishes criminals, is a hotbed for nurturing recidivists. In the United States, after being imprisoned, the offenders are generally returned to the environments in which they committed the crime. Miles Harer studied the prisoners released from the Federal Bureau of Prisons in 1970, 1978, 1982 and 1987, and found that about 44 percent of them rearrested again or had their parole revoked in the first three years (Harer, 1993). Several other studies confirmed Harer's data. In a study of 108,580 inmates released from prisons in 11 states in 1983, 62 percent were rearrested for felonies or serious misdemeanors within three years of release (United States Department of Justice, 1983).

So-called copycat activities are examples of negative socialization. According to the data of the U.S. Department of Justice, in 2005, 47 percent of inmates in state prisons have a parent or other close relative who has been incarcerated (Butterfield, 2002). Of course, difficult social conditions, such as poverty, a low level of education, social inequality, a criminal environment and several other factors are mostly responsible for this correlation. At the same time, we cannot ignore the reproduction of criminality within families.

The Case of Immigrants

Negative socialization is an important phenomenon for new adult immigrants as well as for their children. There is a strong tendency among immigrants to settle in neighborhoods characterized by poverty, substandard housing, poor schools and high crime rates, which was described in the classic work *The Polish Peasant in Europe and America* (Thomas and Znaniecki, 1920). This environment provided immigrants, to use Merton's famous typology of goals and means, with new opportunities to achieve mostly legitimated goals, which are dominant in their environment (Messner and Rosenfeld, 1997). Shaw and McKay found that as soon as the immigrants moved toward a wealthy neighborhood, the criminality rate subsided (Shaw and McKay, 1969).

However, the second generation of immigrants represents a special case. This phenomenon was described by Alejandro Portes and Ruben Rumbaut in their books and articles (see, for instance, Portes and Rumbaut, 2001). According to these authors, the second generation of immigrants from the developing countries assimilate to their new countries mostly under the control of their peers, who are deeply immersed in various sorts of illegal activities. As suggested by Christopher Jencks, a prominent American sociologist who summarized Portes's and Rumbault's findings, the children of poor immigrants often come to resemble the children of poor Americans and many of them join gangs, use drugs and alcohol, have children out of wedlock, get arrested and spend time in jail (Jencks, 2002, 94).

The Refusal to Accept the New Values and Rules

The negative socialization among the new generations of immigrants is particularly strong when the immigrants, for one reason or another, become convinced of the superiority of their native country and its order and culture over the culture of the new country, or if they assume that the culture of the new country is unjust, unfair or discriminates against them. Often both factors work together. The feelings of superiority over the culture of the new country can be detected among Muslim immigrants in different countries of the world (Huntington, 2004, 188, 357–362). This initial hostility partially explains how people from Muslim countries are much more persistent in pursuing their old traditions, and often sacrificing the material benefits that come with better adjustment to a new environment; in some cases, they are even ready to directly challenge the authorities in a new country (Hunt, 2000). Many Muslim immigrants not only do not try to claim to accept the customs of a new country, but also flaunt their differences, as do, for instance, many Turks in Germany or Arabs from African countries in France. The leaders of Muslims in Europe openly reject assimilation, defining it as "cultural rape."[10]

The same feelings of superiority of their culture can be seen among Chechens and Azeris who have immigrated to Moscow and other Russian cities from the Caucasian republics. However, despite the cultural defiance many Muslims prosper in their new countries. The United States 2000 census found that the median income for an Arab family was about 5 percent higher than the median income for all American families. The proportion of Arabs working in management jobs was higher than the American average (42 to 34 percent) (*New York Times*, March 9, 2005a). The place of Chechens and Azeris in Russia in the beginning of the twenty-first century was the same, despite their open hostility to the Russian culture and style of life. Their well-being was much higher than that of the ethnic Russians.

Discrimination is often a cause for negative socialization. The tendency of some immigrant youth to behave badly often occurs, as mentioned before, not because the majority of immigrants do not know the rules and values of the new country, or do not want to know them, but because of the hostility of the native residents who see immigrant peoples as a drain on public coffers, as competition for their jobs or because immigrants assume the superiority of their old culture over the country in which they live (Tienda, 1999, 136).

Mistrust of People and Institutions as an Obstacle to the Positive Influence of Values

A good indicator that offers more evidence of the insufficiency of internalized values in the maintenance of order is the degree of trust of people in their compatriots and in social institutions. Indeed, it is reasonable to suppose that the higher the trust in people and institutions the higher is the expectation that they will behave according to accepted values and norms.

The Mutual Trust of People

You may have correct expectations about the behavior of people whom you suppose are criminals. However, this type of "bad" expectation has nothing to do with trust, which is based on "good" expectations.[11] If you believe that "others" will violate social norms and that you cannot trust them, you will hardly observe the social norms yourself.

The level of trust shows, among other things, how much people believe that their values are shared by others and they can expect them to behave accordingly. The World Values Survey provides us with remarkable data on this issue. It asked the question, "Generally speaking, would you say that most people can be trusted or that you can't be too careful in dealing with people" (Inglehart et al., 2001, question 94). The highest level of trust was found in Sweden. However, even here only two-thirds of the people trust each other. In most countries the level of trust is less than 50 percent. In Turkey and Brazil, the level is 10 and 7 percent, respectively. In America, people were divided almost fifty–fifty (52 percent trust "others") and in Russia only a little more than one-third have faith in their countrymen (in the country 38 percent, in Moscow 34 percent).[12] Putnam cites even less optimistic data about America, which show that only 37 percent of Americans felt that "most people" can be trusted, a decline from 58 percent in 1960 (Putnam, 2000, 73). Francis Fukuyama (1995, 307–321) shares the same view as Putnam in describing the low level of mutual trust in contemporary American society.

In general, as Ronald Inglehart showed with his World Values Survey data, high trust in people is closely correlated with "historically protestant culture," with its typically high level of social order and democracy, whereas the lowest trust was found in countries with Orthodox, Islamic and Catholic cultures (mostly in Latin America), which combine low levels of order and unstable democracies (Inglehart, 1991, 91, 102).

Attitudes toward Public Institutions and Elites

The mechanism that maintains order (which receives help from internal values) demands high respect from the dominant institutions (government, business, church, elected bodies) and especially for the leaders at all levels of society, and first of all the political, business, religious and intellectual leaders. The decline of the moral authority of institutions and the elite has a negative impact on the morals of society, particularly among the youth.

Meanwhile, in contemporary society, the prestige of social institutions and leaders is not very high; in fact, in some cases it is quite low. Let us take, for example, the data of the World Values Survey on attitudes toward the political system. If we ignore the data on nondemocratic countries such as China as unreliable (here positive attitudes are shared by 80 percent of the people), the highest level of positive attitudes toward the political system (if we can trust these data and ignore the desirable values effect) was found in India (58 percent) and the United States (55 percent), whereas Poland reached only 9 percent (Inglehart et al., 2001, variable 285). These data match the data from the question about the ruling elite in the country (is "the country run by a few big interests looking out for themselves, or it is run for the benefit of people?"). Two-thirds of Americans (68 percent) pointed to a "few big interests"; in Mexico, 80 percent. The friendliest attitudes toward the ruling elite were found in Chile (45 percent) and Latvia (35 percent).[13] It is not amazing that in the same survey the trust in government was also quite low: in the United States, 41 percent, and Canada, 20 percent (Inglehart et al., 2001, 289).

The Russian Case

Today, Russia is a country that much more than any other mistrusts almost all social and political institutions. Indeed, there is no one institution that can garner more than 40–50 percent of the nation's trust. Most political institutions enjoy a confidence level of only 10 to 30 percent and some even lower. Using Levada-zentr data (2005), I classified the major Russian institutions in three categories, depending on the trust level among the public: high, middle and low. Even if we suppose that the people's trust in Putin as a personality (but not the presidency as an institution) is higher than 50 percent, as suggested by some polling firms, Russia's lack of confidence in social institutions is still unique. The picture, of course, would be even more astounding if we excluded both Putin and the church from an international comparison (see tables 4.1–4.3).

Table 4.1 Institutions with a high level of trust

Institution	Level of trust (% of population)
Putin	47
Church	41
Army	31

Table 4.2 Institutions with a middle level of trust

Institution	Level of trust (% of population)
Security agencies	25
Media	24
Regional authorities	17
Attorney General's office	16
Courts	15
Federal government	14
Local authorities	14
Police	12
Trade Unions	12

Table 4.3 Institutions with a low level of trust

Institution	Level of trust (% of population)
State Duma	10
Council of Federation	10
Political parties	5

The data clearly show that people have a special mistrust of the new democratic institutions in the country. Among the 15 institutions included in the poll by the Levada-Zentr, the three "pure" democratic institutions ranked at the bottom.

Among the 79 countries in the World Values Survey that responded to the given question, Russia held the sixty-ninth place with regard to the degree of trust in the parliament. Even if the Americans are very critical of all their institutions, their trust in the U.S. Senate and House of Representatives is much higher than the trust of the Russians in their parliament. While both chambers of the Russian parliament (the State Duma and the Federal Council) collected only 10 percent of the people's trust, 53 percent of Americans trust Congress a "fair amount" and 7 percent a "great deal."[14]

It is difficult to imagine how Russians can conform to social values on their own initiative if they hold almost all public institutions, as well as their elites, in contempt. Clearly, with such attitudes toward public institutions, order in societies such as Russia depends mostly on the fear of sanctions imposed by state agencies. It is also clear, considering the level of corruption and collusion of cynical businesspeople and mafias, why lawlessness dominated Russian life after the collapse of the Soviet Union.

The United States

The trust that Americans place in most of their institutions is much higher than in Russia. In May 2005, 74 percent trusted the army (Russia, 31 percent), 63 percent trusted the police (Russia, 12 percent), 44 percent, the presidency (Russia, 47 percent), 41 percent, the U.S. Supreme Court, 37 percent, the public schools, 26 percent, the criminal justice system (Russia, 15 percent), 22 percent, congress (Russia, 10 percent) and 22 percent, big business (Russia, 20 percent). The attitudes toward these institutions have oscillated, but ultimately have not changed over the last three decades (Gallup, 2005d).

Although the Americans have better opinions of their institutions and its elites, they are still quite skeptical about them. Most Americans do not believe that their politicians and businesspeople follow the values that they preach.

CONCLUSION

A major problem with the concept of values as the basis of social order is the existence of a large number of values that play a destructive role in society. Meanwhile, most sociologists operate with the concept of values as if they are only helpful for the maintenance of order. Indeed, many people internalize not only positive values, but also negative ones. Drunkenness, drug addiction, violence, promiscuity, rudeness in behavior, xenophobia, the hatred of minorities, corruption and anti-intellectualism are only a few of the long list of values that play key roles in the value systems of many people. What is more, people are often forced to behave according to these values because of the fear of being punished for refusing to do so.

A major segment of the population in any society is permanently at odds with the law. Their criminal behavior not only produces many victims of violence or the loss of property, but it has a tremendous impact on the minds and behavior of law-abiding citizens. The anti-social behavior of a considerable part of the youth population has become a more and more serious problem in many countries. The place of negative values in the mind of many people is revealed when they find themselves beyond the control of state agencies or various informal groups. Under such circumstances, these people violate the major values that seemingly were internalized by them. These developments occur inside as well as outside the country.

In some segments of society, the negative values that challenge order are espoused by a considerable number of people. This is true in the case of the corporate sector. The corporative (or oligarchic) ideology contains various values that justify rude violations of law by rich people and preach tolerance toward corruption, the manipulation of elections and the media along with the direct violation of law. The manipulation of elections by power and money was considered, for instance, the only way to get reasonable people into the legislature who could work with oligarchs. This ideology does not, in fact, hide its contempt for the masses, democratic procedures and their manipulation by money.

Organized crime is another sector of society that fosters negative values. The ideology of this sector contains values that are deeply inimical to social order: the cult of violence and the contempt for law, the disdain for hard work, a belief in the possibility of corrupting officials and the indifference toward the national interests of the country.

The mistrust of social institutions is a powerful factor that accounts for the spread of negative values in society. Indeed, people who think that their government, judicial system and big businesses are corrupt have little reason to respect honesty or hard work as values.

With the spread of negative values in society, it is evident that they influence the minds of young people when they prepare themselves for adult life. The mainstream in sociology tends not only to neglect negative values, but also has a tendency to avoid such an issue as negative socialization; it is treated only as a positive process. However, negative socialization plays an enormous role in any society. Children digest negative values in families as well as in schools and among their peers. They are taught how to use guns, alcohol, cigarettes and drugs, as well as how to hate people of different races, social status, ethnicities and religions. Unfortunately, along with educational measures, the fear of sanctions is one of the most effective ways to mitigate the influence of negative values on behavior.

CHAPTER 5

National Common Values: Partially a Myth

The concept of common values and internalization lies at the core of the culturological approach to the issue of social order. Only with the assumption that the majority of the population shares the same assortment of positive social values is it reasonable to insist that social order can be based only on values. Common values play the crucial role in Parsons's theory and in the theories of all those who follow his tradition (Parsons, 1951, 41). Although I am critical of the concept of common values as the basis for order, I do not take a nihilistic stance toward the role of national culture and common values. In a society that can be considered socially, ethnically and culturally homogeneous and stable, the existence of common values and even a sort of national character and identity is an empirically proven fact. The ideal society for culturologists, particularly those with conservative orientations, is a nation with a middle class that makes up the majority of the population, belongs to the same ethnic and cultural group and evidently shares the same values, which would almost automatically bring order in society with minimal intervention of the state. In Samuel Huntington's book *The Challenges to America's National Identity* (2004), such a society was not a figment of the imagination, but indeed existed in America before the 1950s.

However, even in a society that is close to Huntington's ideal, values cannot be the main basis for order, because many people do not internalize them to such a degree that they guide their behavior. Even in a society that looks this homogeneous, common values play a limited role since many people with the same ethnic and religious background have very different attitudes toward many important issues. Some authors go so far as to cast doubt on the uniting role of social values. They indeed direct behavior, but they do it differently for different people. Even the members of a family are often unable to come to a consensus on many issues, from the way to spend money to the choice of a TV program. Such are the views of Michael Hechter and his coauthors. They point out that the internalization of values is more likely to sow the seeds of conflict than create order even in homogeneous societies (Hechter et al., 2003, 329; see also Wrong, 1994, 34).

Although the existence of common values in society is an evident fact, it is important to note that many of them are not so much a product of a special culture, which many culturologists insist on, but rather of values of universal character, such as family, religious rituals or incest prohibition, along with the ban on murder or the recognition of some form of property. These values reflect the conditions necessary for the function of any social organism (see Giddens, 1989, 38–39; Murdock, 1954). Furthermore, in many cases, so-called common values are, as noted earlier, indeed nothing more than the rules that are observed, because of the fear of sanctions.

In a heterogeneous society the concept of common values demands even more reservations. In this case, it is impossible to assert that intragroup variation (the differences among various social, ethnic and cultural groups) is higher than intergroup variation (the differences between the nations). Criticizing the theory that defends the consensual nature of social order, as David Lockwood (1992, 15) noted, this theory is ill-equipped to deal with the variability of values and beliefs.

However, if a country is ruled by a strong authoritarian regime for a relatively long time we can see the trend toward the formation of some common values shared by the majority of the population. In such cases, there are objective factors that force people of different groups to accept common values as a condition that allows them to cooperate with the dominant ethnic and cultural group, particularly if this group runs the bureaucracy and sets the rules for economic activity. Many non-German minorities in the Austro-Hungarian Empire or non-Russian minorities in the tsarist and Soviet empires as well as non-English minorities in the United States were eager to learn the dominant language and culture to survive and prosper in their environment.

Debates on the Common Values Concept: The American Case

The intensive debates over the concept of common culture as the basis of social order started in the late 1960s and continued to expand in the next decades. The question of whether America is homogeneous or heterogeneous has played a central role in these debates. In any period in American history, there were those who insisted on the united character of the American nation and those for whom America was an extremely diversified society. Of course, the role of the advocates and foes of the idea of American homogeneity has varied depending on political and social developments. If to take into account only the last 50 years, it is possible to point to the Vietnam War in the 1960–70s and the war in Iraq in 2003–05, which supported the idea of the polarization of the American nation. Certainly, political ideology influences the perceptions of American society. Conservatives tend to focus on homogeneity and their critics on heterogeneity.

Taking into account the views of the diversity (or homogeneity) of American society in the past and present (the second half of the twentieth century and particularly in the last two decades), we can identify four groups of authors.

The Advocates of America as a Homogeneous Society

One group of authors is confident that American society, with a middleclass that encompasses the majority of Americans and with its abhorrence of class ideology, has always been more or less homogeneous. According to this view, the American culture has determined all the major aspects of society. This group is clearly composed of those who insist on American exceptionalism, such as Irving Kristol (1975) and others (see Bell, 1996; Hofstadter, 1989; Lipset, 1996). These authors refer to Tocqueville (1969, 691–692) and Weber (1985, 7–11) as thinkers with great confidence in the homogeneity of America. Some of them, such as Hall and Lindholme, talked about Americanism as a sort of religion combined with ideological vagueness (1999, 82, 84, 86).

Homogeneity is a Myth

This vision of society, as consisting of groups of people who have little in common with each other, became particularly prominent in the 1990s among social scientists with postmodern tendencies and a focus on social constructivism. They were joined by those scholars who studied developments in post-Communist society, and also by those scholars who overcame the fear of being accused of racism or imperialism and began to look soberly at the developments in Africa and Latin America.[1]

These critics of the concept of common values usually operate with rich factual information and assert that in many cases the existence of common values is a myth or an artifact created by social scientists. In fact, as Paul DiMaggio (1997) noted in his survey of the literature, such a view has been developed mostly in the area of cultural studies.

The first critic of the common values concept was probably Michael Mann (1970), but it was Martin (1992) and Taylor (1992; 1995) who made the first great contributions to the analysis. Several authors joined them, including John Higham (1999, 43), who pointed out that, because of the extraordinary diversification of immigration (the immigration to several other countries such as Argentina or Australia has been more homogeneous), and despite the melting-pot effect, American cultural elites, as late as the 1850s, worried about the incompleteness of the national character. He also attacks the ethnocentric universalistic myth that focuses on the core of the predominant American ideology. Another author who was skeptical about the role of dominant culture was Anthony Cascardi. He discussed "a series of separate values-spheres, each one of which tends to exclude or attempts to assert its priority over the rest" (Cascardi, 1992).

In the early 1990's, Beth Hess and her coauthors, talking about America, noted that in this country there are two competing value orientations that are no longer clearly associated with age (Hess et al., 1993, 68). An interesting critique of the common values concept can also be found in the works of Zerubavel (1992).

The presidential election in 2004 brought immense support in favor of diversity. Talking about the culture war that rages in America, many conservatives and liberals described the American society in the beginning of the twentieth century as deeply split (Langer, 2004).

Conservative Pessimists: Homogeneity in the Past, Heterogeneity Now

Another category of scholars—labeled here as advocates of "homogeneity in the past, heterogeneity now"—includes authors with different ideological orientations. Some of them, mostly with liberal or even radical tendencies, bemoan the excessive rise of individualism as the major cause for the differentiation in American society. Here the most known names include Bellah et al. (1985) and Walzer (1994). Close to this group are the advocates of communitarianism, including Taylor who talks about the fragmentation of American society, focusing on ethnic and social enclaves in the United States (Taylor, 1992; 1995).

However, this concept was particularly dear to scholars with conservative orientations, particularly those who had strong anti-Marxist orientations, as well as the adversaries of multiculturalism. They included authors such as Arthur Schlesinger (1991) and D'Sousa (1992, 25–39). In one way or another, their vision of America in the near future is shared by several other authors with the same ideological tendencies (Bennett, 1995; Bouvier, 1992; Lucas, 1995; White, 2003; Wuthnow, 1999).

In the beginning of 2000, it was Samuel Huntington (2004) who became a champion of this view with his focus on the growing influx of Spanish-speaking immigrants who refuse to assimilate. He predicted the total transformation of American society, from its homogenous Anglo-Protestant culture of the past to its current bilingual and bicultural form.

America Was never a Homogeneous Society

In the mid-1930s itself, some American authors, such as Robert and Helen Lynds, discovered the invidious class distinctions in American society. Milton Rokeach (1973, 93), who used as an empirical basis the values survey of 1968, was also inclined to think that values differentiate significantly among groups, varying across demographic and cultural variables. These authors are joined by several British writers such as Linda Coley who insisted that Americans could not develop a sense of nationhood, because they did not have neighboring countries that they detested in the same way as the British detested the French (Colley, 1992). For Ernest May (2004), America has always been "a federation of federations." The radicals and particularly Marxists, with their focus on the social polarization of American society, such as Michael Harrington (1969), have been among the most consistent critics of the cultural homogeneity of America. Much later they were joined by a host of authors who wrote about "two Americas," including Greenberg (2004), Messner and Rosenfeld (1997), Kuper (1969) and Hechter (2000, 156–157).

Long Live Heterogeneity: The Radical View

Among those who rejected the unity of society were Left radicals of various types. The members of the first purely ideological group, which did not pay much attention to factual analysis, were hostile toward this concept, because the idea of common values seemed problematic to them for ideological reasons. Instead, they hailed the demolition of common values if they still existed. They were quite visible among the critics of the United States. The commonality of social values broke down under pressure from competing class factions, social forces and regional demands (Wark, 1999). This group demands that the multiplicity of American society is a desirable development (Tully, 1995). Among these radical critics are feminists such as Iris Marion Young (1990) and literary critics such as Roger Kimball (2002).

America Today Is Less Homogeneous than in the Past

I gravitate toward the members of the fourth group who believe that America today is much less homogeneous than in the past. However, I think that the members of this group, such as Huntington, exaggerate the level of homogeneity in the past. Without denying the role of common national values, I assume that American society has always been significantly diversified and the unity of the country and its order was sustained not only by "the centrality of Anglo protestant culture," as Huntington vehemently argues (2004, 30), but by law enforcement agencies. Indeed, there were always big groups in America who had very little to do with the Anglo-Protestant culture, including black slaves, Indians and, of course, the first generation of immigrants who in no way were able to digest the dominant culture in the country.

In this respect my position is somewhat close to that of Michael Walzer who suggested that Americans are protected from moral anarchy by a shared reverence for the Constitution (Walzer, 1989). Now we discuss the role of national common values in other societies.

THE CRITICS OF THE COMMON VALUES CONCEPT APPLIED TO OTHER COUNTRIES

Several researchers have insisted that cultural heterogeneity is typical for other countries. David Nicholls claimed that recent empirical research casts doubt on the existence of such a set of "common values" in Britain. Eldrid Mageli showed that India, like many other culturally heterogeneous states, seems to hang together precisely *because* no one tries to enforce any kind of common values on the population. He writes that in order to survive as a state, India must continue to be pluralistic with value fragmentation and allow for a number of different kinds and shapes of allegiance.

For the critics of the homogeneity concept, a special role belongs to the regionalists. Among major arguments against the exaggeration of the cultural factor and the role of common values is the great diversity of regions inside each "civilization." Russian or Chinese regions with the same cultural and religious traditions today look like separate countries, a result of the developments in the last decades. It is enough to compare, for instance, Moscow and the provinces in Russia or Shanghai and provinces in China. The comparison of the Italian North and South, or the various Indian provinces would only strengthen the thesis.

THE EMPIRES

The common values concept as an explanation of social order is particularly dubious in ethnically, socially and, consequently, culturally heterogeneous countries. As a matter of fact, most populations throughout history have lived in heterogeneous countries. It is amusing how Huntington disparagingly talked about the major European empires in modern times as "the collections of diverse groups" and "conglomerations," which were held together by "the emperor and his bureaucracy," without mentioning the many centuries of longevity of these empires (Huntington, 2004, 19).

A heterogeneous society such as an empire, with its numerous ethnic groups, by definition cannot have a lot of common values. This is true about continental empires, which existed until the middle of the twentieth century, including the Austro-Hungarian Empire, the Ottoman Empire, the Chinese Empire during the Qing dynasty and to some degree also Arab empires. The ethnic and cultural diversity of continental empires was enormous. Take as an example the Austro-Hungarian Empire. The dominant ethnic group, Germans, made up a minority. The coexistence of different ethnic, cultural and religious groups was a norm in these empires over long periods of time. The heterogeneity of maritime empires, such as the British or French in the seventeenth through the twentieth centuries was, of course, even greater.

The same is true about the Soviet Union in which the core of the empire was a totalitarian regime, which, with its full monopoly of media, education and culture, was able to instill official values on a territory where the Russians made up only-half of the population. However, despite the big successes of Soviet propaganda and the official declaration about the emergence of a new entity (the Soviet nation), most non-Russian people maintained their own system of values and declared their loyalty toward the Soviet values only under the threat of sanctions. It was proved by the fact that literally overnight, after the collapse of the Soviet empire in 1991, the Soviet values lost any sway over non-Russians, particularly people in the Baltic republics, Caucasus and Central Asia (Shlapentokh, 2001).

It is remarkable that Parsons, with all his focus on values as the major regulator of society, noted that the ancient Roman Empire retained a polytheistic religious system but sustained order in the empire with "the concept of law and citizenship" (Parsons, 1964). As Marguerite Yoursenar described in his novel *Hadrian*, the Roman emperor Hadrian wanted as his citizens "the tattooed black, the hairy German, the slender Greek, and the heavy Oriental," with their peculiar clothes and their strange gods, on only one condition: that they will obey Roman rules and enforce the law (see Acocella, 2005, 242–252).

However, the existence of empires is not the only thing that undermines the fundamentals of cultural determinism. We should also consider the fact that in Europe states emerged several centuries before the formation of nations (its self-identity), nationalism and a specific national culture, which Marxists and theorists of modernization, such as Ernest Gellner, are prone to ascribe to industrial revolution and the surfacing of common national markets. Liah Greenfeld (1992) contends that England was "invented" in the sixteenth century. Some authors, such as Gerald Newman (1997), locate English nationalism even in the late eighteenth century. Krishan Kumar (2003) named an even later date: the end of the nineteenth century.[2]

"Primordialists"—the opponents of the late origin of nations—have probably some right to contend that nationalism, as it is most often defined, emerged much earlier than the sixteenth century. The major argument in favor of this concept is the existence of a deep connection between the self-identity of a nation and religion, as Benedict Anderson wrote in *Imagined Communities* (1983). Some authors even talked about a connection between "the umbilical sacred" and nationality, as suggested by Anthony Smith in *Nationalism: Theory, Ideology, History* (2001).[3]

However, it is hardly disputable that in England or France in the fifteenth through the eighteenth centuries there was a development of a system of social values that could not, on its own, determine social behavior, even if we take into account the role of the church in the maintenance of order. It was, of course, only the existing state whose activity determined the level of order in society. The developments in London in the early eighteenth century present a good example of the importance of the state in the maintenance of order in this period. The price of alcohol declined tremendously, which led to widespread drunkenness. The entire social fabric in the capital was almost in shambles. Only the government, which adopted new laws, was able to somewhat diminish the delirium in the capital (see Warner, 2000).

CONTEMPORARY NATIONS: CULTURALLY HOMOGENEOUS SOCIETY

Many contemporary nations are no less heterogeneous than the old empires. A big part of the population continues to live in heterogeneous societies. The United States, India, the Russian Federation, Brazil and several other states, let alone most African countries, are heterogeneous, despite the existence of some common values that have indeed been internalized by a majority of the population. The heterogeneity of these countries is rooted first in the ethnic and cultural diversity of the population in these countries as well as in social differentiation.

The available data show that the commonality of values is to a great extent a myth even for the most homogeneous democratic countries in the world, such as the nations of Northern Europe. This view is not shared by some scholars who believe in the dominance of common values (DiMaggio et al., 1996). However, it is bolstered by those who believe in the essential diversity of society, such as Paul Croce (1993) who insists that issues such as health service, the environment, abortion, race and a host of other controversial issues polarize contemporary Western society.

Evaluating data from the World Values Survey, it is necessary to remember that the discrepancies in behavior in any society are much greater than in the responses to the questions about values. People tend to support what they regard as desirable values and often combine an allegiance toward these values with behavior that contradicts them (conformism at the verbal level and non-conformism in behavior) (Shlapentokh, 1982). The issue of the validity of the answers to these questions is never raised by the authors of the World Values Survey (see Inglehart, 2001), or by those who use these data (see, for instance, Huntington, 2004).

I use the index of homogeneity, which is computed as the number of values among the 123 values in the World Values Survey that are supported (or rejected) by more than 80 percent of the population, or accepted either by less than 20 percent or by more than 80 percent. The index of heterogeneity is computed as the number of values that are supported by 40–60 percent of the respondents.

The data that describe the degree of values consensus in various countries are given in tables 5.1–5.3.

As can be seen from table 5.1, in general no more than one-third of the values in developed countries are supported by the majority of the population, with Japan as an evident and expected exception.

Our data show that the highest level of consensus on values can be found in developing countries. Indeed, the index of consensus is 50 percent or higher in 4 out of 16 developing countries, including Bangladesh (65), Ghana (60), Nigeria (59) and Colombia (55). None of the countries in two other groups—developed and post-Communist countries—have such a level of consensus. However, even more remarkable is the fact that among developing countries, the majority have a level of consensus that is lower than 50 and some are very low: Mexico 12,

Table 5.1 Developed countries (in percentage of all the values included in the survey)

Country	Index of homogeneity (0–20 and 80–100)	Index of heterogeneity (40–60)
Britain	24	19
Finland	34	26
Norway	35	21
Sweden	38	
Spain	34	20
United States	38	21
West Germany	38	27
Australia	31	27
Japan	45	18
Switzerland	31	27

Table 5.2 Post-communist countries (in percentage of all the values included in the survey)

Country	Index of homogeneity (0–20 and 80–100)	Index of heterogeneity (40–60)
Armenia	36	25
Azerbaijan	41	21
Belarus	32	28
Bulgaria	33	27
Estonia	33	23
Georgia	33	24
Latvia	27	27
Lithuania	37	18
Moldova	31	24
Poland	43	17
Russia	32	26
Ukraine	28	28

Table 5.3 Developing countries (in percentage of all the values included in the survey)

Country	Index of homogeneity (0–20 and 80–100)	Index of heterogeneity (40–60)
Argentina	31	24
Bangladesh	65	17
Brazil	39	27
Chile	28	28
Colombia	55	13
Dominic Republic	39	22
Ghana	60	8
India	30	23
Mexico	12	32
Nigeria	59	12
Pakistan	31	31
Peru	39	23
Philippines	36	27
S. Africa	38	19
S. Korea	48	20
China	38	20

Chile 28 and Argentina 31. It is remarkable that of the 26 developed and former Communist countries, only 5 countries have an index of homogeneity that is lower or higher than the interval between 30 and 40, where the absolute majority of countries are located (21). None of the 5 countries differ from the main interval by more than 6 points: Britain (24) and Japan (45) showed the maximum differences.

America

Now let us dwell on American society. On the whole, according to the data from the World Values Survey, only 38 percent of the 123 values included in the survey can be considered as consensual, and 21 percent of the values are strongly polarized (between 40 and 60 percent of the Americans held the same views on these values). In terms of the level of homogeneity, the United States is behind Japan (45), but ahead of Great Britain (24) and Russia (32). In a further analysis, I use data from other sources also; first, from the two surveys of 4,000 Americans conducted by the Pew Research Center in 2003.

Consensual Values

As a rule, most values with respect to which Americans hold a consensus are universal values. But even these values, with few exceptions, are not shared by a significant number of Americans. We separate universal values, which are supported in almost all countries, from the limited universal values that find endorsement in many nations. Finally we single out those consensual values, strong and weak, that are specific only to America as well as to a few other countries.

Consensual Universal Values are represented by values such as "the family": 95 percent support it in the U.S.; 88 percent in Norway; 91 percent in Japan; 84 percent in Russia; 98 percent in Turkey; and 96 percent in Nigeria. The same consensus was found with other values related to the family, such as respect for parents or marriage.

Religion is probably the most important value for Americans. As Huntington contends, religion in America is not only important but a central value. He wrote: "Americans have been extremely religious and overwhelmingly Christian throughout their history" (2004, 83). In 1999, 86 percent of Americans believed in God and 8 percent in a universal spirit. In 2002, 65 percent of Americans said religion was very important in their life (U.S. Bureau of Census, 2002).

When it comes to the degree of religiosity, according to the World Values Survey America is surpassed only by Nigeria, Poland, India and Turkey. Quite close to America in religiosity are Ireland, Brazil, Chile, Mexico and Italy.

Other consensual values in the United States, which may be considered universal, do not enjoy such universal support as family or religion. Patriotism is supported by 79 percent of the American respondents (Pakistan, 85; Peru, 80; Venezuela, 94; Germany, 12; Taiwan, 17; and Switzerland, 26). The same is true about such a value as "good compensation for doing one's job": 88 percent of Americans voted for this value along with 81 percent in Japan, 83 percent in Nigeria, 91 percent in Russia, 90 percent in Turkey (in Norway as well as in other North European countries the support for this value was much lower at 58 percent). Friendship belongs to the same category of universal values, which is spurned by a considerable number of Americans: 76 percent of Americans supported it, accompanied by 96 percent of people in Japan and Norway, 99 percent in Nigeria, 84 percent in Argentina and 86 percent in Russia.

The support of specific (nonuniversal) consensual American values is also limited. Americans belong to a small group of nations that strongly support all the institutions and norms related to individual activity. However, a belief in the advantages of private property enjoys the strong support of only 59 percent of the Americans. The figures are similar in Turkey (44 percent strongly support), but this is quite different from the 30 percent of people in Norway and 10 percent in Russia who believe the same. Only two-thirds of Americans are active supporters of competition (60 percent), similar to Brazil (61 percent) and Nigeria (70 percent). In contrast, only 31 percent are strong supporters in Japan, and 35 percent in Chile.

Values that Polarize America

Along with the values that are supported by the majority of Americans (and only rarely by the absolute majority) there are many values that deeply divide American society. By the beginning of the 2000s, Americans were strongly divided; that is, they were fifty–fifty in their attitudes toward several values that are important for social relations, including the relative role of order and freedom, the relations between the church and state, the relative role of civil liberties, the fight against terrorism, the right of the federal government to control much of our daily life, the government regulation of business, people's ability to influence the government, equal rights, the role of military strength to ensure peace, the role of technological progress, employment, the importance of ecological concerns and the control over books that contain dangerous ideas.

The polarization of values is characteristic of the American middle class. Alan Wolfe surveyed 200 families in various American suburbs within the framework of the "middleclass morality project" in the late 1990s. He tried to demonstrate the unity of the American middle class, but ultimately realized the deep ideological gap within it (Wolfe, A., 1998, 319–322). He found strong differences on religious issues: 50 percent of Wolfe's respondents lamented America becoming an atheistic country whereas almost 40 percent disagreed with such a diagnosis (46–47). His sample was deeply divided on the attitudes toward family. Whereas 22 percent of respondents voted for the traditional family and the same number supported the new forms of family, 58 percent were ambivalent on this issue (100). Almost half of the respondents were against it, whereas 37 percent supported it and 15 percent took a neutral position (102). People's attitudes toward immigrants were also polarized: 16 percent expressed "welcoming attitudes," 19 percent expressed negative attitudes and the rest took an ambivalent position (140). David Brooks, in his book *On Paradise Drive*, described the American middle class as divided by "enormous gulfs in values, aspirations, understanding of the world and food preferences" making a stronger argument than Wolfe (Brooks, 2004c).

An explanation of the diversity of values in American society is beyond the goal of this text. Those who recognize the high diversity of American society differ in terms of their views of the causes. Many authors look for traditional explanations, referring to the major social and demographic factors, such as material and social status, race and ethnicity, age, education, family status and place of residence. All of these factors are included in the description of "the American political portrait" as it was described in the aftermath of the presidential election of 2004 (*New York Times*, November 7, 2004b).

In the last decades several authors, without denying the role of socio-demographic factors, discussed the phenomenon of the culture war and advanced as the major psychological and ideological latent variable the concept of "worldview," which is thought to explain the views of Americans, the psychology of the individual and even hints at the genetic structure (see Evans, 1997; Green et al., 2002).[4] Indeed, the same data that characterize the voting behavior of Americans show that people with the same material standing or the same education share opposite views. This cannot be reduced to one or even a few socio-demographic factors using the most sophisticated methods of correlation analysis.

However, whatever the cause of the values segmentation of American society, it is not a homogeneous nation in terms of values, and therefore values, by themselves, cannot serve as the single basis of order in the country. As David Brooks wrote, "if you look just around the United States you find amazing cultural segmentation. We in America have been 'globalized' (meaning economically integrated) for centuries, and yet far from converging into some homogeneous culture, we are actually diverging into lifestyle segments. The music, news, magazine and television markets have all segmented, so there are fewer cultural unifiers, such as *Life Magazine* or Walter Cronkite" (Brooks, 2005b). It is evident that with such differences in the attitudes toward many crucial issues, social order can be maintained only with respect for law.

THE SOVIET AND POST-SOVIET CASES: FROM RELATIVE HOMOGENEITY TO HIGH HETEROGENEITY

The Soviet Society

Unifying the people living in the territory of the Soviet Union was one of the main tasks of the Communist regime. The same was the case in Communist Yugoslavia. The complete control of the Kremlin over media, education, culture and science, and the migration of the population from one republic to the next were all factors that indeed created a sort of "new Soviet nation" (Fedoseyev, 1974, 305–306). This thesis was launched by Soviet ideologues in the 1970s.[5] It was not a simple ideological artifact, as several liberal intellectuals of this period contended. The pressure of the Soviet totalitarian state was so great that common Soviet and pure Russian values, such as patriotism, collectivism, the hostility toward the West, were indeed quite influential in the Soviet times.

However, still despite the efficacy of Soviet ideology and the fear of repressions, the Soviet society was far from being homogeneous. Throughout Soviet history, and particularly in Stalin's time, the people lived in three separate mental worlds. In the first world, the people supported the regime; in the second, they hated it; and in the third, people tried not to think about ideological matters and spent very little time, emotion or thought on any world beyond everyday life. These three worlds intersected only partially. The people of each world had only a superficial idea about the minds of those who belonged to other worlds. They were often amazed when they came into contact with people from other worlds (Shlapentokh, 2001).

Post-Soviet Russia

The developments in Russia and other post-Communist countries provided the critics of the common values concept and cultural determinism with plenty of arguments. As mentioned earlier, the distinctions between different social and ethnic-cultural segments of society are so great that it is difficult to speak about a single set of values shared by the majority of the population.

Contemporary Russia, for instance, is polarized on almost all values in almost all socio-demographic groups (social, territorial, age and nationality).

Keeping some sort of consensus on old and mostly universal values, such as "patriotism" or "family," Russians are strongly divided on all new values. Let us start with private property. On one hand, no less than two-thirds of the Russians changed their attitudes toward private property as a general value, and now support it as a social institution (Fund of Public Opinion, 2001). On the other hand, only a minority endorsed private property for large companies, particularly in areas of the economy close to the country's natural resources (ROMIR, 2003). Forty-eight percent of Russians think that a reconsideration of the results of privatization would benefit the country (39 percent say the opposite). Russians are also split on the value of competition. According to the World Values Survey, 43 percent of the Russians strongly support competition (30 percent showed moderate support). These figures are close to several capitalist countries (in Spain, for instance, 40 percent strongly support the market economy, 26 percent, support it moderately).

The Russians are deeply split when they compare the socialist and capitalist systems. In March 2004, 53 percent of the Russians voted for "the economic system based on state planning and distribution," compared to 34 percent who preferred "the economic system based on private property and the market" (Levada-zentr, 2004a). Many Russians suppose that the state bears the major responsibility for their material life. In the global survey of values, only 14 percent of the Russians (as against 71 percent in America) believed that poor people can themselves "escape from poverty" (in April 2004, 41 percent of the Russians considered themselves "poor"). One-half of the Russians voted for an increase in the state's responsibility for the material life of their citizens; only 12 percent of Americans and 17 percent of the Swiss did the same (Inglehart et al., 2001; see also, Fund of Public Opinion, 2004a; Levada-zentr, 2004a).

No less remarkable are the attitudes of the Russians toward political values. In March 2004, 24 percent of the Russians endorsed Western-style democracy (Levada-zentr, 2004a). Many Russians accepted as important several political freedoms, particularly the freedom of speech and migration inside and outside the country. Two-thirds of the Russians enjoy participating in elections (Fund of Public Opinion, 2003). However, in an August 2003 survey, in which the Russians were offered 24 values, "democracy" was not among the ten most-popular ones (family, 46 percent; security, 43 percent; wealth, 37 percent; peace, 36 percent). "Democracy" was supported by less than 15 percent (Petrova, 2003). Further, 41 percent of the Russians would like to return to the Soviet system (Levada-zentr, 2004a; Sedov, 2001; 2002). Two-thirds of the Russians (according to the global survey of values) are convinced that democracy is bad for order in society (60 percent), and particularly for the economy (64 percent) (Inglehart et al., 2001). According to another study, by the end of the century, only 5 percent of the Russians assessed "democracy" as "very good," compared to 55 percent in the United States, 44 percent in Japan, 66 percent in Nigeria and 43 percent in Peru. On the whole, in 2004, no more than one-third of the Russians described themselves as supporters of "the reforms," whereas 50 percent were adversaries of the reforms (Fund of Public Opinion, 2004b).

Values and Order: The Debates

An analysis of the attitudes toward key values in three societies—America, the Soviet Union and post-Soviet Russia—showed that the degree of heterogeneity in all of them was so high that it was simply impossible to base social order on consensual values, particularly if we suppose that the surveys exaggerated the positive attitudes of people to the dominant values. Not only big societies, but even a small department in a university cannot function on the basis of the members' consensus on major values and rules. Small units of society demand the fear of punishment in all cases when a statute is violated. A tenure position, regardless of the security it provides, cannot protect them from the opprobrium or even harsher sanctions if they trespass the rules of the game. The bigger the social unit the more important is the fear of sanctions for the maintenance of order.

Even in a totalitarian society, the state could not achieve consensus on many values. How is it possible to believe that such a phenomenon can exist in a democratic society based on pluralism? There have been fierce theoretical debates between those who focus on values pluralism and those who focus on liberalism and freedom. The first group assumes that one value can be replaced by another and the second insists on the autonomy of values, liberty in the first place and the crucial role of choice in human life (see Berlin, 1969; Berlin and Williams, 1994; Galston, 1999; Gray, 1995). However, regardless of which side is taken, is values pluralism always compatible with Berlin's negative freedom (the lack of external coercion)? Or, is the combination of values pluralism and liberalism, as suggested by John Gray, not universal? The sociological data showed the validity of the second point of view.

It is quite unreasonable to develop new initiatives in social life based on the assumption of society's consensus on values. John Rawls's liberal proposal on justice is a typical example. Rawls recognizes that "the diversity of views will persist or may increase" in democratic society and assumes wrongly that "a single general and comprehensive conception could be maintained only by oppressive use of state power." However, he believes that it is possible to find "a general and comprehensive conception" that "might be supported by an overlapping consensus." Did Rawls indeed believe that it is possible that in American society the absolute majority of the population will support (on the condition that it will understand it), for instance, the idea that "each person has to have" an equal right to a fully adequate scheme of basic rights and liberties compatible with a similar scheme for all (Rawls, 1987, 3–4, 227). It is remarkable that the debates between communitarians and liberals are also going on with an implicit assumption that it is possible to achieve consensus in society with good arguments (see Bellah et al., 1986; Kymlicka, 1988; McIntire, 1987; Paris, 1991).

At the same time, with skepticism about the moral consensus, I strongly support moral education in school and the use of media and arts for this purpose. However, Americans are not united with respect to their attitudes toward values in education. Indeed, according to the World Values Survey, only 47 percent are confident that their children should respect "hard work," 56 percent, "independence" and 59 percent "determination." The degree of consensus on the values that make up social order is one of the most important cultural, social and political issues, and demands a sober and realistic approach.

CONCLUSION

Values can play a major role in the maintenance of social order if they are shared by the majority of the population. There are big debates in the sociological literature about the degree of homogeneity (or heterogeneity) of American society and other societies. I join those authors who are inclined to see most societies as heterogeneous in terms of the people's attitudes toward the major values that influence social order. This is not only true about all empires that existed in the past, but also about such relatively stable countries as Norway or Sweden. An analysis of data from the World Values Surveys in the 1990s supports this view. I elaborated on this subject with a detailed examination of the attitudes toward values in contemporary America and Russia. This analysis showed that in both countries stability cannot be based on social values alone, because in many cases people are polarized in their attitudes toward them.

CHAPTER 6

Changes and Stability of Social Values and Norms

The goal of this chapter is to develop another argument against the overestimation of social values as the primary basis for social order by analyzing the stability of values. Indeed, the concept of culture, as it is used by many social scientists, supposes that values (an essential part of culture) persist in an almost unadulterated form over long periods of time, even centuries. These values, once internalized by people, have lasting effects, according to Rokeach (1973, 5–6). They withstand many developments and are handed down from generation to generation. The concept of cultural determinism supposes that values are stable, and that their relative role, despite the permanent conflicts among values, does not change. However, if this thesis is flawed, if values can change quickly, if culture or even parts of culture can be transformed quite fast, if it is able to adapt to the changing reality, a belief in the crucial role of the current culture and current values in social life seems to be an exaggeration. At the same time, it is undeniable that the "current culture," as one of several factors of "social reality," plays an important role, but mostly (not always) as a force of inertia and an obstacle for change in the social process.

Theories on the Stability of Values

The assumption about the strong fortitude of social values and their hierarchy is based on two premises. The first premise assumes that most social values, like genes, are stable and impervious to any external impact, such as the influence of economic, social and political factors. This premise is crucial for Parsons and his contemporaries, who describe culture as an entity descending upon society from above, from new religious and philosophical systems, almost totally independent of other developments (political, economic or international), which shape all major dimensions of society.[1] This belief in the crucial role of culture (or civilization, a term often used as a synonym for culture) has an impressive pedigree that includes such names as Spengler, Toynbee and Sorokin, to name only a few.

The whole spirit of Parsons's theory was the high stability of values and the existence of a strong mechanism that restores the equilibrium in the motivational structure of society as soon as some strain emerges. Parsons's belief in the high permanence of major elements of culture has become part of the works of many contemporary social scientists. Some focus on the deeply rooted, almost genetic feature of single cultures in the world. Some are even inclined to underscore the perennial character of culture.

Alan Fiske and his coauthors in *Handbook of Social Psychology* (1998) tend to describe culture as *deus ex machine*, which is able to determine human life with the same values and patterns of behavior over centuries, but is, itself, mostly impervious to the impact of ecological, economic and political factors as independent variables whose influence on human behavior is secondary.[2] They compare various cultures—for instance, American and Asian—without ascribing the differences in culture to specific political and economic behaviors. Talking about such a feature of European–American culture as the individualistic approach to personhood and the inclination of people to make their choices in various spheres of life, and contrasting it with the East Asian culture, these authors do not mention that the freedom of choice was imbedded in the social, political and economic structures of one society and is absent in the other (Fiske et al., 1998, 921).[3]

Even more questionable are the attempts of Nisbett et al. (2001; 2003) who, on the basis of dubious experiments, suggest that there are radical differences between "Westerners" and "Asians." He ignores the profound differences inside each macro group and tries to explain people with this dichotomy.[4]

Denying the derivative origin of most cultural values, which crystallizes the patterns of adaptation, these authors ignore the existing political and economic conditions, as well as geographical and climatic realities, as the major factors shaping the life of any society including its culture. It is evident that the works of Jared Diamond, who ascribes great importance to geographical factors in shaping contemporary Western civilization, are an anathema to culturologists.[5]

THE IMPACT OF SOCIAL AND POLITICAL REALITY ON VALUES

Culturologists and those who support them are not only in deep conflict with the materialist school in social science and psychology (behaviorists or evolutionary psychologists), they are also at odds with the strong tradition in the sociology of knowledge, which recognizes various forms of interaction between the substructure (reality) and superstructure (mind). These structures were offered by Marx and adopted by most of the representatives of this school (see Berger and Luckman, 1966, 6).

Further, the cultural determinists, who, like Parsons, think only in terms of the macrocultural system, ignore the important role of single social institutions, which directly enforce people who voluntarily join institutions and accept the rules and only later the values of the institution.

The primary character of rules over values is typical for people who chose the army as a career and then appropriate the traditions and values of military institutions as their own. Quite often the rules and values of the army take over the cultural system as a whole. David Lipski (2004), opposing two values systems—first, that of military institutions (values such as discipline, self-sacrifice, duty, honor, courage and "controlled but savage violence") and second, that of American society as whole (values such as freedom, self-expression and pleasure)—evidently points to the prevalence of the first system of values over the second within American military institutions.

Robert Sampson and John Laub (1994, 64–99) argue against the exaggeration of "crime determinism," as developed by Gluecks (1950) and several other authors (as discussed earlier). They showed that "turning points" in the life course could interrupt the personal tradition of criminal behavior. They name two turning points: marriage and jobs. These two institutions, with their rules, are in some cases able to influence the social behavior of people. Another author who writes about crime, Donald Garland, rejects cultural determinism even more explicitly, suggesting that "culture must be viewed as inextricably bound up with material forms of action, ways of life and situational conditions." He continues, "We can thus talk about culture as a dimension of social life and a shaping context of social (and penal) action" (Garland, 1990, 194).

At the same time, there is no doubt that national culture plays a very important role and I do not want to be in the camp of those postmodernists and social constructivists who deny the "supra-individual" character of culture and see it at best as a conglomerate of various beliefs and values that people, in the process of "deliberate cognition," can choose from (see DiMaggio et al., 1996, 265–266, 271).

THE FLEXIBILITY OF VALUES

I assume that many social values and beliefs are very flexible, because they serve individuals and society as mechanisms of adaptation and survival. Not only instrumental values but even terminal values, which describe the goals of human behavior, are strongly influenced by the change in environment. The values and beliefs that belong to the ideological level of mentality are particularly flexible. These values and beliefs can be removed and replaced with surprising speed. We might refer to this as the "cassette mentality," given the ease with which viewpoints are changed by the individual. As Huntington (2004, 338) noted, not without sarcasm, "in 2000 there could well have been in Dresden people in their eighties who in their youth were sincere Nazis, then became sincere Communists, and after 1989 were sincere democrats."

Significant transformations in the political, economic and social order, particularly revolutions, bring radical changes in the value systems and in the relative weight of certain values in society. Several scholars with different theoretical views have reported data showing the great flexibility of values. Among them were Bellah et al. (1986) and Robert Putnam (2000), who lamented the decline of civic duties in the United States, and Francis Fukuyama, who described the major changes in the attitudes of the West toward the family and the obligations toward society and the declining role of trust as a value (*The Great Disruption*, 1999).

However, it was Ronald Inglehart who made changes in values his major preoccupation since 1970. Developing his theory about the postmodernist shift in values in the second half of the twentieth century, Inglehart joined the camp that supports the idea of the high flexibility of culture under the impact of external variables, and first of all economic processes. He talked about "the rise of new values and lifestyles," and even "the emergence of a new culture" "throughout the advanced industrial society." He focused on the concept of the scarcity of economic resources (and also on the related concepts of declining marginal utility and productivity) as the main factor that produced changes in values in developed countries. With the rise of the economy, the decline of the scarcity of resources and the rise of economic security, people moved from materialist values to postmaterialist values and now have less interest in economic factors (Inglehart, 1997, 25–28, 31–33; see Abramson and Inglehart, 1998, 9).

It is possible to accept Inglehart's conclusion about the tremendous impact of economic processes on culture without ignoring, of course, the initial influence of culture, including religion and other traditions on any "take off" in the economy. However, political changes can be an even more powerful factor in changing values and beliefs, which was evident as early as the Middle Ages. The famous statement "cuius regio, illius et religio" (he who reigns establishes the religion) reflects this experience. In this respect, I can find allies in scholars, such as Skocpol (1985) or Jackman and Miller (1996), who focus on the influence of the institutional changes on culture, which they considered as an endogenous variable.

The Inertia of Values and Beliefs

However, if the same political and economic order is sustained in society over a long period of time, even for centuries, the people inside the country create a very conservative society sustained by strong centralized power and the dominant ideology, most often religion. It creates the impression that such a society could "never" change, at least not radically. For both insiders and outsiders, the culture in such a society appears to be a crucial factor that is able to resist any external or internal factors of change. In fact, history shows how the strong conservative forces of the current culture will yield to the pressure of external forces, and quite quickly, if the elites, old or new, promote change. A comparison between Turkey, in which Kamal Ataturk changed Muslim society radically, and Saudi Arabia, whose leaders were able to preserve the existing order over a long period, suggests that culture is only one of the variables that influences the course of events, being itself the object of change.

I do not deny the inertia of several values, particularly those that we consider here as "individualistic" values. Values and beliefs are a sort of emotional and intellectual investment, which people try not to deflate, even if their stubbornness damages their ability to adapt to a new reality.

Learning values and cognitive constructions exclude access to "other values" and "other paradigms" and decreases one's ability to adjust quickly to the changes in their environment. The opportunity cost of accepting the given system of values and cognitive constructions, and the cost of rejecting other values and constructions, with their usefulness for adaptation, became evident during the radical transformation of society in the Communist world after 1989, and after the immigration to a country with a very different culture. These costs are much higher for old people with their declining ability to change and their resistance to new values and cognitive constructions. These costs are much easier for young people for whom a poorer life experience and a lower level of education turn out to be an asset in the process of adapting to new conditions.

People are formally forced to choose between various opportunities because they cannot live without some values and some ideas about the world. Once acquired, values and cognitive constructions have a serious impact on human life.

In a stable group or society, loyalty to the dominant culture is a manifestation of the adjustment to the environment. In an unstable group or in a new one, culture is an obstacle to adaptation, except when some elements of the old culture turn out to be in line with the new culture and even accelerate the adjustment, a case seen in the adaptation of the Chinese and Koreans to life in America.

Without denying some elements of biosociology and the influence of cultural variables on social processes, I, however, can cite myriad data that show how cultural patterns swiftly change with the developments in political and economic reality.

The Key Role of Elites and the State in the Creation of New Values and their Implementation

The elites create new values and quickly transform them into laws. Using the state as a coercive instrument, they force the masses to accept the new values and implement them, either because they finally internalized them, under pressure from above, or simply because of the current fear of sanctions. However, the same elites, using the power of the state, religion, education and arts, can successfully protect the values necessary for their dominance for centuries.

An approach that ascribes the origin of new values and beliefs to elites is deeply hostile to those who espouse ideas of self-regulation of society in both forms through culture from above, a la Durkheim or Parsons, or through individual interactions from below. Those who belong to the traditional cultural school usually tend to advance the spontaneous "mass" origin of new values and beliefs and reject the creative role of elites. Parsons talks about leaders, but only in the context of the division of roles and in no way does he link leaders to the creation of new values and new order in society (Parsons, 1951, 100, 135–136, 190). Indeed, with his specific attitudes toward changes in the social system, Parsons denied the ability of "one or inherently primary sources of impetus to change in social systems" (an allusion to Marxism). He believed that "new values patterns" emerge as a result of "the development of cultural configuration," including the development of science, or of religious ideas. Parsons left no room for the leaders, reflecting the new trends in society, to emerge as the creators of new values and beliefs. Parsons discussed several revolutionary movements (among them the Nazi movement), but he talks about the emergence of a new subculture; he mentioned the leaders as only playing the "expressive" role (Parsons, 1951, 492–493, 520–525). Among the opponents of the elitist approach are authors such as Dahl, who with his belief in the pluralism of American society does not single out social groups that take a leading role in social processes (Dahl, 1989).

New Left thinkers, including postmodernists, see the elites only as actors whose activities lead to the perpetuation of its dominance. In their view, the creation of new values and rules is a process in which all participants participate as equals, like the ranchers in Ellickson's county in California (1991, 152–153).

Even such a balanced author as Inglehart is generally inclined to ignore the role of elites in the creation of the values necessary for maintaining order in society (Inglehart, 1997). However, in one of his publications, with Paul Abramson as a coauthor, he points to the active role of the leaders of mass movements "in challenging forms of political action that helped to bring down authoritarian regimes in East Europe and the former Soviet Union" (Abramson and Inglehart, 1998; Inglehart, 1997, 26, 53).

The Elites as the Motor of Change
and the Bulwark of Conservatism

In their activities as creators and defenders of social values, elites use them in their own interests as well as in the interest of the social constituency, from small segments of the population to the whole nation. The difference between the egotistical interests of elites and the interests of the nation can be as great as it was, for instance, in Mao's China during the cultural revolution or in Yeltsin's Russia, or as small as it was in Stalin's Russia during the war against Nazi Germany. There is no doubt that in defending their interests, which may or may not concur with the interests of the masses, the elites resort to the most intricate means to create an ideology and values that are useful for them. Only the two-prong approach to the role of elites, which rejects the commendation of ruling elites as selfless "servants of society," as well as the disregard of their positive role in society creates a basis, in my opinion, for the sound analysis of their role in society and in the maintenance of social order.

As a matter of fact, only the elites are engaged professionally in the process of constructing ideology. Only elites are producers of values and beliefs as opposed to the rest of the population, which consists of consumers. The elites not only create values and beliefs, but translate them into laws and rules, as well as remove old values and beliefs. Controlling various social institutions, elites possess the instruments to persuade the masses about the validity of the dominant values and beliefs.

Rejecting the system-integrative approach, which is close to culturological theories of social order, I suppose that a segmented vision of society is a better fit for explaining social order. This approach supposes the special role of elites in the various segments of society—political, economic, cultural, ethnic and religious—in the maintenance and creation of values and beliefs.

Elites maintain and develop values in their own segment of society, but also try as much as possible to turn these values into national ones and transform them into laws. The competition among elites to make their values influential is a primordial phenomenon in almost all societies. The struggle is going on first of all between the key values of elites. Of course, the elites always have to take into account the views of the masses. In different societies and periods they do this in different ways, but the initiatives in forging order and sustaining it belong always to the elites. In most cases, the influence of the elites on the values of the masses is much stronger than vice versa.

In creating new values and norms (which are often brought in from other societies) and maintaining old ones, a special role is played by the educated class and its intellectual elite (i.e., intellectuals and people in media who possess the skills to justify the new laws and values and disseminate them). A special role is played by religious elites who have enjoyed throughout history more autonomy, influence and direct power than other groups of educated people. Religious elites have, in some cases, even seized political and economic power from other elite groups.

The relation of intellectuals (the true producers of new values and beliefs) to the political and economic elite is a subject of perennial debate. However, only a few authors claim that some intellectuals have total autonomy when compared to other types of elites, political and economic ones in the first place.[6] Either in the capacity of the independent stratum of the population, as Mosca or Mannheim suggested, or as the servants of the dominant class, intellectuals, on their own initiative or at the order of others, always have a monopoly on the articulation of new ideologies and new values.

The approach that I support is close to the spirit of Hobbes and John Stuart Mill who believed that only intellectual elites (and not blind forces) are able to prevent society from becoming a "stagnant pool." Pareto and Mosca are among the other authors who are close to my thinking. Hobbesian logic suggests that in most cases only a "few" people, such as the ruler, the government or the initiators and leaders of public movements, are able to coordinate the activity of people with the help of persuasion and coercion. It is the "few" who create most values, turn them into laws and force people to observe them.

The Allies

To some degree, these views are close to those of neo-Marxists, who focus on the cultural capital or media (Gramsci, Bourdieu and Habermas) as the major instruments of the dominant class in capitalist society.

The problem with contemporary Marxists and neo-Marxists is that they totally deny the positive role of elites in the creation and sustenance of order in society, an idea that was evident for Friedrich Engels in his *The Origin of Society and State*, written 150 years ago.

In one or another form, the elitist approach has found support outside the neo-Marxist camp. Much before the emergence of the neo-Marxist school, Tocqueville observed that the elites ("authorities" in Tocqueville's terms) "at first enforce obedience by constraint: and its laws are not *respected* until they have been long maintained" (Tocqueville, 1969, 255; italics in original). Amusingly, the same train of thought can be found in the text of Gentile, a notorious fascist philosopher, who insisted, in a rather normative fashion, that coercion precedes the process of internalization of values, saying that law "immanent in compulsion should become the conscious will of the person subject to it" (Gleason, 1995, 18).

Norbert Elias, in his book on the building of European civilization with its values and norms, demonstrated that the motor of change was the state and the ruling elites. He suggested that the bearers of civilization consist of a tiny aristocratic upper class, which rules over the rest of the world. He ascribed special attention to the role of "manners books," whose dissemination was very important to "civilizational processes." He underscored a tightening and a differentiation of the control imposed by society on individuals.[7] Elias directly relates the civilizing process to the formation and growth of the state, which monopolizes violence on its territory (Elias, 1978).

Some support for the elitist approach can be found among those contemporary social scientists who are critical of the theories that insist on the spontaneous "mass" origin of values. In an obvious critique of this theory, Hechter and Opp (2001b, xi) pointed to the fact that legal norms are created by design. The same view was held by Edward Banfield who insisted that "the amorality," or amoral familialism of Southern Italy, can be changed only by the intervention of outside forces: the political Left, the church and the industry of the North (Banfield, 1965, 164). Benjamin Schwartz was sure that the process of assimilation in America was directed by the Anglo elite, which was able "to stamp its image on other people coming to this country." He continues, "the elite's religious and political principles, its customs and social relations, its standards of taste and morality, were for 300 years America's and in a basic way they still are—despite our celebration of 'diversity' " (Schwartz, 1995, 62).

Some support for the elitist approach to the origin of new values can also be found among those scholars who study the role of law in social processes and who ascribe to the central administration an important role in value changes (Sunstein, 1993; see also Lessig, 1998).

The view of elites developed by Samuel Huntington in *Challenges* (2004, 151–153, 157, 171–174, 199–200, 325) was interesting. On one side, as a typical culturologists, he talked about the Anglo-Protestant culture and the Protestant religion as the major factors of American life, since the inception of the nation. However, on another side, he recognized the crucial role of "denationalized elites," as he labeled them. These elites are, as he asserted, "almost three times as liberal as the public on the whole." Since the 1960s, they pioneered changes in the value system of America, coming up in favor of multi-culturalism over "Americanization," and against religion and many other core American values, underscoring the radical differences in the views of the bulk of the population, which is still devoted to protestant ethics and the elites who try to destroy it by all possible means. Neil Ferguson ties the successes of the British Empire in the Middle East and the gloomy future of "the American empire" in this region to the different types of British and American elites. The first type was deeply involved in international affairs, whereas the second did not want to "bear the personal cost of international governance" (Ferguson, 2004).

A large group of defenders of the elitist approach consist of scholars from the non-Western world who observed the expansion of Western values and laws in their society. For these scholars, the leading role of the elites in this process is more than evident. Among them are, for instance, those who studied India. Sunil Khilnani, in *The Idea of India*, discussed democracy in this country as "imposed by political elites on the masses after the centuries of rule by invaders and empire builders" (Khilnani, 1997). The role of British elites in imposing democratic institutions in India (as well as in other British colonies) is also significant despite the brutality of British imperialism (see Shama, 2003; see also Zakaria, 2003).

I illustrate the high flexibility of values and the role of the elites in this process, using as examples Russia and the United States, as well as postwar Germany and Japan.

CULTURE AND ELITES: THE RUSSIAN CASE

There were two cases in twentieth-century Russian history when the elites created a new system of values and beliefs.

The Victory of Bolshevik Values

Despite resistance from "the old mentality," the Bolsheviks were able to instill several new values in the public mind after the October Revolution in a very short period of time. Ronald Inglehart (1997, 19) was very wrong when he asserted that Stalin's program of changing Russian society failed.

Let us take as examples private property and religion, two central values in prerevolutionary Russian society that dissolved during the Soviet era. Indeed, the Communists were not only the first in world history to destroy the foundation of traditional private property, but they convinced the people to loathe this form of property. This alone was a grandiose ideological success, even if we take into account some of the "communal traditions" that existed in Russia before 1917. In 1993, two years after the fall of the Soviet system and five decades after Stalin's terror, after the ideological brainwashing and after Yeltsin's official propaganda against public property, more than 50 percent of the Russians demonstrated in various polls their allegiance to the concept of public property.[8] They advocated public property for large enterprises and a regulatory state role in the economy, while expressing their suspicion of private property and private businessmen. Even Gorbachev, the great reformer and destroyer of Communist society, did not express any positive words about private property until one year before the collapse of the Soviet Union (Shlapentokh, 2001).

The Communists were also quite successful in downgrading the importance of religion in Soviet society. There were widely divergent views on the degree of religiosity of the Russian people before the revolution (from the praise of prerevolutionary Russians as "the single God bearers in the world" to the assertion that they had always been indifferent toward Christianity). However, it can hardly be denied that the church played a significant role in the lives of most Russians before the revolution.

In the 1920s and 1930s, the Bolsheviks managed to recruit hundreds of thousands of Russians to destroy many thousands of their churches. With the educational system and propaganda machine based on the glorification of science, the Bolsheviks greatly decreased religious beliefs in the public mind. In the 1970s, according to a sociological study, no more than 25–30 percent of the population (mostly old people) considered themselves "religious."[9] In comparison to the mid-1930s, this number dwindled by two times. According to the national census in 1937, this number stood at 57 percent (Zhiromskaia, 1998). Besides the energetic atheist propaganda, the worldwide trend of secularism was also accountable for these changes and the dominance of atheism in the country. Those who were developing their careers in the Soviet Union adapted to official atheism extremely quickly (after 1991, the same people declared themselves to be religious).[10] People with higher education too were less likely to hold religious beliefs.[11]

According to Yurii Levada's study of the Soviet people's religious views in 1989: "en mass the non belief in God surpasses the belief in God," and "it is possible to speak about the non-religiosity of Soviet society." By 1989, the people understood that their religious feelings would not hurt their social status. In fact, much of the media favored religion. And still, 35 percent of the Russians declared themselves "nonbelievers"; less than 20 percent reported that they followed religious rituals (Levada, 1993, 216–218).

The First Attack against Soviet Values

The next case is related to the offensive against Soviet values, which were deeply embedded in the Soviet mind. Again, the attack did not come from the masses, from below, but from the liberal intellectual elite from above.

The attack against Soviet values was started by liberal intellectual elites in the 1960s itself. The objects of its attack were specific Soviet values. Since the early years of Soviet history, the official ideology proclaimed its opposition to universal (or in the Soviet lexicon, "all-mankind") values, favoring its own specific Soviet values, based on Marxism and the class approach. By universal values, Soviet ideology usually refers to humanistic values, such as altruism, kindness, friendship and respect for tradition.

Following Stalin's death, the intellectuals began a general offensive against the class approach and in support of universal values. Perhaps more so than in any other activity, intellectuals were united in this movement, regardless of their ideological propensities. In addition, the intellectuals were able to take advantage of the political elite's growing desire to achieve respectability on both the domestic and international fronts.

The major message that the intellectuals, particularly the writers, wanted to get across to the Soviet people was that without respect for universal, and to some degree Christian, values, they were doomed to moral degradation. Given the insignificant influence of the church on the Soviet people, the intellectuals essentially became the single group striving to raise the moral standards of behavior in the country.

Since 1953, Soviet literature has been active in the struggle to advance new universal values. Two basic themes can be identified in this regard. The first was related to the defense of universal civic values, such as openness, political freedom and equality. The second stressed more universal humanistic values, such as love, friendship, honesty and devotion to parents and family.

These themes have gained momentum in different periods, depending on a number of circumstances. In the late 1950s and early 1960s, both themes were promoted equally, when measured by the popularity of writers representing them. In the mid-to-late 1960s, civic values took a leading role; in the 1970s, with the intellectuals' increasing political apathy and the rise of the Russophile movement, humanistic values prevailed.

The intelligentsia's strong interest in classical Russian literature is important here as well. Soviet ideology has generally favored writers who stressed social conflict and thus generated negative attitudes toward universal values. By contrast, my survey of *Literaturnaia Gazeta* readers, conducted in 1968, found that the intelligentsia was becoming attracted to the older Russian writers who addressed the more eternal problems of human life and universal values. When asked about their preferred Russian authors, the respondents gave 36 percent of their votes to Tolstoy, 32 percent to Chekov, 21 percent to

Dostoevsky, 18 percent to Kuprin and 17 percent to Bunin (the figures do not total 100 percent since some respondents endorsed several authors). Writers oriented toward social issues were much less popular.

Preferences regarding foreign authors also indicated support for those addressing universal values. Most popular were those writers focusing on issues of humanity and individualism, such as Ernest Hemingway, Erich Maria Remarque, Heinrich Böll, Graham Greene and J.D. Salinger.

The advancement of universal values went ahead with much less vigor in the social sciences than in literature and the arts. Nonetheless, Soviet philosophers and sociologists made significant steps in this direction. After 1986–88, it became possible to recognize publicly that universal values, such as mercy, compassion and kindness, were among the most neglected in Soviet history. This recognition, in turn, legitimized the creation of associations designed to assist the elderly, the handicapped and children.

The Second Attack against Soviet Values: After 1991

In 1985–87, the new leader of the Soviet Union joined the struggle against old values. The major targets of the campaign, launched this time by the general secretary of the party himself, were the highest sacred cows of the Soviet ideology—the state as the supreme value along with public property and the planning system, the Soviet empire, the army and the KGB. Fierce attacks were directed also against the major Soviet beliefs about Lenin, the October Revolution, collectivization and others.

Under Gorbachev's impetus, liberal media advocates became committed enemies of the state. They completely denounced the state, which represented a major value and a real icon in Soviet ideology. Media highlighted the advantages of liberal capitalism while condemning the Soviet ideology. The public was bombarded with the suggestion that only privatization could save the country in a brief period of time. Many propagandists of liberal capitalism suggested that the destruction of socialism would make the people owners of the means of production.

As the new ideology evolved, Gorbachev declared a war against the Soviet totalitarian state on many fronts. After 1986, the Kremlin tolerated and then sanctioned the growing attacks against other sacred cows of the Soviet value system: the party as the leading institution and the party apparatus. Of particular interest was the evolution of attitudes toward the army, an institution that had been sacred for 1,000 years in Russian history.

A Special Case of Changing Values: The Army

The army was a highly respected institution among all strata of the population. The occupation of officer was among the ten most-prestigious jobs in the country. This opinion had already been established by the first sociological studies of male teenagers conducted in the 1960s. On a scale from 1 (low regard) to 10 (high regard), the position of officer was rated by young males with a score of 6.36 (in 1965); four years later, this number increased to 7.55. Army officers enjoyed higher levels of prestige than the majority of occupations that demanded a college education (i.e., engineers, doctors and teachers). Among rural teenagers, the profession of officer reached second place on their list of the most-favored jobs (Tarasov and Kotunov, 1984, 25–81). Even in 1994, when the prestige of the army decreased, the profession of officer was still rated with a 5.87, much higher than such occupations as professor, journalist, politician, actor or scholar.[12]

The respect for the army was so strong that in 1985, on the eve of perestroika, draftees were still willingly going to the army, and the farewell party for them was indeed a manifestation of joy and pride. Nikita Mikhalkov's film *Kinfolk* (1982) depicted the farewell party for a young man going to the army as a celebration.[13]

In post-Soviet Russia, the media treated draft-dodgers like heroes. Army cadets had no prestige in society. After the strong ideological campaign launched in 1987 by liberal media and then continued by the new rulers of the country after 1991, the attitudes of the population toward the army changed drastically. According to a 1997 survey, only 18 percent of young Russians wanted to serve in the army.[14] Bribing recruiters and falsifying medical records are considered legitimate strategies for avoiding army service. Avoiding army duty was seen as a form of civic protest. Young people who are not able to skirt recruitment are viewed as misfits or failures because they do not have the resources (intellectual or financial) to avoid service. After 1991, one would be extremely hard-pressed to find a rich Muscovite in the Russian armed forces. Russian families are no longer willing to sacrifice their children for any war, regardless of its official justification.[15]

The American Case

The high flexibility of values is typical of American society. As in Russia, all major changes in values in the United States, as well as social reforms that are usually based on new values, were initiated by American elites and institutions such as the courts, media, the congress, labor unions and organize public movements, civil rights organization, feminists, consumer activists and environmentalists, as well as a host of single-issue groups headed by prominent individuals such Betty Friedan, Martin Luther King, Bayard Rustin (Bellah, 1991, 124; D'Emilio, 2003). John Judis insists that "elites and elite organizations have served as a repository for a set of values that have been essential to American democracy."[16]

In the last half century, it is in fact difficult to find any change of values in America that was not initiated by political and cultural activists. We see the same thing in all other countries in the world.

The swift changes in values in America since the 1960s are indeed remarkable. Let us compare Williams's list of 15 values, which described society in the 1950s–60s with a list of values from the 1990s. Some key values for Americans in the 1990s are simply absent in Williams's list, including ecology. According to Inglehart's study of values in 1995–97, 48 percent voted for the priority of ecology over economy; 77 percent voted for job security, the active role of women in the economy (37 percent), order in society (49 percent) and freedom (51 percent). As John White (2003, 12) writes, "The value consensus that existed previous to the sexual revolution of 1960s forbade premarital sex, saw divorce as a horror to be avoided, and never, ever discussed homosexuality in polite company."

A comparison of the values survey conducted by NORC in 1968 (and used by Milton Rokeach) with the World Values Survey conducted in the late 1990s showed the same differences. Among the 18 terminal values in the first survey, it is impossible to find such values as "environment," "hard work," "state of health," which appeared in the survey on values 30 years later (Inglehart, 1997, ix–xiii; Rokeach, 1973, 57).

The data brought by Ronald Inglehart in his studies of postmodern values also show the significant changes in American values. In 1974, using 12 values—postmaterialist ("more say in government," "more say in job," "less impersonal society," "freedom of speech," "ideas count more than money," "more beautiful cities") and materialist ("economic growth," "strong defense forces," "maintain stable economy," "fight rising prices," "fight against crime," "maintain order")—he found that the number of people with a materialist orientation surpassed the number of people with postmaterialist orientations by 35 percent, but in 1994 the number of people with postmaterialist orientations was higher than the number of people in the other category by 12 percent. The same drastic changes were discovered in all West European countries. In Denmark, for instance, the corresponding numbers were 35 and 22 percent (Inglehart, 1997, 140; see Abramson and Inglehart, 1998).

The cases of homosexuality or smoking are probably even more eloquent indicators of the ease with which each society can change its attitudes toward social issues. Until the mid-1980s, attitudes toward homosexuals were almost unanimously hostile. However, it took less than one decade to polarize America in their attitudes toward this issue.[17] In the early 1990s itself, only 57 percent of Americans said that "homosexuality is never justified" and only 39 percent of Americans were against having homosexuals as their neighbors (Inglehart et al., 1998, 80, 307).

The German and Japanese Cases

Postwar Germany and Japan offer excellent examples of radical changes in values taking place in a short period of time and from above. Indeed, in both countries, new constitutions, containing new values (most of them directed against the past), were issued by the occupying powers, changing the psychology of both nations considerably.

In West Germany, it was the higher commissariat headed by John McCloy that was the major motor that changed the rules, laws and ultimately the values in this part of Germany. Two other Western occupying powers—England and France—cooperated with the American administration in the democratization of West Germany, adopting in 1946 the Basic Law as a substitution for the constitution. The first section of this document enumerated the civil and political rights of all citizens. With an eye on the Weimar past, and in order to protect democratic institutions from extremists, the Basic Law banned all political movements that could endanger the new democratic order. The Basic Law was apportioned a crucial role in governing the German parliament, the Bundestag. The electorate law adopted later established the election—"personalized proportionality"—which combined the proportional system of representation with elements of the constituency system, similar to the system in Britain and the United States. The electorate law avoided the flaw of the election system of the Weimar republic, which forced people to vote only for the party, but not for the individual. As one of its major tasks, the American administration and its allies wanted to persuade Germany about the criminal character of the Nazi regime, and that the Nuremberg trials were fair, along with the restitution to Jews and the state of Israel. The military administration saw its most important tasks in the decentralization of the government, the increased role of states (Land) and the decartelization of the economy. The Basic Law also created a Constitutional Court, which, in the spirit of the Anglo-American principle of judicial review, could challenge the constitutionality of any law or measure taken by the government (Schwartz, 1991; Turner, 1992).

It took probably one decade for the majority of the West German population to accept the new values introduced by the allies despite the significant resistance of the old generations, which, for a long time, was far from the condemnation of the Nazi regime, its racism, anti Semitism and the endorsement of the Nuremberg trials. The cold war climate, which was used by Adenauer's government, did not encourage the democratic process and denazification. The conservative forces in West Germany concentrated mostly on the Christian Democratic Union and tried to hinder the Westernization of Germany, for instance, by fighting the liberation of women (see, for instance, Hohn, 2002).

At the same time, Germany's experience with democracy in the past—even before the Weimar republic—helped impose new principles of political and economic life in Germany. Some analysts, such as Donald Kommers, even asserted that "the bottom–up" process of democratization in West Germany was as important as the "top–down" process.[18]

The role of the military administration in promoting new values in postwar Japan was even greater than in Germany in view of the weak democratic traditions in the country. The General Headquarters of the American army in Japan headed by General Douglas McArthur was the same as the high commissariat headed by John McCloy in Germany. It declared a policy of demilitarization and the eradication of "the will to war," as well as the democratization of Japanese society, which was reflected in a new constitution endorsed by the occupiers in 1947. The changes introduced by the occupiers were so strong that, as the American author John Dower wrote, "although not all of the early reforms survived intact, their durability was ruefully acknowledged by Yoshida Shigeru, the dominant conservative politician of the early postwar period, whose own cabinets were forced to introduce much of the legislation for the victors' agenda." It was, as Dower suggests, "one of the most audacious experiences in social engineering in history." Even "the counterreforms," "the reverse course" imposed in the 1950s under the impact of the cold war could not essentially change the democratic transformation of Japanese society (Takemae, 2002).

It was the American military administration that, despite tremendous resistance, managed to diminish the cult of the emperor in the country. The Constitution of 1947 guaranteed basic civil, political and other fundamental rights to Japanese citizens, and created a judicial system that was committed to upholding these liberties. The postwar reforms liberated women from traditional roles and granted them the same legal rights and entitlement as men. With the prompting of the Supreme Commander of the Allied Powers (SCAP), Japan adopted a new electoral law that made the first free general election possible. SCAP created also a sort of multiparty system, which—far from the Western model named the one-and-a-half party system—still represented major progress in comparison to the political system in Japan before 1945. All the more, in the 1990s there were some positive changes in this area and in other political parties, besides the Liberal Democratic Party, which dominated Japanese political life, and the Socialist Party, which became much more active. The American occupying authorities did much to weaken the feudal *zaibatsu* (the elite conglomerates in the economy), and the redistribution of property, the promotion of local autonomy, the decentralization of education, land reforms and labor rights (Takemae, 2002, 516–560).

The reforms introduced from above changed immensely the mind of the majority of the Japanese population, particularly the new generations that looked at the world from a radically different perspective than their grandfathers. I am not suggesting that General McArthur and his administration fully changed the minds of the Japanese people and eliminated the influence of the old culture. As one author who surveyed the impact of the occupation on the Japanese mind underscores, "many old traditions remain, especially in the social and psychological areas" (Hane, 1996). Some Japanese traditions seem strongly opposed to the Western values that were imposed on Japan after 1945, including the notorious Japanese bureaucracy (see Scalapino, 1989). Other Japanese traditions are valuable to other countries, including Western countries, as Vogel contends in his book *Japan as Number One* (1979).

However, caveats aside, it is evident that the average Japanese person, by the end of the twentieth century, had a new mentality, and widely accepted democratic values in comparison to the mind of his ancestors before 1945. As an American authors contends, "on the whole, the Americans were successful in convincing young Japanese that 'democracy' was good and 'feudalism' was bad" (Duus, 1976, 247; see also Passin, 1992). The new attitudes of the Japanese toward many political, economic and social values were to a great degree the product of the developments that occurred after 1945 under the guidance of SCAP, a sort of "planned political change" (Kawai, 1960; see also Baley, 1996, 4; Ishida and Kraus, 1989). The crucial role of SCAP cannot be diminished even if we label it as "benevolent colonialism" (Duus, 1976, 239), or if the Japanese input in the reforms is taken into account (Ward and Sakamoto, 1987) or if we accept the view of a tiny group of scholars who suppose that the reforms were built up on prewar developments, such as the liberalism of the Taisho era (Ward, 1968).

CONCLUSION

The weakness of Parson's culturological concept of order, which is shared by most contemporary sociologists and social psychologists, exaggerates the stability of values. Indeed, for values to play the role ascribed to them by Parsons they would have to be steady and impervious to the current political or economic processes.

Without denying the inertia of several values and beliefs, I join those scholars who assume that social values are highly flexible, as well as culture in general. The dynamism of social values should be ascribed to the activity of the elites, which, in order to maintain order and protect their interests, introduce new laws and values. As an illustration of the high flexibility of social values, Russia in the twentieth century presents a particularly interesting case. In a relatively short historical period, the Russian people radically changed their value orientations twice: first, after the Communist revolution in 1917, when they abandoned their allegiance to religion, private property and the market economy, along with several other values; and second, after the anti-Communist revolution in 1991 when the Russians began to respect the same values again. The major changes in the attitudes of Americans to various values in the last 50 years represent another example of the shaky basis of order, when it is based only on values. Of special interest is Germany and Japan after their defeats during WWII. The American military administration was able to radically change the role of values in both societies, setting both on the road toward democratization and demilitarization.

CHAPTER 7

Fear as a Neglected Variable

In previous chapters, I tried to show that culture and its core (social values) cannot serve as the only basis of social order. The mechanism of rewards and particularly the fear of punishment are necessary for the maintenance of order. Meanwhile, the social role of fear is mostly downgraded in contemporary sociological literature.

FEAR: A DEFINITION

I define fear as a basic negative emotional reaction to a threat, real or imaginary, and an expectation of pain (see Barbalet, 1998; Petty and Wegener, 1998, 353–354; Zajonz, 1998, 594).[1] Fear as an emotion is deeply linked to uncertainty and the future, an issue that was raised by John Dewey in his classic work *Quest for Certainty*, and developed by Andrew Ortony and his coauthors who defined fear as a "prospect based emotion" (Ortony et al., 1990, 109–114).

The fear of the future has always been an important part of human life. In some periods of history—for instance, in the Middle Ages in Europe—the most intensive fears in society were fueled by eschatological predictions of the end of the world, which played a major role in people's lives (Bloch, 1961).

As any other emotion, fear can be encouraged or stifled by the individual or society. The adaptation mechanism can have the opposite effect on fear. It might stimulate it as a warning about danger, or soften it to the point of eliminating it from the mind of the individual or society, if nothing can be done to prevent the nefarious event.

Whatever the type of fear, it is not a "material object," but a signal of a possible event that can damage the individual, group or nation. The cognitive school in the psychology of emotion returns to the Stoics, who viewed emotions as linked to beliefs and rational judgments (see Dixon, 2004, 3–4; Solomon, 2003; 2004; Sunstein, 2003).

The "objective character" of a perceived threat is crucial, but it represents only one factor.[2] I reject both extremes in the treatment of fears: "naive realism" on one side, and the postmodern "total relativism" on the other. My point of view is that people's fears more or less reflect real objective dangers in society ("hard reality"). I also recognize that fears are mental constructions that can be influenced by "soft reality" (ideology, historical memory and various individual psychological characteristics) as much as by any emotion, such as love, envy or even physical pain. Imaginary fears that have no "objective basis" (the fear of a nonexisting foreign enemy, for instance) are as "objective" as "real" fears. Henrich Heine noted that "imaginary pain" is also "pain." Adam Smith in his *The Theory of Moral Sentiments* even defined fear as "a passion derived altogether from imagination" (Smith, 1982, 30).

The anticommunist hysteria in the United States during the cold war period was an excellent example of the mixture of "rational" and "irrational fears" (see Barson and Heller, 2001; Pry, 1999; on the fear of war—"real, pretended or imaginary"—in the postrevolutionary years in America, see also Emma Rothschild (2004). Another example was the Soviet fears of the war in the 1920s and 1930s and during the postwar period. There was the same mixture of fear produced by propaganda and real facts (Shlapentokh, 2001). A more recent episode, the developments surrounding Hurricane Katrina in New Orleans in September 2005, also confirmed this observation. As generalized by two journalists who studied the criminal activities during this period, "What became clear is that the rumor of crime, as much as the reality of the public disorder, often played a powerful role in the emergency response" (Dwyer and Drew, 2005).

Fear does not play such an enormous role in the life of human beings as it does in the world of animals, where this emotion competes only with the permanent quest for food. Darwin paid much attention to fear, focusing on flight as the major reaction to threats (1965). As Erich Kahler noted, man alone sleeps (in most instances) without fear (1967). However, fear dominates human psychology at several different levels of awareness (from direct alarm to deeply repressed anxiety). Fear as an essential part of human existence has been underscored by a few philosophers such as Hobbes, Kierkegaard, Heidegger and Sartre, as well as by Freud and particularly Eric Fromm and Karen Horney.[3] Fear is clearly not ignored by classic writers, such as Homer and Ovid, or by recent authors of quality fiction and bad horror novels, as Joyce Carol Oates (1998) suggested in her article in *Salmagundi*, where she discussed the "aesthetics of fear."

The Existential and Social Fear

Several intellectual traditions have helped to entrench the concept of fear in the literature as a mostly existential, internal psychological and individual phenomenon, as opposed to an external, social one. Only a few authors, such as Barbalet, make a clear distinction between social and nonsocial fears (Barbalet, 1998, 149).

In the opinion of several authors who focus on the existential character of fear, people should be able to control their fears. It is impossible to deny that the transformation of fear in the human mind and the ability of individuals to cope with fear is an extremely important aspect of human life. It is also true that fear has deep physiological roots and in many cases can emerge, along with other emotions such as jealousy, as an all absorbing emotion that does not have "objective grounds." World literature is full of novels that describe the irrational outbursts of fear. Recently, it was two British authors, Julian Barnes (2004) and Ian McEwan (1999), who very vividly described how fear can take control of human beings.

Drawing on the purely psychological concept of fear are Greek philosophers such as Aristotle, religious philosophers such as Augustine or Thomas Aquinas and philosophers such as Spinoza (1949, 131), Kant (1959, 67) and Michel Montaigne, up to the last representative of the eighteenth century, Tocqueville.[4] Among the thinkers of the Enlightenment, it is probably only Montesquieu (even if he did not share Hobbes's belief in the positive role of fear), in *The Spirit of the Law*, who "externalized terror," that is, insisted that the fear of terror has an external origin, stemming from the activity of the despot.

Among contemporary authors, the psychologization of the concept of fear has been quite popular. Some authors repeat Montaigne's elegant phrase about the crucial role of "the fear of fear" (Shklar, 1987). They went so far as to proclaim that terror is a "psychological reaction" to overweening physical danger (Robin, 2004, 9; Shklar, 1987, 84).

Most fears, unlike purely existential ones, have a social origin. They are engendered by society, its institutions and developments.[5] The proportion of existential versus social fears, which are not separated from each other by an iron wall, varies a great deal. Yurii Levada attempted to measure the relative role of both types of fear in post-Soviet Russia. He discovered that existential fears (the fear of death of close relatives or one's self) are the leading fears on a 5-point scale (1 minimal, 5 maximal). The Russians assessed them in 2003 as 4.17 and 3.57, respectively. Fears that have social origins were ranked somewhat lower: the fear of criminals (3.48), the fear of poverty (3.36) and the arbitrariness of the authorities (3.35) (Levada, 2004, 17). Similar data can be found in the case of France in a survey conducted in 2004, and in the United States in 2005.[6]

Here I deal with fears that originate under social conditions. Images of fear change in the course of history. For example, the nature and variety of fear in the Middle Ages were in many respects different from those of the present. The content and repertoire of fears change from one culture to another and further still from one period to the next within a given culture.

Here, I do not consider individual existential fears, such as the fear of death or the fear of losing a beloved family member, unless these fears are used by social institutions or social actors for their purposes.[7]

In addition to a medley of historically and culturally influenced fears, there are also a number of apparently universal fears that recur with little variation through time and across cultures. Among these anxieties are the fears of natural disasters, war, the dispossession of independence imposed on one's ethnic group or nation, starvation, drastic degeneration in one's standard of living, anarchy and crime in society. The similarity between fears across history and across cultures enables modern scholars to understand the documents of the past and address various impending catastrophes.

HOBBES, LOCKE AND PARSONS

Contemporary sociology tends to ignore or downgrade the role of fear as a crucial factor in the maintenance of social order, in the decision-making processes of individuals in their everyday lives and in the quality of life. This disregard of fear is combined in the literature with the underestimation of the role of Hobbes in social science. In no way do I expect that Hobbes, with his numerous contradictions and obscurities, can be taken as a source of wisdom on all social issues. In fact, the Hobbesian model of society, created in the seventeenth century and strongly influenced by the antidemocratic predisposition of its author, should not be seen as a major basis for the analysis of social order and other aspects of social life. As Barbalet aptly noted, "One does not have to eat the whole Hobbesian pie to savor one of its cherries" (1998, 150). With all my respect for Marx, I would reject the attempt of Orthodox Marxists to look at contemporary society through the lenses of only this thinker. Though extremely creative, his works belong to the nineteenth century. However, both Hobbes and Marx made their contributions to social analysis and offered important independent variables that have passed the test of time. These variables should not be treated in a monistic or reductionist way, that is, as the only variables that determine social life—this being the usual strategy used by their critics as an argument to dismiss their contribution to social analysis.

Hobbes demands that we take into account people's fears and general mistrust of each other, along with the fear of the state. These variables have been mostly ignored by the mainstream of social science in the analysis of democratic societies. On one side, most sociologists, discussed in detail later, do not see the difference between positive fears, which are useful for the maintenance of order, and negative fears, which diminish the quality of life and political freedoms. On the other side, there is a tendency in sociology to make no distinction between the state in totalitarian society and the state in democratic societies. Although there is some overlap between the functions of both types of states, they are radically different. One is deeply hostile toward its citizens, whereas the other is, with all its flaws, an essential factor for the prosperity of the people.

As a materialist and someone who experienced the English civil war, Hobbes focuses on self-preservation as the major reason for action, and offered (along the line chosen by Machiavelli a century before) a gloomy picture of human beings as solitary entities in the state of nature. This view in no way contradicts the spirit of theories of rational choice, as aptly observed by Ross Harrison (2003, 65). Hobbes's picture of human beings includes also a belief in their rationality and such goals of human beings as power in the first place (later Nietzsche develops this idea), but also wealth, honor and glory (or reputation). He believed that "during the time when men live without a common power to keep them all in awe, they are in the condition which is called war, and such a war is of every man against every man." He demonstrated high perspicacity in his reflections on the nature of society and the cause of conflicts, and he focused on the dearth of resources (Hobbes, 1996, 66, 84).[8]

Hobbes's pessimistic view of human beings roused the anger of the next generation of thinkers, among them Rousseau, even if his critics contended that Rousseau's concept of the "common will" was not very far from the idea of the Leviathan, as noted by Benjamin Constant in 1815. Hobbes and Rousseau both supposed that people are born equal, but they drew different conclusions from this first premise.[9] In regard to Rousseau's polemic against Hobbes, the liberal thinkers who sided with the French author were inclined to accept the image of the "noble savage," rather than the Hobbesian individual who assessed others only in terms of power (Hobbes, 1996, 10).

Remaining skeptical about the ability of people to reconcile their perceptions of what is good and what is bad, Hobbes saw the powerful state as the embodiment of the single will (in the person of the king, or in a governing parliament), which, with the promises of punishment for the violation of law, creates the basis of order. "Where there is no common Power, there is no Law: where no Law, no Injustice if there be no Power erected, or not great enough for our security; every man will and may lawfully rely on his own strength and art, for caution against all other men" (Hobbes, 1996, 10). Hobbes's sober analysis of the state and power is still enlightening. As Ross Harrison noted, Hobbes prevents us from the illusions of "the argument of power." "As the Mafia might put it, after placing the horse's head in the bed, it is an argument that cannot be refused. The horse's head threatens death to the person whose bed it is, and thereby gives him a reason to act" (Harrison, 2003, 46).

Hobbes mocked liberty from law as totally absurd (Hobbes, 1996, 85,141). In his deep penetration into the concept of order, Hobbes was the first to pay great attention to the period of transition of power—a particularly dangerous period for people in nondemocratic societies. This issue has been ignored by most analysts who study societies of the Soviet type (Hobbes, 1996, 123–132).

Over three centuries only a few prominent figures since Hobbes dared to join him in expressing a similar view on the role of the state and coercion in human society. Among them was Goethe who was not afraid to say that "order is more important than freedom, because without order there is no freedom."[10] Freud too belongs to this group. Referring to the "aggressive inclination of human beings," he said that only a powerful state can prevent society from self-destruction. Almost repeating Hobbes, Freud wrote that "civilization expects to prevent the worst atrocities of brutal violence by taking upon itself the right to employ violence against criminals" (Freud, 1930). Albert Einstein concurred with Freud on this issue, as we can see from their correspondence (Einstein and Freud, 1964, 199–121). Hobbes was evidently close to Weber, whose definitions of the state and political power, with his focus on coercion and the importance of using physical force against those who do not obey the state, is similar to the spirit of *Leviathan* (Weber 1947, 154).

Without mentioning Hobbes or other relevant authors, Locke offered a milder view of human nature and gravitated toward a utilitarian theory, focused not on the Hobbesian state of nature and the war of all against all, but on a state of nature that does not suppose that people harm each other "in his life, health, liberties, or possessions."

Locke believed that self-interest and the rationality of the human mind were sufficient grounds for order. "Two men who pull the oars of a boat do it by an argument and convention," and without resorting to help from Leviathan. Locke did not ignore the role of fear in social life. He treated fear as a particular form of "uneasiness," and believed that human rationality would urge people not to permanently fight or fear each other. Locke also did not ignore the importance of political power, which guaranteed freedom and the right to property. Locke also endowed political power with the "right of making laws, with penalties of death, and consequently all less penalties for the regulating and preserving of property and of employing the force of the community in the execution of such laws, and in the defense of the commonwealth from foreign injury, and all this only for the public good" (Locke, 1988). However, in Locke's philosophy, the state yielded to civil society and was dependent on the free will of people who contracted with it, whereas Hobbes's political machine emerged with "tacit" (not active as Locke supposed) acceptance of the people (Locke, 1959, 305, 316, 333). Locke was followed by Leibniz who accused Hobbes of exaggerating the importance of Leviathan (Leibniz, 1988, 118–119). Kant, belonging to the next generation of thinkers, was even harsher in his critique of Leviathan, where people were presented as "immature children who cannot distinguish what is truly useful or harmful to themselves" and "would be obliged to behave purely passively and to rely upon the judgment of the head of state as to how they ought to be happy" (Kant, 1970, 74).

Locke would come to be seen as more attractive to Anglo-American social scientists than his pessimistic antagonist who was directly linked to Social Darwinism by most of his critics, an accusation that in the 1990s might seem even more terrible than in the past (see about this accusation in Wrong, 1994, 7). In the second half of the twentieth century, Hobbes was accused of being a moral relativist, atheist, socialist, an advocate of totalitarianism and a precursor of National Socialism and Stalin's regime. In some ways, these accusations have grounds, because Hobbes focused on the obeisance to the ruler, as well as the ruler's right to confiscate the private property of his subjects (see Hampton, 1986; Rogow, 1986, 234, 245; Sommervile, 1992; Tuck, 2002, 130). Carl Schmitt (1938), whose sympathy to Nazism is beyond doubt, tried to use Hobbes for the substantiation of National Socialism as the alternative to the decaying Western society. However, to assess Hobbes's intellectual heritage in one way or another depending on how he was used in history is as wrong as evaluating Marx only through the prism of the Soviet experience.

It was Parsons who expressed the dominant views on Hobbes in Anglo-Saxon literature in 1964. It is true that Parsons paid a lot of attention to Hobbes and even labeled the whole issue of social order as "Hobbes' problem." Parsons had the same claim to look at society as a system. As Michael Oakeshott noted, Hobbes "stands out, and not only among his contemporaries, but also in the history of English philosophy, as the creator of a system" (1975, 11).

Parsons accused Hobbes (incorrectly in the opinion of Wrong, 1994, 74) of "proto utilitarianism" (as a matter of fact, he and many other contemporary authors did not make the distinction between Hobbes's and Locke's "utilitarianism" and the classic utilitarianism of its authors, such as Bentham and Mills),[11] and with some reason (but also with some exaggeration), disregarding culture and values as influencing human behavior (see Parsons, 1975, 88). Of course, there are grounds to name Hobbes as an advocate of individualism, a Wrong version of the not-too-over-socialized human actor.[12] Parsons did not believe that many elements of culture—"civil associations" (see Slomp, 2000, 6) among others—play an important role in Hobbes's picture of society. Parsons maintained that macroculture in general, its "normative elements," or moral values, is enough to answer "the Hobbesian problem of social order." Parsons did not deny that Hobbes's solution to the problem was possible. Rather, he regarded the solution (the establishment Leviathan) as unstable. Only order based on internalized values and culture in general would be stable. This view was shared by his illustrious contemporary Robert Merton (1949; Parsons, 1960).

Parsons, who was much more sympathetic to Locke than to Hobbes, did not like Lockean "proto utilitarianism" either (Parsons, 1982, 97–99). Parsons did not want to see human beings at war with each other, but he also did not want to see human beings coming to agreement with each other because of their mutual exchange and complementary human interests, which are useful to them. Parsons supposed that moral social values are imposed on people from the top by a macroculture.[13]

After the 1960s, the mainstream in sociology refused to recognize Hobbes's contribution to understanding how society works. Many authors used as a pretext the fact that Hobbes belongs to political philosophy, as if Locke and Marx do not.[14]

The compendium on Hobbes contains 14 articles devoted to various facets of Hobbes's heritage, but none of them treats Hobbes as a social scientist and discusses his contribution to the understanding of social processes (Sorell, 1996). Quentin Skinner in his numerous works on

Hobbes over four decades also treats Hobbes mostly as a political theorist, even if he underscores Hobbes's contribution to "humanitatis" and "civil science" with his special focus on morals and history (see Skinner, 2002, 50–55; 1972a,b, 109–142; 1972c, 136–157; 1978). Several authors treated Hobbes with condescension and without due recognition of his contribution to social and political theory. They criticized him with arguments from the contemporary world, as if the author of Leviathan is equal to his critique in their historical experience (see Kavka, 1986, 437–452).

One way of degrading Hobbes as an original thinker was to suggest, as Helen Thorton showed, that Hobbes's theory is simply a description of the Biblical hell, ignoring the experience of the civil war in England, which provided Hobbes with sufficient "stuff" on the "state of nature," as well as Hobbes's necessity, with his reputation as an atheist, to substantiate his non-Orthodox views of church authority (Thornton, 2005, 4–8, 164–168). For instance, Sheldon Wolin, along with many others, called Hobbes's state of nature "a kind of political version of Genesis" (Wolin, 1970, 264). Leo Rauch seconds this view, saying that Hobbes's political theory repeats the religious myth about the Fall of Man (Rauch, 1981, 89–102). Only Dennis Wrong, in "The oversocialized concept of man in modern sociology" (1961), stretched his hand to the Hobbesian image of human beings (see also Wrong, 1994, 90–92). Wrong's pieces on the same subject in 1961 and his later work in 1994 were unique. This sociologist deserves great credit for his attempts to keep Hobbes a part of social science as well as for his attempt to persuade the sociological community (mostly in vain, as demonstrated by the experience of four decades after the publication of his famous article).

To my best knowledge, only a few social scientists since the 1960s showed their interest in Hobbes as a source of inspiration for the analysis of social order and society in general. It is possible to cite only a few articles and books on Hobbes that take a rather positive stance toward his contribution to social science. But even they tend to place the focus on Hobbessian reflections on contract as the basis for the establishment of the sovereign (the weakest part of Hobbes's "sociological" heritage) to treat him mostly as one of many "contractual" political scientists, obliterating Hobbes's major contribution to social science. Among these are Jean Hampton with her sophisticated analysis of the Hobbesian concept of covenant in the light of the prisoner's dilemma and game theory (Hampton, 1986). Having high esteem for Hobbes, I, however, found that Hobbes explained the emergence of the sovereign with a complicated and unrealistic, or even "fantastical" (to use Ross Harrison's adjective) procedure that supposes the existence of binding contracts between citizens in his favor and presents them as "the author" of a sovereign (Harrison, 2003, 108–113, and 132–188). The same "contractual" focus on Hobbes can be found in other contemporary authors (see, for instance, Levine, 2002, 15–54). Like Hampton, Gabriella Slomp looked at Hobbes through the prism of game theory, but unlike her she applied it in order to show that Hobbes was correct in his description of the human individual, and was not afraid to compare Hobbes's *Leviathan* to Orwell's *1984* (Slomp, 2000, 6–18).

However, some authors see Hobbes as a social thinker who penetrated deeply the fabric of society. Garrett Hardin, in "The tragedy of the commons" (1968, 1243–1248), as well as Peter Kollock (1998, 202–203), highly appreciated Hobbes's shrewdness in understanding the difficulties of maintaining order in any society (see also Black, 1983, 41).

Hobbes is definitely not disregarded by experts in international relations who belong to the school of political realists. Few authors deny that the mutual threat of nuclear destruction was a key factor that accounted for international security in the cold war period. Since 1945, the old purely Hobbesian idea about world government, with coercive power, found many supporters. As David Gauthier noted, at the peak of the cold war, "the advent of nuclear weapons brought the state of nations nearer to the true Hobessian state of nature"; the world government (the international Leviathan) was the single way to create international peace (1969, 207, 210). The Hobbesian vision in international relations outlived the cold war and continues to influence the authors who gravitate toward "the realist theory" of international relations. This approach is challenged by the liberal, Lockean vision of the world, which is based on the idea of the crucial importance of peaceful interdependence of states as the major factor defining international relations, on the assumption that people are "basically good" and behave rationally. "The pure realists" inspired by Hobbes and to some degree also by Marx, with their focus on the political economy of inequality and uneven development (the conflicts between nations as another driving force along with class struggle), are also challenged by those who focus on the role of institutions and ideas in international relations, even if they tend to incorporate "the Hobbesian premise" in their studies (see, for instance, Keohane, 2002, 3, 7, 43, 63–87, 246; see also Kagan, 2003; Keohane, 1986). At the same time, there has also been quite a few intellectuals, such as Kenneth Boulding (1962, 335), who admonished nation states, even during the cold war, to follow

Parsons's vision of society based on common values and "create a social contract and to agree to machinery that will give the contract stability."

It is remarkable and amusing that although Hobbes is mostly ignored by sociologists and political scientists as irrelevant to contemporary society, for the media and the public Hobbes is a part of folklore, a symbol of order and the forces against it. A Google search on September 23, 2005, revealed that Hobbes was mentioned 4 million times; Leviathan, 2.8 million times (for comparison, Parsons received 300 thousand; Weber, 4.8 million; Durkheim, 1.8 million; Spencer, 2 million). It is only natural that David Brooks, *New York Times* columnist, in his description of life in American society, wrote, "It's already clear this will be known as the grueling decade, the Hobbesian decade. Americans have had to acknowledge dark realities that it is not in our nature to readily acknowledge . . . the thin veneer of civilization, the elemental violence in human nature, the lurking ferocity of the environment, the limitations on what we can plan and know, the cumbersome reactions of bureaucracies, the uncertain progress good makes over evil" (Brooks, 2005c).

THE STUDIES ON FEAR: ONLY AT THE MICRO LEVEL

The downgrading of Hobbes as a social thinker has been deeply intertwined with the disregard of fear as a major social issue in the sociological literature. Fear has been studied not as a big social issue, but as a specific, mostly isolated phenomenon that does not have broad implications for the fabric of society. It is true even about the studies of the fear of war (see Slemrod, 1988; Villaume, 1996).

After September 11, there were a lot of studies about the fear of terrorism and people's attitudes toward it. The fear of terrorist acts became a part of life in many places in the world, and we have seen a growing literature on this issue (see Acharya, 2004; Barber, 2003; Henderson, 2004).

Another area of study where fear plays an important role is the study of people's fears of disasters of non-terrorist events. The works of Enrico Quarantelli are prominent among these works. Most studies are concerned with post-catastrophic situations, such as the way societies, organizations and communities respond to technological or ecological disasters, or how individuals and the public adapt to disasters (see Demerath and Wallace, 1957; Dynes, 1966; 1970; Hodgkinson and Stewart, 1991; Janis and Mann, 1977; Kreps, 1978; 1983;

Mileti et al., 1975; Mozgovaia, 1994; Perry, 1985; Rose, 1982; Wright and Rossi, 1981).

Other popular issues include the fear of pollution, the fear of toxic and nuclear waste sites (Gelbspan, 2004; Gerrard, 1994), the fear of food (Diamond, 1997; Mooney and Bates, 1999; Nottingham, 2003; Viscusi, 1992), epidemics (Markel, 2004, 16), venereal diseases, AIDS (Doka, 1997; Lego, 1994) and poisonous foods or illnesses from foods.

It is remarkable that the torrent of books on the various threats generated a countervailing force, that is, many authors devoted their publication to de-masking false or exaggerated threats in each sphere mentioned here. Douglas Powell and William Leiss (1997) published a book about the exaggerated perceptions of danger in various spheres of life, particularly when it comes to food (Powell and Leiss, 1997). Ronald Bailey (2002) and Roger Bate (2000) published collections of articles that denounce fear mongers in ecology. Several other authors joined the club of alarmists in various areas (Arnold, 1990).

With its strong connection to uncertainty, fear is also a subject of the many studies on risk, which is directly related to the research on disasters. Most of these studies deal with the issues on the micro level and stay away from big social issues. Most also deal with experts' perceptions of dangers, the assessment of risks, or the probability that dangerous events will occur (see among recent publications, for instance, Paul Slovic, 2004, 137–153). Some studies deal also with ordinary people's perceptions of risk along with emotional factors that influence these perceptions (see Loftstedt and Frewer, 1998, 116, 240; Sunstein, 2003, 45–46, 61–62; Viscusi, 2003, 1–22).

THE DISREGARD OF FEAR
AS A SOCIETAL ISSUE

It was Franklin Roosevelt himself who, in his inaugural speech, rephrasing Michel Montaigne's statement, uttered the famous words that "the only thing we have to fear is fear itself." Fear, as a societal issue (i.e., as a major problem of macro society), is ignored in most sociological textbooks. This was the case in the *Handbook of Sociology*, edited by Neil Smelser (1998), in Smelser's textbook *Sociology* (1994), as well as in most other textbooks (Andersen and Taylor, 2002; Macionis, 2004). In one of the recent texts, fear was mentioned only in the discussion of love and courtship, because "fear breeds love" (Henslin, 2004, 332).

Fear is ignored totally in various sociological dictionaries, such as *The Blackwell Dictionary of Twentieth Century Social Thought*

(Outhwaite et al., 1994), *The Blackwell Dictionary of Sociology* (Johnson, 1995) and *The Concise Oxford Dictionary of Sociology* (Marshall, 1994). Fear as a concept is absent in the numerous publications of Ronald Inglehart, even if his theory of value changes in developed countries explains to a great extent the increase of "the sense of security" when "risk became a central political issue" in society (Inglehart, 1997, 32–34, 36, 43). It is not amazing that this term was absent from the big project, Human Values and Beliefs, carried out by the University of Michigan in the 1990s. This study included 370 variables describing various aspects of human life (Inglehart et al., 1998). The term fear cannot be found in this large-scale research project, "The 2004 Political Landscape," conducted by the Pew Research Center, included more than one hundred variables.[15]

Only a few theoretical books have dealt with the issue of fear. Among them are Pitirim Sorokin's *Man and Society in Calamity* (1968) and Albert Cantrill's book (1971). It is necessary to mention also the chapter "Fear and Change" in Barbalet's *Emotion, Social Theory, and Social Structure* (1998). The author recognized that "the relevance of fear to constructive aspects of social processes is almost wholly ignored." However, talking about social fears, Barbalet concentrated most of the chapter (20 pages) on the fears of elites, as a major cause of changes in society (149, 151).

The number of sociologists who devote their empirical studies to fear as an independent variable is relatively limited (Biderman et al., 1967; Ennis, 1967; Garofalo and Laub, 1979; Gordon et al., 1979; Hindelang et al., 1978; Reiss, 1967). The sociologists who are close to this subject are those who have been working under the umbrella of the "threat hypothesis of the conflict perspective," as it was formulated by Allen Liska (1992), the editor of a book in which various studies on the subject were published ("threat of lynching, threat of police brutality, threat of minority riots and others"). Generally speaking, Samuel Prince's statement seven decades ago still holds true today: catastrophic thinking remains "a virgin field in sociology" (Prince, 1920; see also Bailey, 1958).

It may be supposed that fear is an important topic in social psychology. But this does not hold true in the textbook *Social Psychology* (Taylor et al., 2003). Fear was mentioned only perfunctorily in relation to "fear-arousing messages" (153–154), punishment and retaliation in individual relations (416) and with regard to the existential fear of death (120). Fear was slighted even more in another textbook with the same title, *Social Psychology* (Michener et al., 2004). The term was mentioned only once, again in connection with fear arousal messages (203). Even the prestigious two volumes of *The Handbook of Social Psychology* (Gilbert et al., 1998) almost ignored the subject. In the first volume, which runs almost 900 pages, fear was mentioned (and not as a special subject) on only 9 pages; in the second volume, it is never mentioned (Gilbert et al., 1998). It is not amazing that fear is treated in a book by McMahon et al. (1995) as a purely individualistic issue in the context of Watson's experiments. The book's treatment of the social nature of fear can be found in its descriptions of the vagaries of love (190–569). Theodore Kemper's book *A Social Interactional Theory of Emotions* (1978), with its focus on fear as determined by "un sufficient power," is a rare exception, because several other authors dealing with emotions almost completely ignore fear and all the more its social importance.[16]

Surprisingly, even authors who study societies of the Soviet type mostly ignore the role of fears, as if Orwell is irrelevant to the study of Soviet society. Certainly, those who reject the concept of totalitarianism either ignored the issue of fear as a major element of Soviet society (Siegelbaum, 1997), or they reduce its significance to families with "bad social origins," without describing it as a part of everyday Soviet life (Fitzpatrick, 1999). However, even the advocates of the totalitarian model, such as Martin Malia (1994, 269 and 1999, 3), were far from Orwell in their understanding of the omnipresent fear in totalitarian society, that within such a society "no emotion was pure, because everything was mixed up with fear and hatred" (Orwell, 1949, 105), and where "the espionage, the betrayals, the arrests, the tortures, the executions, the disappearances will never cease" (Orwell, 1949, 221). But probably even stranger is the absence of fear as a major issue for many developing countries, such as Mexico, in which fear of criminals and particularly fear of drug dealers and corrupt officials is a major concern for the majority of the population.

The Literature on the Role of Fear as a Factor of the Quality of Life

The role of fear as a crucial factor for quality of life is beyond the subject of this book. However, I still find it necessary to mention that contemporary sociological literature pays little attention to this issue.

Indeed, the literature on the quality of life (or standard of living) ignores fear as an important factor influencing the mood of the people. It is surprising that, since their emergence in the 1970s, studies on the quality of life, which are oriented toward research on how people feel about various elements of their lives, mostly ignored the role of fear and its impact on the quality of life (Allard, 1972; AMA, 1974; Andrews, 1986; Campbell, 1971; 1981; Campbell et al., 1976; Fradier, 1976; Michener, 1970; Sirgy et al., 2003).

How the Fear of Crime Is Treated in Literature

Though paying a lot of attention to crime and deviant behavior, mainstream authors tend to underestimate the fear of crime as a powerful factor that determines the quality of life. This is often ignored by the authors of sociological textbooks in the sections that describe deviance and even in the sociological literature devoted to these subjects on the whole (Shlapentokh and Shiraev, 2002, 5–6). The term cannot be found in works that deal with norms and laws.[17] It is amusing that some authors who discuss crime try to avoid the term fear.[18] Alex C. Michalos, in *Essays on the Quality of Life*, offered an exception to this tendency in his studies on the quality of life. This issue is analyzed in several chapters of his books, such as "Perceived crime increases and fear" (2003). The article "Fear as a social fact" by Allen Liska and his coauthors (1982) also should not be forgotten.

The disregard of fear is rather amazing in view of the major role of fear in people's choices of residence, schools for their children, entertainment and vacations. It is also remarkable how few sociologists pay attention to the fear of discrimination of women (see Laushway, 2000; Walklate, 2004), African Americans' fears of the police (see Brooks, 1999; Russell, 1998; Sulton, 1994) and the fear of discrimination of various groups of the population, such as illegal immigrants, homosexuals, handicapped people and the elderly. Sociologists do not pay much attention to the fear experienced by the majority of the population, such as the fears of unemployment, diseases, bankruptcy, eviction, crime and several others.

The Focus on Criminals and Disregard of Victims

The tendency to ignore the fear of crime as a key factor of the quality of life can be attributed to the inclination of contemporary sociologists to concentrate their attention on the perpetrators of crime, and almost totally ignore the consequences of crime on its victims and society as a whole. In fact, the cost of crime for society can be presented as a sum of two elements: the transformation of many people into criminals, with all their social deprivations (incarceration, the permanent fear of police and the low quality of life), and the losses of victims (from the loss of life and property to the permanent fear of crime).[19]

The point of view defended here with respect to the attitudes toward the crimes of immigrants was eloquently supported by an Italian criminologist, Luigi Solivetti. Speaking about the mainstream study of crime, he wrote, "many of them (researchers) perceived as politically incorrect the hypothesis that immigrants—a category of vulnerable, often exploited people, victims of injustice—could in turn be regarded as responsible for acts of injustice and high crime rates. Others, intrepidly combining Foucault-derived epistemes and labeling theory concepts, rejected the very idea of taking into consideration non-nationals' crime rates, looking at them as merely a by-product of power" (2005).

Bemoaning the criminals who commit crimes under the impact of adverse social conditions, the authors of sociological textbooks and other general texts do not lament the products of crime: fatalities and losses. Meanwhile, even if a criminal is a pure product of society and has to be treated mercifully, the damage that he or she does to society is many times higher than his or her personal losses as an individual. Describing "gangs as one way that illegitimate opportunity structures beckon disadvantaged youth," Henslin said nothing about the impact of gangs on people living in cities (Henslin, 2004, 140–148; see Federico and Schwartz, 1983, 181–225; Robertson, 1987; Shepard, 1990, 148–166).

The responsibility of society for crime and the disregard of the impact of crime on society were typical for so-called conflict theorists. These theories, in their Marxist or non-Marxist versions, suggest that crime is a natural product of class struggle as well as of "imperialism, racism, capitalism and sexism and other systems of exploitation" (Federico and Schwartz, 1983, 183, 187; Taylor et al., 1975, 113–146). In this respect, Gary Becker set the bar high in his now famous Nobel Prize speech in which he contended that "theft is socially harmful" only because it forces criminals to "spend on weapons and on the value of their time in planning and carrying out their crime," which is "socially unproductive" (Nobel Lectures, 1997).

These theories imply that crimes are dangerous only for the dominant groups that define crime as any behavior that is against their interests. These theories often contend that in a truly egalitarian society the rate of crime would decline substantially (Vold, 1958).

Fear attracts greater attention among criminologists as well as researchers of urban life, who discuss the fear of crime and the fear of minorities. However, they tend to discuss the subject without focusing on the general perspective about the role of fear in society (see, for instance, Ditton and Farrall, 2000; Lane, 2002; Maher, 2003; Pantazis, 2000).

FEAR IN ECONOMICS

With the low attention to the role of fear in sociology and social psychology it is not amazing that economics with its tendency to ignore social issues in their picture of the economy is almost not at all concerned about this issue. The general picture of economics, as a terrain free of social issues, remains the same, even after some progress in economic psychology in the last decades. In any case, the major textbooks on macro- and microeconomics do not even discuss fear as one of the major motives of "homo economicus." Gregory Mankiv, in *Principles of Macroeconomics* (2001), ignored the fact that economic behavior is dominated not only by incentives based on cost–benefit calculations but also by people's fear of losing what they have. Speaking about unemployment, Mankiv, like most of his other colleagues, ignores the fear of unemployment and the fear of managers of being ousted from the market or going bankrupt. The same focus only on "positive incentives" is typical for the text book *Principles of Macroeconomics*, written by Karl Case and Ray Fair (1996) and several other textbooks on economics.

HOW TO DOWNGRADE THE ROLE OF FEAR IN MACRO SOCIOLOGY

There are three groups of authors who try to downgrade the role of fear in social life or even cast doubt on the term itself. The first group justifies, as I found in my discussion of this issue with my colleagues, the almost total disregard of the concept of fear in the textbooks of sociology, social psychology and political science by citing either the vagueness of this term or the existence of parallel concepts, such as dread, fright, angst, concern, anxiety and awe. This nominalistic approach, which casts doubt on the use of abstract terms such as fear, can be applied to any concept used in the social sciences, including values, attitudes, norms, power, influence, socialism, capitalism, globalism, democracy and so on.

The second group treats "fear" as an individual psychological phenomenon, a sort of "anxiety" related mostly to existential fears, such as the fear of death and illness. These fears do indeed play an important role in human life. The term "fear" and "anxiety" overlap, even if they are often treated separately (anxiety is vaguer than fear, which is a more specific emotion) (see Riezler, 1944, 491). There are several data showing the scope of these fears, but it is wrong to ignore the crucial role of social fears in human life. It is interesting that other emotions besides fear, such as love, altruism, compassion, even hatred, are treated by social scientists. In the project, Human Values and Beliefs, carried out by the University of Michigan in the 1990s, fear could not be found among the 370 variables describing various aspects of human life; the study did include such emotions as love and sorrow (Inglehart et al., 1998; 2004).

The third group of authors recognizes the social character of fear, but tries to present it as mostly irrational and generated by media. Glasner's book is a typical example. The major flaw in Glassner's methodology is that he ignores this perspective in analyzing fear in America. He seems most interested in telling us that we have nothing to fear. The author, for instance, informs us that "only one in ten public schools reported any serious crime" (1999, xiv). By the author's estimations, the media's concern about "babies having babies" has been blown out of proportion because "only about one-third of teen mothers were younger than eighteen, and fewer than one in fifty was fourteen or younger" (88). The author talks about the "confected" fear of crack in the 1980s, and explains that "fewer than 33 percent of those who try crack become addicted" (134). He is sure that media maximize claims about youthful drug use, because a survey shows that "only about one in four twelve-year-olds was willing to speculate about a friend or classmate having used hard drugs" (142). Glassner was followed by Michael Welch, Eric Price and Nana Yankey (2002), as well as Marc Siegle (2005) and James Walsh (1998) who also accused the media, the government and businesses of "manufacturing menace" and creating moral panic in society, without attempting to measure the degree of the real threat to people from criminals. At the same time, there is no doubt that, as these authors point out, there are several forces in any society that are interested in spreading fears and profiteering on it.

Without the inclusion of the fear of sanctions for violating the law or norms, it is impossible to answer the Hobbesian question and explain how nondemocratic as well as democratic societies sustain order.

Positive and Negative Fears

It is necessary to make a distinction between good and bad fears, not unlike the difference between good and bad cholesterol. Some concerns, such as the fear produced by racial or religious intolerance, criminal activity or the repressions of an authoritarian government harm society and should be eradicated as much as possible. At the same time, fears that bolster "positive" social values are also "positive," as a condition for the maintenance of social order.

There are many people in this country, drawing on various political ideologies, who often do not make a distinction between "positive" and "negative" fears, and ignore the radical difference between law-abiding states and corrupt or totalitarian ones. Therefore, they denounce any measure that instills fear in those who violate the social order. Any action the state takes to improve order often evokes in their minds the specter of either Hobbes's Leviathan or Orwell's Big Brother, as if social order can be created and maintained without a strong state. I now discuss the attitudes toward the state and other types of formal control later.

What could be better than living in a perfect fearless society? In societies built in the imaginations of the authors of the great utopias—Tommaso Campanella at the end of the sixteenth century or Edward Bellamy in the late nineteenth century, among others—there was no fear in human relations. The same was the dream of the famous Russian anarchist Prince Peter Kropotkin, who was well-known prior to the Russian revolution in 1917. In Kropotkin's fantasy society, order was established by altruism and mutual help. The state and fear did not exist. However, the reality of social life in the early twenty-first century shows that society cannot be based only on the good intentions of its members. We still need a strong and democratic state that is able not only to penalize each violator of the law, but also to maintain in the mind of each member of society, whatever his or her social or ethnic background, the fear of violating the social order.

Fear of Sanctions as an Important Guarantor of Order

I believe that social order is shaped not only by processes inside the human mind, stimulated by moral internalized values, but also by the pressures on human beings from outside. This pressure from "outside" stems not so much from what is going on in micro worlds—the interaction of people on the individual level—but from above, that is, from the state, the church, other organizations and public opinion.

It was shown earlier that the values mechanism by itself is too weak to be a guarantor of social order, although its role is quite significant. Even in a homogenous society, the internalization of good social values per se does not guarantee social order. Many values that people internalize are deeply hostile to social order. It is evident that the arguments in favor of the values mechanism as the basis of order look even weaker if we think about a heterogeneous society in which most people have lived. As this book suggests, it is the fear of sanctions for violating laws, rules and values (or the desire of reward) that is mostly, but not entirely, responsible for the observance of values and norms and ultimately for social order in society. In fact, fear, much more often than compunctions (the romantic Freudian conflict between the superego, which embodies civilization, and the egotistical ego, a product of the violation of internalized values), forces people to abstain from violating values, norms and rules. Thomas Aquinas, with his unlimited belief in a perfect God, as if preempting Hobbes's famous definition of human nature, talked about three kinds of appetites or inclinations that humans share with all other creatures, including the concupiscible appetites, love and the desire for pleasure. Believing in divine control (even if it is limited because of free will) over human beings (the law of God) and assuming the universal religiosity of people in his time, Aquinas did not trust religious values and proclaimed the importance of natural law, which he mostly identified as civil or human law backed by sanctions and the fear of their violation, as a necessary condition of organized social life (Arrington, 1998, 142–143).

Even internalized values should be sustained incessantly in a given social milieu by ideological as well as by coercive means. As soon as the milieu stops doing this, the withering of these values begins almost immediately. The backing of values by law supposes sanctions against those who violate the law and the fear that the sanctions engender.[20] The famous explanation of Bill Clinton (2004) about why he had an affair with Monica—because "I could do it"—was brilliant evidence of the role of fear in the observance of morals. In the same style, Russian oligarchs, explaining the illegal origin of their wealth, usually answer, "such were the times," as if bribing officials in order to secure a big oil company for an almost symbolic price was not evidently illegal at the time (Shlapentokh, 2004c).

David Callahan, in *The Cheating Culture, Why More Americans Are Doing Wrong*, asserts that "high payoffs for winners and weak punishments for offenders have combined to encourage dishonesty among students, doctors, lawyers, taxpayers, auto mechanics, job applicants, stock analysts, file sharers and corporate executives" (Callahan, 2004). Indeed, most social values play their regulatory role only because they are now, or were in the recent past, backed by outside forces, such as the laws and norms installed by the state and its law enforcement agencies, as well as by other social institutions: first of all by the church, the family and by various other groups and public opinion. The relative role of these institutions as a source of fear varies from society to society and from one time to another. We can easily cite the cases when each of these institutions played a dominant role.

It is important to note that the universal observation of certain values (even those values, positive or negative, that have a presumably genetic basis or a long cultural evolution) demand in each country a law that punishes those who neglect these apparently deeply rooted values. Incest is a good example. It is evident that the number of incest cases (or neglected children) would be much greater if people were not afraid to behave according to their immediate wishes. Other indicators about the weak impact of internalized (biologically and culturally) values that have to regulate the behavior of parents toward their children are the statistics on abused and missing children. Over 3 million children in the United States are at risk of exposure to parental violence each year.

In the United States, more than 2,000 children flee home each day. The large number of child rapists is also an indicator of the zero influence of social values on the behavior of those who force girls and boys into sexual relations. Of all the violence offenses committed in the United States between 1998 and 2002, 11 percent were by members of the family; 10 percent of these offenses were against daughters or sons; 4 percent of all offenses against daughters or sons were rapes (Bureau of Justice Statistics, 1998–2002). In 2003, 5 percent of all murders in the United States were committed by parents against their children, or by children against their parents (Department of Justice, Family Violence Statistics, 2003). The number of children killed by their parents is also formidable. In Russia during the 1990s, for instance, each year parents murdered 1,000–3,000 children (Russian TV, 2005).

The Unconditional Rejection of Fear as a Negative Phenomenon

The tendency to ignore the positive role of fear in society is nurtured by two almost mutually exclusive visions of society. One vision, as mentioned before, simply denies the presence of social fear, positive or negative, in society, claiming that the perceptions of fear are artifacts created by media and politicians.

Another vision of the world supposes that all social fears are hostile to society and accuses the state and other hierarchical organizations of being the main producers of fear. This vision implies the summary rejection of punishments of any sort as activities that generate fear.

The classic representative of this line of thinking is Judith Shklar. In her famous essay, "Liberalism of fear," written in 1989 (it is included in her book *Political Thought and Political Thinkers*, 1998), she introduced the concept (one that is close to Isaiah Berlin's "negative liberty") that the major preoccupation of contemporary democratic society is the "liberalism of fear," which is more important than the "liberalism of natural rights" or the "liberalism of personal development" (8–9, 12). In her book *Ordinary Vices* (1984), she singled out cruelty as a major vice and regarded the state and its agents as the greatest perpetrator of cruelty. She said nothing about numerous other perpetrators of cruelty, such as criminals, racists, family members, bosses in business, peers and dozens of others. Essentially, she saw a threat to the fabric of society coming only from the enemies of liberalism, and said nothing about other destructive forces. Peter Berkowitz (1998) noted that for Shklar liberalism is always "smug and tidy"; Shklar did not believe that individualism, which she praised, can generate dangers to society. In fact, the extreme of liberalism prompts anarchism and chaos in society.

Corey Robin was Shklar's follower. In his 300-page book, with the appealing title *Fear: The History of a Political Idea* (2004), he mentioned the fear of sanctions only in a negative way. It is amusing that he was able to ignore the fear of sanctions when he discussed the role of fear in the Old Testament, suggesting that fear has only an ethical dimension (Robin, 2004, 7).

David Garland is also strongly hostile toward the fear of sanctions. He starts his book *Punishment and Modern Society* (1990, 1, 288) with the statement, "the punishment of offenders is a peculiarly unsettling and dismaying aspect of social life." The last paragraph in the book commences with words about "the tragic quality of punishment," suggesting that we should try to do without it.

Fear in Hierarchical Organizations

The view that fears in contemporary society should be treated only as negative phenomena pushes its advocates to see fear in hierarchical organizations (or in any social unit, such as the family or a congregation) as always evil. Although it is important to diminish the role of fear in any sphere of human life, it is, at the same time, populist and utopian to ignore the positive and indispensable role of fear in the functioning of any social group.

The call to "drive fear out of the work place" is suggested in the title of a book by Ryan and Oestreich (1998, 3–4). The authors enumerate all sources of fear in the work place:

- Having one's credibility questioned
- Being left out of decision making
- Being criticized in front of others
- Not getting information necessary to succeed
- Having a key assignment given to someone else
- Having disagreements that might lead to damaged relationships
- Getting stuck in a dead-end job
- Not getting deserved recognition

The authors of the book categorically reject the concept of "an acceptable level of fear," and they bluntly assert that "fear undermines the potential of any organization." The authors are also confident that the cause of fear is ultimately found in the lack of trust between supervisors and employees (10–11, 18, 25–30).

They seem to sincerely believe that a hierarchical organization, company or university department can function without any trace of fear. They devote most of the book to elaborating a recommendation on how to build up trust between managers and employees. There is no doubt that many of their recommendations are quite sound. However, the assumption that in many cases fear in hierarchical organizations plays a positive role totally escapes their rather idealistic vision of the world. Such a sophisticated author as Tony Judt also accepts the view that "the American workplace is . . . a site of managerial coercion and workers' fears," even if does not think that the situation in other Western countries is much better, as Corey suggests (Judt, 2004, 40; see Rimer, 2005).

All these authors evidently confused the necessity to diminish fear in the work place as much as possible with the inevitability of the fear of sanctions for any organization. In Fellini's sarcastic movie "Orchestra," the director was ousted by the musicians who did not want to tolerate his commands and threats.

REALISTIC VIEWS ON THE ROLE OF FEAR OF SANCTIONS IN SOCIETY

Meanwhile, many authors in the past have cast doubt on the idea that values are enough to influence human behavior. Jefferson wrote that it made no difference to him whether his neighbor affirmed one God or twenty, since "it neither picks my pocket nor breaks my legs"

(Jefferson, 1967). Weber once noted, "Even a 'brotherly admonition,' such as has been used in various religious sects as the first degree of mild coercion of the sinner, is 'law' provided it is regulated by some order and applied by a staff" (Weber, 1978, 35).

There are a number of contemporary authors who also cast doubt on the moral basis of values and laws. Authors such as Hechner and Opp, who are critical about the focus on values as the main basis for social order, recognize that "the state, of course, is also responsible for regulating behavior in modern society," and that "legal norms are different from social norm" (Hechter and Opp, 2001b, xi). Robert Bellah (1991, 10, 111) and his coauthors, even if they ignore the term "fear" in their "good society," nevertheless insist on the crucial role of "social sanctions, both positive and negative, in this society." As David Bayley suggested, we can talk about the hierarchy of sanctions and fears of them to which the individual is exposed. The highest level is taken by the state, and the lowest level by "proximate authorities" with the intermediate institutions between them (Bayley, 1969, 27; see Barkun, 1968).

Claude Fischer said that we live in "the world of strangers" and bluntly declared that "order can be sustained without a moral consensus." As she writes, mocking the moral consensus concept as the basis for social order, "We must deal, at least tacitly, with people whom we do not recognize, and, most importantly, who are obviously different from us in many ways." She continues, "In such encounters among people from different subcultures, behavior expectations are neither shared nor certain" (Fisher, 1999, 214, 220; see also Lofland, 1973).

In his turn, Edward Banfield's famous study of the community Montegrano in the Italian South vividly described the life of people, all Catholics, who supposedly lived in a Hobbesian state of war, and who were unable to perform common actions. Order in the community was maintained only by the state and its carabinieri (1965, 20, 30, 38, 87), or by mafia, "which create a primitive social order," as Arthur Stinchcombe (1997, 6) suggested, joining Banfield's verdict. Observing the postwar Italian South Banfield was blunt in asserting that people there observe law only when they are afraid of being punished for its violation. He notes also that in such a society "the weak will favor a regime which will maintain order with a strong hand" (Banfield, 1965, 92, 96). As some researchers note, many kinds of behavior in the second half of the twentieth century moved from the realm of private morality to criminal law (Sheleff, 1975).

It is remarkable that among libertarians there is a clear tendency to avoid the moralization of human behavior (for instance, the role of what Friedrich Hayek calls "positive duties," demanding a sort of altruistic action in favor of others), as well as the concept of internalized values with the clear emphasis placed on rules.[21]

It is a typical tendency of "cultural determinists" (or "culturalists," to use the terminology of Jeffrey Alexander and Neil Smelser, 1999a, 4) to see law only as a manifestation of common values, while ignoring the importance of the coercive component of law (Gibbs, 1989, 397). There is also a strong tendency among scholars to regard values as the cause of laws.[22]

THE DECLINE IN CRIME IN NEW YORK:
THE ROLE OF VALUES AND FEAR

The fast decline of crime in New York City in 1990 deserves special attention as an argument for a sober assessment of the role of values and the fear of sanctions in the maintenance of order. Reported index crimes dropped from a high of 6,300 per 100,000 people in 1990 to a rate of less than 3,100 in 2000 (Jenny, 2002). During this period, in New York City the murder rate dropped by 45 percent and other serious crimes by 36 percent (*The Economist*, October 12, 2002).

There are different theories that explain this almost miraculous fall in the crime rate. One theory attributes it to the "get tough" policy carried out by former mayor Rudolph Juliani and his so called "broken windows" approach (a term coined by criminologist George Kelling) to law enforcement, which supposes no tolerance toward small disorders (Kelling et al., 1996). Most experts agree that the major factor that prevents crime is the arrest rate. Felony arrest rates (except for motor vehicle thefts) rose 50 to 70 percent in the 1990s. When the number of arrests for burglary increased by 10 percent, the number of burglaries fell from 3.2 to 2.7 percent. When the arrest rate for robbery rose by 10 percent, the number of robberies fell from 5.9 to 5.7 percent.

Close to this theory is another one that links the developments to the growth of the police force in New York by 35 percent in the same period and the rise of the number of prison inmates by 24 percent in the same period.

The third theory explains the phenomenon as a response to the economic boom of the 1990s and the decline of unemployment by 39 percent between 1992 and 1999. The fourth theory credits a change in drug habits, with crack users switching to heroin, which does not induce violent behavior and is fairly cheap these days.

According to a fifth theory, demographic trends clearly explain a great deal. Crime rates exploded in the 1960s and 1970s as baby-boomers began to enter the high-crime ages. After rising nearly 80 percent between 1960 and 1980, the number of white males in high-crime ages started to decline. This demographic shift contributed to a modest decline in crime rates. Then, in the 1990s, the number of nonwhite males in these age groups also started to fall and crime fell sharply.

Finally there are theories that explain the decline of crime by the rise of education, immigration ("poor but highly motivated immigrants, at least of the first generation tended to commit fewer crimes than other poor folks"), the quality-of-life, initiatives to reduce litter, fix broken windows and beautify neighborhoods and even, as suggested by the iconoclastic criminologist Andrew Karmen (2000), "the death of bad guys."[23]

None of these theories even remotely ascribed the developments to the learning and internalization of social values. It is evident that theories that focus on the efficacy of police activity, on the role of the state of the economy or on demographic changes in the population totally disregard the role of moral values in the case of New York.

Fear and Socialization

The fear of sanctions plays a crucial role in the socialization and learning of the prescription of the dominant group or societal culture, a circumstance that is highlighted by a few authors, mostly in social psychology, whereas most sociologists ignore it.[24] Further, the internalization of social values is often deprived of the moral dimension and does not differ from learning the rules (or laws) supported by the educational system, media and arts.

The learning of values produces not so much people who are committed to values but conformists who are afraid to violate them because of sanctions. Indeed a great simplification lies in Parsons's magisterial postulate that "the culture provides standards of selective orientation and ordering" (Parsons, 1951, 327).

In fact, these values, which in many cases are nothing more than rules, such as those that regulate traffic, can be considered as induced, which means that they function as long as the outside forces exist (the state, religious institutions or reference groups). These forces bolster the values and punish those who do not conform. Coming back to values such as tolerance, which was discussed earlier, as Jackman and Muha noted (1984), the value changes wrought by education are not internalized. Instead, they represent a superficial socialization that is just strong enough to allow people to fit in comfortably with college expectations and, I will add, to avoid sanctions in their environment.

Education merely "polishes" and qualifies a person's negative attitude expressions. The fear of sanctions continues throughout adult life and it is a permanent part of the human mind for people from all walks of life and for all societies.

CONCLUSION

As shown in previous chapters, social values, with all their importance, cannot, contrary to Parsons and his followers, maintain social order, even in a relatively homogeneous society. In fact, order in society cannot be preserved without the "material rewards for good behavior" or the fear of sanctions for bad behavior. Meanwhile, the mainstream in sociology tends to downgrade the role of fear—"positive fears," that is—as an important condition for the maintenance of order. It tends to treat the fear generated by the state and its agencies only as deleterious and bad for the population. The disregard of the positive role of the fear of sanctions is correlated with the underestimation of the role of social fear (different from individual or existential fear) associated with the quality of life, such as the fear of crime or the fear of unemployment (negative fears). In treating crimes, most authors focus only on the perpetrators of crime and the social conditions that push people to commit crimes, ignoring the victims of crime and the damage to social order.

Fear as a concept is mostly ignored in sociological textbooks and dictionaries, which represent the state of sociology, as do textbooks in all sciences. It is even more remarkable that the major works in social psychology tend to ignore fear. Several authors try to downgrade the role of fear in society, suggesting that these fears are fomented by media for the sake of sensationalism.

It is not amazing that the disregard of the role of fear in society by many authors is combined in sociological literature with praise for Locke's focus on self-regulation and the refusal to recognize the importance of Hobbes as a thinker who made a strong contribution to the analysis of social order, underscoring the role of the fear of sanctions to prevent anarchy in society.

CHAPTER 8

The Leading Role of Formal
Control as the Basis of Order

FORMAL AND INFORMAL SOCIAL
CONTROL IN CONTEMPORARY SOCIOLOGY

In my opinion, and several scholars agree, the state plays a crucial role in the maintenance of order by instilling the fear of sanctions. However, the majority of social scientists, if you judge them by their textbooks and other publications, denies the positive role of the state in maintaining order and are hostile toward formal social control in general.

It is remarkable that with the changing ideological climate in the United States, the interests in social control as a subject significantly declined in the 1990s in comparison to previous decades when Park and Burgess proclaimed that "social control should be . . . the central fact and the central problem of sociology" (Park and Burgess, 1924, 42). It is possible to find textbooks that simply do not contain a section on social control (Macionis, 2004). For Parsons, "social control" was an important issue, but he described it as a very weak mechanism that plays a minimal role in dealing with people who do not behave according to expectations, and who do not have "adequate motivation." It is remarkable that he considered a criminal and a sick person as almost identical types of people who deviate from the equilibrium in their behavior (Parsons, 1951, 27, 29, 312–313).

In the last decades, two schools of thought—a Parsonian cultural determinism and postmodernism with its "bottom–up approach"— narrowed the positive role of social control to only the activities of society toward marginal groups of the population. In the case when members of these schools recognize the role of social control, they identify informal control as its leading part, or even consider, as Mead did, the feelings of self-criticism and guilt, in the Freudian spirit, as the main instrument of social control (Mead, 1934, 253–257). Very few contemporary authors could, as Messner and Rosenfeld did (contrary to most scholars with the same Leftist and liberal orientations), explicitly discuss the crucial importance of the formal system of social control, pointing to its weakness in America as a main cause of the high level of crime in this country (Messner and Rosenfeld, 1997, 76–79).

The authors of various sociological textbooks and special works on crime and social control devote minimal attention to formal control, placing the emphasis on informal control, or, to use the term of several authors, "the third party," but not the state. As Rodney Stark (2001, 213) suggests, "the most common mode of social control is informal, consisting of direct interpersonal pressure." Informal control looks much "nicer" than formal control, which is associated with brutal policies and the hell of prison (Janovitz, 1975). Formal control is accepted by many sociologists only with reluctance. It is usually treated as dealing only with criminals and generally irrelevant to the life of most people (Cohen, 1985, 230).[1]

INFORMAL CONTROL AS BASED PARTIALLY ON THE FEAR OF SANCTIONS

The mainstream tends to idealize informal control, as if it is based only on persuasion and the influence of dominant values (religion in the first place), and authority without fear of sanctions (or the loss of benefits or prestige).[2] "The principal source of enforcement of social control is the informal sanction of group members," declares a sociologist, referring to authorities such as Coleman and Hechter (Horne, 2001, 19). The most common mode of social control is informal, and consists of direct interpersonal pressures (Stark, 2001, 213). Robert Sampson and John Laub (1994) also reject the concept of social control as closely related to the state. They "adopt a more generalized conceptualization of social control as the capacity of a social group to regulate itself according to desired principles and values, and those to make norms and rules effective" (18).

Dan Lewis and Great Salem reasonably noted that when "the sociological literature revolves around the notion of community and social change in the city, there is a noticeable absence of thought about government and politics." They added that "city government and the politics of the community are treated as secondary matters that do not affect social control." However, to address the issue of social control without thinking about the role of political institutions is to give only a partial analysis of the problem.[3] Those who focus on informal social control look for examples among communities that are idealistic cases of a well-regulated society that does not need intervention from outside. Praising informal control, most authors, such as Rodney Stark, implicitly assumed that it is based on internalized values and therefore is better than formal control, which is based on the fear of coercion. In the case of Japan, Rodney Stark, referring to a study by Michael Hechter and Satosho Kanazava, describes a system where order was based on "local group solidarity," and the three principles— "dependence" (many people depend on their group as the single source of survival), "visibility" (the almost total lack of privacy) and "extensiveness" ("teachers encourage students to inform on one another" and bankers can refuse to give a loan if "applicants do not show proper respect for their parents") (Stark, 2001, 215–218). The same rosy picture of informal control, as if based only on "the expression of approval or disapproval by significant others," can be found in many other textbooks (see Hess et al., 1993, 132; Horne, 2001).

Meanwhile, in many cases, informal, non-state, control, such as the control implemented by the family, a job, public opinion or peers, is also based on the same fear as formal control, only it is inspired by the authorities of local communities (nonreligious or religious), which try to scare its members and force them to conform to the most inhuman and cruel rules, as Americans learn from their childhood reading of *The Scarlet Letter* or *Salem Witches.*

Robert Sampson and John Laub argue that informal control, based on persuasion and affection, is much better than formal control based on repressions. However, contradicting themselves, they support Gerald Patterson's "coercion theory" (1982), which ascribes ineffective socialization to the inability of the family to "provide effective punishment for transgressions" (16, 67).

Even the sanctions imposed by one's peers are often extremely cruel and nurture intense fears (Eckstein and Gurr, 1975). Robert Ellickson is somewhat of an exception among those who hail informal control. Although he thinks that informal control is superior to formal control, he recognizes that sanctions are an organic part of both informal and formal control (Ellickson, 1991, 76–81, 124).

Still, the role of informal control in society is quite significant. There is no doubt that this role is changing from time to time, from society to society, with a clear tendency toward decline in the last centuries, due to the urbanization of society, in favor of formal control, with the transition from Gemeinschaft to Gesellschaft. In some rural societies, considering the strong personal ties of people living in small communities, informal control can be as strong as it is inside a family.

It is true also that the central administration often relegates its formal control over its citizens to the lower levels of the hierarchy or even directly to communities of people. However, in all of these cases, central, national or federal laws cover the most important spheres of life and mete out punishments to the gravest violators of order.

Science is another example that shows how sanctions are important for the functioning of institutions. Science can supposedly be ruled by "the ethos of science" without any fear of sanctions and coercion. After Merton, as Steven Chapin states, "the Hobbes/Parsons social order problem" was solved on the basis of "the regulative principles of social order in science," which "were furnished by scientific knowledge itself" (1995, 301). In fact, it is conventional wisdom that the high quality of scientific work is sustained not only by the internal values of scholars (first of all by their willingness to enhance their self-respect as well as the respect for science), but also by the fear of peer reviews, by the fear that their experiments will be impossible to repeat and finally by the fear of damaging their reputations.

The history of the world knows many self-regulated communities that were free from authorities and the role of fear (besides the fear of being excluded from the commune). These communities appeared in different countries and in different times but usually had a short life.[4]

The leading institution and major source of positive fear is, of course, the state and its agencies. In almost all societies, with the exception of pure theocratic societies, the central administration was the major guarantor of social order.

HOSTILITY TOWARD FORMAL CONTROL AND COERCION

The praise of informal control and the belief in internalized values are combined with deep hostility toward coercion and law enforcement agencies. As the author of a textbook wrote, describing the assortment of various instruments of social control, "coercion is usually a short term tool, for it tends to generate resentment and resistance." It also "ensures conflict" and "people resent the use of power." The author, without separating totalitarian and democratic systems, goes so far as to assert that "if coercion must constantly be used people will withdraw support from official government" (Taylor et al., 1973). Another author adds that "formal processes by their very nature generate deviance and dissent" (Turner, 1985, 125, 126). His colleague names a section in his chapter on deviance in his textbook, "The law as an instrument of oppression" (Henslin, 2004, 152). L. Stone (1987) talks about prison as "a vestigial institution." Following him a decade later, David Garland denounces prison as an institution that "fails to achieve the ends of crime control" and lost its "basic raison d'etre" (1990, 288). Hostility toward formal control (the state and formal law) manifests clearly in the definition of deviance, in purely psychological symbolic terms as "any behavior which violates social expectations" (Federico and Schwartz, 1983, 183).

Other social scientists insist that "punishment does not deters crimes," either because people cannot be rehabilitated by sanctions, or because the penitentiary system always works badly (Shepard, 1990, 163–164). They maintain that the intensive use of coercion erodes the legitimacy of the state (Jackman, 1993, 16), and has very high costs, because it restricts "personal choice and freedom" (Stark, 2001, 214), as if anarchy is the best condition for the maximization of both. The most hostile force against coercion was "new criminology," which describes the punishment of crimes only as if it was done in the interest of the dominant class. Many authors who oppose coercion as a leading element of social control in fact do not make a distinction between the scope of real coercion and the fear of coercion (Jackman, 1993, 35).

Negative Attitudes toward the State as a Source of Fear

Of all the institutions of formal control, the state is the major object of hostility in the sociological literature. It is possible to single out several groups of scholars with regard to their attitudes toward the state in Western society as the guarantor of order.

The Radical Left

The first group describes this role in society in only a negative way. It embraces mostly Left sociologists of different types (Marxists, neo-Marxists, Left radicals and others). All Orthodox Marxists, neo-Marxists as well as so-called post-Marxists almost completely ignore the importance of order for "the toilers," "the proletarian or working class" and the masses. In their publications, the concept of "social order" is simply absent (see, for instance, Domhoff, 1996; King, 1986).

However, when Marxists of all types express their views on the state in Western society they are strongly hostile toward it. Marc Neocleous declared his complete agreement with Marx's view that "bloody legislation" and "bloody discipline," which created a class of wage labor, was a product of "the police methods to accelerate the accumulation of capital by increasing the degree of exploitation of labor" (Neocleous, 2000, 17). In his textbook, James Henslin (2004) joins Marxist conflict theory and summarizes his attitudes toward the state and its law enforcement agencies as follows: a contemporary "legal system . . . has been designed by the elite (capitalists) to control workers, to keep themselves in power, and, ultimately, stabilize social order"; "from this perspective, law enforcement is a cultural device through which the capitalist class carried out self-protective and repressive policy" (153). John Macionis (2004, 143), also in a textbook, conveys this vulgar Marxist message about the essence of the American state. He writes, "people who directly challenge the capitalist system, including the inner-city 'underclass' and revolutionaries—Merton's innovators and rebels—are controlled by the criminal justice system or, in the time of crisis, military forces such as the National guard."

Along with scholars with evident Marxist influences, radical authors, seen as structuralists and poststructuralists, also look at the state as a monster that is deeply hostile toward ordinary people. The role of Michel Foucault and his *Discipline and Punishment* and *The History of Sexuality* is of special importance. This philosopher is evidently an adversary of the "bottom to top" approach and the belief in the resolute role of the masses in social processes, a fact that postmodernists, his admirers, tend not to note. In fact, Foucault (1995) described the gradual expansion of the state's power from the time of feudalism as promoted only by the almost sadistic desire of the state machine itself to increase its control over human beings—"not to punish less but to punish better . . . to insert the power to punish more deeply in the social body"—by all possible means, including science. Being rather close to the old Marxist description of the state as the instrument of oppression of the masses, Foucault almost totally ignored the strengthening of social order as a purpose of the extension of punitive actions in an almost anarchic society.

He describes the order imposed by power as a deeply hostile phenomenon to human beings, whether it be in schools, factories, army barracks, hospitals or, of course, in prisons. Foucault insists that "punishment did not restore justice; it reactivated power," and sees the processes started by the Enlightenment as a gradual offensive. For Foucault, "The mind is a surface of inscription for power, with semiology as it tool" (1995, see 1976).

This hatred of the state accounts for the cult of Michel Foucault in the United States in the 1970s–90s. Many American social scientists were pleased with his almost Orwellian image of the state as a monster that has subjugated ordinary people with numberless regulations since the Middle Ages and that fully controls knowledge in society, making "objective truth" impossible.[5]

Corey Robin's *Fear* presents a typical case of the hatred of the state by the contemporary American non-Marxist Left. He cannot contain his absolute, in fact, anarchistic hatred of the state in all its forms. For him, the state, whose power is always abused by elites against the masses, is always a "counterrevolutionary force" that is able to sow fear amongst its oppressed, powerless subjects (Robin, 2004, 47–48, 161–163, 181–191, 200).

Several other authors are closer to Robin's view. David Garland declared that social science has always focused on the protection of the individual "from the state" (2001, 12). Rodney Stark talked about the "taming of the state," describing the state as "a constant threat to its citizens," and as a dominant question in political thought in the last 2,000 years (Stark, 2001, 438–439). John Irwin describes the American state as guilty of "overcriminalization," and sending people to prison for "nonconformist life styles" (Irwin, 1985, 40–41). Nanette Davis and Clarice Stasz, the great admirers of Foucault, joining his diagnosis, contended, "it is the modern state that is the most instrumental in creating and sustaining a violent social environment," and that the police "have proven to be problematic in democratic states, as official intervention can exacerbate preexisting collective grievances, rather than settle them in nonviolent ways" (Davis and Stasz, 1990, 71, 277, 290). Quite often the critique of the state is performed by people outside the scholarly community whose publications present some interest as reflecting the mood of radicals, who in their hatred of the existing society stretch to absurdity their attacks on the state as a social institution.[6]

Liberals

The liberals' negative attitudes toward a strong state and the fear generated by it was shaped under the direct influence of the totalitarian regimes in Europe and in the Soviet Union, and to some degree under the impact of McCarthyism in the United States. The debates over Orwell's *1984*, which have continued since the year of its publication (1949), are noticeable from this point of view. For many intellectuals in America and England the book was about the growing totalitarian threat in the Western world (and not about the Soviet totalitarian society). For some of them it was an indication that "Big Brother" was already celebrating victory in the United States by the 1940s (see Shlapentokh, 2004b). Being influenced by the atrocities of the

Nazi and Soviet regimes and the dangerous tendencies of the state's intervention in social life in the West, these intellectuals refused to see the difference between states in totalitarian versus democratic societies, and consequently declared any fear stemming from the state activity as purely negative.

Apprehensions about the state as a negative institution were also fed by the popular theory in the 1940s–50s about "the flight from freedom," developed by Eric Fromm (*Escape from Freedom*, 1967), a book by T.W. Adorno et al. (*The Authoritarian Personality*, 1950) and one by Hanna Arendt (*The Origin of Totalitarianism*, 1976). This theory suggested that the majority of the population in any society tends to fear freedom without any objective grounds.[7] This idea was based on the assumption that people are the victims of a crippling internal anxiety, not an external danger, as if people's fear of unemployment, poverty and anarchy during either the Weimar republic or in America during the Great Depression were only figments of their imagination, which Roosevelt recommended to his compatriots to remove from their psyche (Inaugural Addresses of the Presidents of the United States, 1985, 235). Of course, none of the defenders of the "fear of freedom" concept cite such an interesting episode from the Middle Ages known as "commendation," that is, when peasants saved themselves from anarchy by exchanging their freedom for bondage in order to be protected by the feudal lord (Bloch and Benjamin, 1939).

By 1949, Arthur Schlesinger saw the greatest threat to American freedom as being not from the Soviet Union, but from the fear of freedom in the soul of his compatriots; he appealed to the frightened individual to free himself from fear (Schlesinger, 1988). In 1990, it was Judith Shklar who became the most-known liberal critic of the state as an institution. She linked fear in society only with the state, but said nothing about fears of criminals, of corrupted businesspeople and bureaucrats and the role of the state in combating destructive forces in society.

Libertarians and Postmodernists

Along with those authors who see the state only as a source of evil, several writers tend to dismiss any role of the state in creating social order. The core of this group is made up of sociologists and economists with libertarian tendencies. The old liberals from the eighteenth and nineteenth centuries, with Locke as their idol, were very strongly against state intervention in social and economic life, but appreciated the role of the state as "night guardian."

The root of libertarianism probably can be found first of all in the works of Herbert Spencer and his doctrinaire form of anti-statism. Spencer would even forbid government, either local or national, to assume responsibility for the paving, lighting and sanitation of cities. Even the less-doctrinaire Bentham's sole advice to the state was to "Be quiet."

Parsons gravitated to a sort of Spencerian libertarianism and almost completely ignored the state as a social institution and an instrument of social control. Mentioning punishment for deviant behavior, he did not link it to the state or to its law enforcement agencies. The courts and police were almost totally ignored in his *Social System*. He talked about laws only as a synonym of regularity, but not at all as a means of control (Parsons, 1951, 201–207). Friedrich Hayek, 50 years after Spencer, was also hostile toward the role of the state in maintaining order. For him "order" means first of all a state of society in which "expectations have a good chance of proving correct" (Hayek, 1973, 36). Hayek insisted that the best order in society emerges only "spontaneously." He, a contemporary of totalitarian states, also pointed to various possibilities of the Western state to "be released from the restraint of rules" and expand its activities at the expense of the private sector, without bothering about the function of the state against deviant behavior. His concern about law is reduced to the protection of private property and contracts (Hayek, 1973, 35–46; 1976, 33–35; 1979, 36).

The intellectual line of Parsons and Hayek was sustained in the last two decades by authors who downgrade the role of the state as a generally weak institution or simply ignore it.[8] The state is not seen as an important institution by Coleman in his *Foundation of Social Theory* (1990), nor by the authors of a collection of articles edited by Munch and Smelser (*Theory of Culture*, 1993). Robert Ellickson, with his high appraisal of the market as a regulatory mechanism and his attack on "legal centralism," belongs to the same group. In his major book, he said nothing positive about the role of the state in Western society. He cannot forgive the rank and file authors who see the state as a crucial agent of order (Calabresi and Melamud, 1972). Ellickson cannot forgive also Ronald Coase, who dared to say, in his famous article "The problem of social cost," that "changes in law might have effects on human interactions" (Ellickson, 1991, 138–139, 280–281).

Paradoxically, the libertarians, the great admirers of liberal capitalism, in their downgrading of the role of the state as the instrument of order are joined by the postmodernist thinkers, harsh critics of contemporary society. The postmodernist negation of the state represents another special type of hostility toward this institution. Some authors went so far as to advance almost absurd theories that the state is "an invention." They confuse the modern "nation-state," which indeed was a relatively new development, with the "state" in general, asserting that the state appeared in history only as a result of the crisis of feudal society. As an invention, as Neil Smelser and his two coauthors directly implied under the influence of the postmodernist ideology, "it cannot be seen . . . as a priori more effective than other forms," and is a response "to specific issues" and a "specific cultural context." They boldly declared that the state, as "a universal institution" "became a source of tension and exclusion." Further, these authors describe the "state" as "a Western model," and muse about the possibility "to invent" "a political system better suited to the problems and cultures of newly independent societies" (Smelser, 1994, 60–61, 70–71).

Had the authors been old, Orthodox Marxists, with their mythology about "the withering state," which was derogated by Stalin, their harangues would have been more or less comprehensible. Otherwise, it is difficult to interpret them as anything but a demonstration of hostility toward the state as an institution. Dario Melossi went so far as to proclaim that the whole concept of the state is an ideological artifact. He wrote, "The state is more than a powerful rhetoric device" (Mellossi, 1990, 6, 169).

A Balanced View on the State as an Instrument of Order

There is a group of authors who recognize the positive role of the state in the maintenance of order. It contains people from various ideological trends. I belong to this group. Karl Polanyi was one of the first Western authors to be influenced by Keynes's *General Theory* (1936) with its apology of state intervention in the economy. He praised the role of the state as the bulwark of order. In *The Good Society*, he suggested that the strong nationalist state was indispensable for coping with the disruptions that emerged in the early capitalist economy, even if this state could transform into a powerful destructive force (Polanyi, 1944). Between the two wars, several authors, predicting a decline or even a collapse of Western civilization, looked at the powerful state as the sole savior of the Western world. These authors included Spengler, who saw in a new Caesarism the way to save the world from collapse.

After the war, U.S. attitudes toward the state deteriorated immensely, mostly because of the Nazi experience and the new information about the nature of the Soviet state. However, in the 1950s–60s, we saw more confidence in the Soviet state's economic progress, which seemingly was strongly buttressed by the miracle of the first Soviet sputnik in 1957 and by Gagarin's flight to space in 1960. The Soviet achievement was behind the high popularity of the theory of convergence, which in one way or another recognized the positive role of the state in society. Even if convergence theory talked about the dissipating differences between two systems and paid high attention to the market, the state still played an important role in Soviet society. It was a very important agent. In the 1950s and 1960s, the major proponents of convergence theory were people with a Marxist past, such as Daniel Bell (*The End of Ideology*, 1960), as well as several other authors such as John Galbraith (*The New Industrial State*, 1967).

Since the late 1960s, the state was the object of attacks from the Left as well as from the Right. Not until the 1990s do we see the appearance of some authors, such as Michael Walzer and Robert Bellah, who mock their colleagues for their "distrust of power." They derogated those liberal thinkers who presume "a society in which equality and liberty have been established and disruption controlled through the use of reason" (Bellah et al., 1991; Walzer, 2002).

With the growth of international terrorism, the debates over the role of coercion in society have taken a new dimension. Robert Kaplan, summarizing his rich experience in traveling in Asia and Africa, sees the gradual withering of the nation-state everywhere, especially in the countries of the Third World. It is the most destructive process of our times, portending growing chaos, anarchy and the "re-primitivization" of society (see Kaplan, 2000). Further, as Kaplan suggests, with the growing number of people living in areas exposed to natural disasters, the role of the state and the army is to save people in the cases of hurricanes or earthquakes, and not being only the protector of people against lawlessness (Kaplan, 2005).

THE STATE AS THE ENFORCER OF LAWS AND VALUES

When I use the term "state," I have in mind the "central administration," or "central government," which is recognized by the population as well as by foreigners as a sovereign legitimate body that runs the given territory and enforces its laws. Most debates about the source of unity

of the population on the given territory are based on either the awareness of the national or religious identity.

I agree with those who operate with the concept "state" as a
combination of the institutions that are run by elites and control the
whole territory, which is considered as "one society," a federation, an
empire or as one political entity. The perspective of the analysis
described here supposes that the state operates on a certain "imperial"
or "national" territory with clearly cut borders that are more or less
accepted by neighbors and the international community.[9] In the
1980s, when Somalia was in a state of complete anarchy, it was still a
"Somali society" because its neighbors did not invade it and did not
annex chunks of its territory. If this had happened it would have
meant the disappearance of this society, which indeed occurred in the
case of many defunct societies in the past. This definition was developed
by Weber and later by Samuel Finer (1975, 84–163). However, there
is a subtle difference between this approach and that of Weber. Weber
correctly talks about the state as a set of organizations vested with the
authority to make binding decisions for people and organizations
located in a particular territory and implement these decisions using,
if necessary, force. However, his definition does not assume that even
a strong state has a limited ability to impose its will on its own territory, which has radical implications for social life (Jackman, 1993, 15).
I agree with Joel Migdal (1988, 22) who evidently recognizes the
inability of the state to completely enforce its laws, talking not about
the violation of law as a normal pattern of behavior, but about the
state as a "contradictory entity that acts against itself."

The "statist" perspective in the study of social order implies the key
role of national (or imperial) laws issued by central state bodies
(as opposed to rules installed by various social actors, such as regional
leaders or the heads of firms or families) as well as the ability of the
state, with its judiciary system, to enforce laws in the given territory.[10]

Law and Values

As previously noted, the state manages to maintain order mostly by
issuing laws in general terms and demanding the observation of laws
by citizens and bureaucracy. By law, I mean directives that are issued
not only by the parliament but by the highest central authorities of the
given national territory. It was Weber who insisted on the broad concept of law, which can be issued in a general way, as simply an "order"
that has to be executed.[11] In Soviet society, laws and directives were
issued by the Supreme Soviet leader, or those to whom he delegated

this work (see Shlapentokh, 2001). In Western democracies, laws or similar norms are issued by legislators as well as by the two other branches of power.

For me, law plays a crucial role in creating order in any society. The centrality of law, and consequently its violation, can be challenged from two angles: formal and substantial. First of all, it is easy to argue that law can be interpreted in different ways. However, this thesis is definitely repudiated by the practices of law enforcement agencies in any society for which the different interpretations of law or deviance are not a serious obstacle for the functioning of these agencies. Criminology, a close relative to sociology, without ignoring the issue of the interpretation of law and crime, successfully functions as a part of the social sciences and tends to make a distinction between social and criminal definitions of law and deviance (see Bohm and Haley, 1999, 24–25).

The emergence of many laws can be traced to the values that are accepted first of all by elites and to some degree also by the masses. Many laws in history have been generated by a sort of "civilizing process." In this respect it is reasonable to agree with scholars such as Dennis Wrong (1994) or Zygmunt Bauman (1989) who talk about the barbarism and incivility often hidden from superficial observations, but which are always ready to rise up and destroy civilizational norms.

Indeed, almost all current values that are vitally important for society are bolstered by law and by the fear of sanctions. Among these, if to take American society as an example, are values such as freedom, health, life, dignity, property, privacy, a clean bureaucracy, the fulfillment of obligations in transactions, patriotism and the readiness to defend the country, individual achievements, material independence and self-reliance (Horatio Alger's ideal), progress and efficiency, hard work and honesty, material comfort, the necessity to protect the security of the state, the necessity to obey the decision of courts, respect for democratic institutions, the rejection of drugs and several others.[12] The case of "freedom," which is regarded by many authors as the main American value ("an essential ingredient in the definition of a good society") (Bellah, 1991, 9), is defined very carefully by many laws. Alan Wolfe, with his tendency to look at American society as a believer in the crucial role of self-regulation, noted that in society morals cannot be maintained without the fear of sanctions for violating laws (Wolfe, 1989).

Americans themselves are very critical of the moral feelings of their compatriots and are skeptical about whether these feelings alone can be the basis of order. As a Gallup Poll found in May 2004, only 18 percent of Americans thought "the state of moral values in this country today is good or excellent," whereas 40 percent thought that it is "poor" and another 40 percent said "only fair" (*New York Times*, May 23, 2004a).

THE CRITERION OF AN EFFICIENT STATE

With the acceptance of the centrality of the state and the laws issued by the state, it is reasonable to discuss an issue such as the efficiency of the state. This subject has not been ignored in contemporary socio-logical literature. However, most authors who wrote on this issue avoided the ability of the state to enforce laws as the major indicator of "the strength of the state" or the "efficacy of the state." For Martin Carnoy, for instance, "the larger is the public sector, the stronger is the state" (Carnoy, 1984, 3; Jackman, 1993, 49). Several other authors gravitate to the same perception of the "strong state," some-times using other versions of the same indicator, such as a ratio of government expenditure to the GNP.[13] Jackman offers "the autonomy of state" as a criterion (Jackman, 1993, 62–65). Krasner supposes that the strength of the state depends on the consensus of the elites: the higher this consensus the stronger the state (Krasner, 1978). Smelser and his coauthors Bertrand Badie and Pierre Birnbaum, making a distinction between a "strong" and a "weak" state, are in fact talking about the democratic and authoritarian (or totalitarian) states. They focus on the degree of autonomy of the subjects. They and many other researchers ascribe a big role to the state in social life and discuss its "capacity"; however, they almost never mention the observance of law, and the fight against corruption and crimes as its major task (Smelser, 1994, 63).

Closest to my understanding of the efficiency of the state are so-called "statists," the scholars who focus their social analyses not so much on "society" but on the "state," even if most of them do not make such a radical distinction between the laws and rules issued by the national institutions and the ordinances issued by any other bodies. Samuel Huntington, in the late 1960s, was close to this concept when he talked about the importance of making a distinction between "moral communities" and "immoral societies," which roused the anger of social scientists with Left and liberal leanings (Huntington, 1968, 28; see also Hopkins, 1972, 275–276). Not very far from this view is the position of Edna Ullman-Margalit, one of Huntington's stu-dents. On one hand, she recognizes the centrality of the state in society. But, on the other hand, she calls for acknowledging the "limitation of the state," and that the state confronts many other centers of power in society and focusses on the intermingling of corrupt state apparatuses with criminals (Ullman-Margalit, 1977, 12–15, 20–25).

With some reservations, it is possible to include in the same group the author Joel Migdal. Despite his use of the Weberian definition of the state he does not even mention in his big book *Strong Societies and Weak States* the terms order or law. He did not talk about their importance for the population. Still, he compares states according to their ability to take social control in their hands, which makes it possible to put Migdal in this group (Migdal, 1988, 3–39, 258–286).

I can also recruit to "my camp" those authors who talk about "the fragility of political order" and the legitimacy of government, supposing that the higher the legitimacy (as well as the greater the longevity of the political institutions, since they enhance the legitimacy of power), the higher "the amount of compliance and consent that the leaders are able to engender" (Jackman, 1993, 156).

LEGITIMACY OF THE STATE AS THE BASIS OF ORDER

The crucial importance of the efficiency of the state relates to its legitimacy in the eyes of the elites and the masses. The nature of legitimacy is a subject of great controversy in the social sciences, political philosophy in particular. With *cum grano salis*, it is possible, as Habermas showed, to extend the concept too much, turning "legitimacy" into a concept describing attitudes toward the social system as a whole and all its institutions.[14] However, here I talk mostly about the legitimacy of political power, or the state, leaving aside all other types of power that Mann (1986) described, following the Weberian tradition: economic, ideological and military.

The different of views on this issue is closely intertwined with the debate over the relative role of fear versus internalized values in the maintenance of social order. The authors who belong to the Lockean–Rousseauan tradition insist that the legitimacy of political authority is based on the social contract between it and independent individuals organized into civil society.

The second school follows the spirit of the Hobbesian approach. It sees legitimacy not as the result of a real negotiation between rulers (or those who offer their services for this role) and the population, but rather as the recognition by the population that the existing social order and its institutions, is legal and right, because they do not see a viable alternative ("default principle") that can maintain order under the given conditions. The ideological indoctrination and the fear of repression help the existing state force people to see the state as legitimate and that there are no possible alternatives.

Since the population accepts the dominance and legitimacy of political power, we can interpret this as a sort of social contract endorsed implicitly by the population. This fundamental circumstance, which blurs the distinction between the two cases and confounds the two dimensions of power (the capacity to impose its will and "the right" to do it), has created in the minds of even prominent thinkers the feeling that the nature of legitimacy is the same for both purely democratic and nondemocratic societies. It is natural that such was the view of Parsons (1969, 361), for whom power was a legitimate product of collective action, supported by the absolute majority and with the exception of the "recalcitrant minority."

It is remarkable that even such experts on totalitarian society as Hanna Arendt (1976, 352–353, 382) and Theodore Adorno and his coauthors (*The Authoritarian Personality*, 1950) followed the same line of reasoning. This group also includes Eric Fromm who was inclined to see the Nazi regime as a product of the consent of the population, which consisted mostly of "authoritarian personalities," yearning for totalitarianism and ignoring the capacity of the Hitler regime, as soon as it took control over the political machine, to impose its will and ideology on the masses. All these authors were orthogonal to their contemporary George Orwell, who saw in *1984* the origin of fear as coming from above and as being bolstered by mass terror.[15]

Furthermore, even Hobbes himself could create the impression that his Leviathan could be born as a result of a priori rather than the implicit consent of the individuals and not as a result of the ruler who took the initiative to save people from their "natural state" and the war of all against all. In fact, Hobbes's assumption about the tacit, implicit consent of people, that is, about the existence of some Covenant between ruler and ruled as the single way to save people from "the state of nature," in no way undermines the real essence of the Hobbesian social philosophy, with its focus on the crucial role of the Leviathan in the maintenance of order. At the same time, Hobbes's discussion of the Covenant gives authors some grounds for considering him a contractual theorist. Hobbes, contrary to Locke, who focused on the natural right of people to be free, declared that the sovereign is in no way bound by obligation toward his subjects and is not even interested in the thoughts of his subjects (1996, 227–228; see also Hindess, 1996, 35–43, 60, 70).

The first approach has some validity to societies with genuine democratic procedures, even if the validity is limited, because people in these societies do not choose the principles of their economic, social and political systems. They take them for granted or endorse them because of the lack of viable alternatives.

The second approach, which I accept, gives a more general explanation of the origin of the legitimacy of political power, particularly in totalitarian and authoritarian societies, as well as often in conquered countries.

Certainly, the recognition of the right of the given power to control people is often bolstered by cultural traditions that urge people to accept what they find when they enter social life. It is noticeable that Weber, the greatest authority on the concept of legitimization, did not pay much attention to order in connection with legitimization (Weber, 1978, 213) as did several other authors who wrote on this issue.[16]

In many cases in history, legitimacy was created not by the cultural traditions and not as a result of the support of the masses or elites, but mostly from power itself. As soon as somebody manages to gain access to the buttons of power and nobody challenges him, the leader acquires almost immediately a sort of legitimacy that will grow with time. It is power that creates an ideology with varied links to cultural traditions (sometimes strong, sometimes not) and justifies power. With the help of sanctions, this ideology is almost always able to persuade people to accept the current power as the single force able to maintain order in society and defend the country from foreign aggression. This ideology is able to develop emotional and rational support among the masses, or "love of Big Brother."

It is important to note that legitimacy is so important for order that the population does not recognizes the legitimacy of the current leaders only under extreme circumstances, as it occurred in Russia in 1917. People generally see a legitimate leader as a vital condition for order in society, even if they disapprove of many aspects of his or her domestic or international policy. This legitimacy absorbs the brunt of the people's anger just as it has protected the most infamous rulers in history, such as Henry the Eighth of Britain and Ivan the Terrible in Russia, both of whom were suspected of having mental disorders.

Legitimization, as a promise for order, was a powerful weapon in the political struggle in many countries in the past. This was particularly true of monarchies, since the people assumed that the higher the legitimization, the higher the support of heaven in the maintenance of order. Various branches of the royal dynasty in medieval France, or even later in the nineteenth century (for instance, the fight between Bourbons and Orleans), fought each other by claiming their superior legitimacy and hoping to find support among the people.

The Soviet Union

The Bolsheviks were able to legitimize, at least partially, their power within a few years after the end of the civil war, showing the population its ability to end the chaos and atrocities, despite arousing the hatred of the majority of the people living on the territory under their control. However, the yearning for order was so great that even the most ardent enemies of the new regime were grateful to Lenin for establishing order in the country, which had been destroyed by two wars. In 1923 itself, even a fervent foe of the Soviet regime, the famous monarchist Vasilii Shulgin, who visited Russia, acknowledged in his book that most people in Soviet Russia had awarded the Bolsheviks legitimacy (Shulgin, 1991). Russian Communists were considered as the holders of order until the end of the Soviet system, a circumstance that was not understood by most authors with strong anti-Communist leanings (see Malia, 1994; Pipes, 1993). The "state," as a central value in the ideology, advanced the political police, the army, the military–industrial complex and the ideological machine as the country's priorities. The official ideology's focus on the leader and the state was supported by the public who saw the strong state as a guarantor of order inside the country and a protector against foreign enemies. The leader was the symbol the regime's order, unity and legitimacy and therefore the cult of the leader was considered a necessary condition for the functioning of the society.

Post-Soviet Russia

The case of the two Russian presidents in post-Soviet Russia is quite eloquent. After the collapse of Communist Russia, a long period of disorganization, high crime rates and corruption began. Against this backdrop, social order became a major asset for the Russians. In 1989, when the Soviet system began to disintegrate, only 18 percent of the Russians responded to the question, "What should be done for the improvement of life?" by answering, "Encourage private entrepreneurship under state control"; 50 percent demanded "firm order" (Levada, 1990, 70, 83). Ten years later, order continued to take priority over any other value. Only 2 percent of the Russians, in a 1998 survey, mentioned the "priority of the individual's interests" among the major principles of new Russia; 27 percent pointed to "order."[17]

Let us start with the first post-Communist president Boris Yeltsin. During his rule, he bombed parliament (killing dozens of people), initiated a war against Chechnia (which killed many thousands), ostensibly funded his 1996 reelection campaign with money from the state coffers (costing the taxpayers one billion dollars), covered up corruption (helping inglorious bureaucrats and oligarchs avoid persecution), presided over a vast decline in real income (down no less than 30–50 percent since 1991), confiscated Russian savings accounts on two occasions (in 1992 and 1998) and lied to his people without hesitation or constraint.

The Russians had a sober image of their president. According to the best Russian public opinion firms in the country, in July 1999 only 3 percent of the Russians "trusted" Yeltsin. He was despised not only by ordinary people, the army, the police, most media and the Communist opposition, but even liberal politicians. Under such circumstances, how could Yeltsin survive? As an answer, many people referred at the time to the KGB, the Ministry of Internal Affairs and the special divisions of the army under his control. However, the real shield that protected Yeltsin was the legitimacy of the regime. The fundamental fact was that Yeltsin was elected as president of Russia two times (in 1991 and 1996). Regardless of his personal qualities, he was a legitimate ruler of the country and nobody wanted to take the risk of removing a legitimate leader from power.

What is more, the many analysts who at that time were sure that Putin's support of Yeltsin could only decrease his chances to be elected as a new president were wrong. The Russians saw in this development not so much a violation of democracy and a throwback of monarchism, but the Kremlin's effort to guarantee the continuity of power, and so they elected Putin as a new president.

A later stage in post-Soviet history again highlighted the role of the legitimacy of power. In 2003–05, Russians disapproved of almost all sides of Putin's domestic policy. However, his general rating was very high. This contradiction confused a lot of analysts who could not see in Putin a symbol of order for the Russian population for whom anarchy and chaos were the major threats to their country (see Shlapentokh, 2005).[18]

LEGITIMACY OF POWER IN CONQUERED COUNTRIES: THE FRENCH CASE

But even more remarkable was the speed with which the population in the conquered countries recognized, even if with many reservations and mostly by default, the legitimacy of the power of the occupiers, an observation made by Hobbes when he defended the de facto power of the conqueror in *Leviathan* (Hobbes, 1996; see also

Somerville, 1992, 165). This happened during WWII, as well as in several other European countries, including the Netherlands, Belgium and Ukraine, though not in Poland or Yugoslavia. The same is true about Korea where the population was quite conformist toward the Japanese occupation.

It is well known how collaboration was widespread during the German occupation of France in 1939–44. In the last decades, the authors of numerous books discussed this painful subject. The resistance was an important development in occupied France. Even if only a minority of the population participated in it, many French were silently on their side and held collaborators in contempt. Still, those who collaborated with the Vichy regime in "zone libre" and the Nazis in "zone occupee," even if to consider the passionate defense of French pride by some authors (the most passionate defense was offered by Vercors in his famous novel *Le silence de la mer*), made up 20 percent of the whole country in 1940–41, and 25 percent in the free zone (see Burrin, 1993, 183, 188; for a less sanguine view of the collaboration in France, see Bernanos, 1948).

These data strongly underestimate the scope of collaboration, according to many authors. A book entitled *Suite française* (2004), by Irène Némirovsky, who was killed in Auschwitz in 1942 and who watched the developments in France in 1940–41, gave a much more sober account about the behavior of French people toward the Nazis than many writings done several years after. Her book makes clear the vast extent of the cooperation of the French with the occupiers (Némirovsky, 2004).

Facing the Germans who were ready to repress those who defied them, the French people had no option, besides heroism. Millions of collaborators justified their behavior or cohabitation (if to use a euphemism in circulation at that time in France)[19] by the fact that Germans controlled the country and their communities as well as those of Petain's government. They saw the Nazi machine and Petain's regime as legitimate under the given circumstances, as a condition for order as an "almost inevitable consequence of the occupation" (Ousby, 1997, 139; see also Gordon, 1980; 2004). As a French author suggested, the root of the collaboration was made up of "passion" (sympathy and admiration for Nazi Germany), "acceptance" and "self-interest" (Defrasne, 1982, 55–88). Another author was more inclined, in comparison with many other French and American writers, to downgrade the level of collaboration. The author suggested that the collaboration was justified by many of his countrymen as "realistic" and "expedient," or even as "the requirement of civility in the contacts with Europeans" (Burrin, 1993, 183–184, 196–197). The famous writer Claude Moriac, explaining his contacts with Germans, resorted to this argument (Moriac, 1990, 361). The ideology of order, along with a belief in the Nazi victory and the victory of "the New Order in Europe," was particularly strong in 1940–42 when the German army was at the peak of its victories. The ideology of order represented the essence of the submission to Vichy and to the German occupiers (Burrin, 1993, 193–194, 198–199). This ideology also included slogans of Petain's "National revolution," phraseology denouncing the corruption and weakness of the Third Republic, which was unable to maintain order in society and defend the fatherland.

The belief that a new ideology will bring the defeated France a chance for survival as a nation inspired the famous French poet Paul Claudel to praise Petain almost as a God in 1940 (later the poet, as Nazi Germany weakened, seemingly changed his sympathies; see Davies, 2001, 28). Petain was indeed perceived by the defeated nation as "a father who has to reassure, guide and discipline" "a nation of children" (Ousby, 1997, 91).

The collaboration of ordinary French people with the Germans was broad. It included flirting with Nazi officers, drinking together in bars, common participation in entertainment activities, even the invitation of German officers to private homes. This in no way denies the strong resistance and the hatred of the Germans among many French people (Burrin, 1993, 202). The number of prominent collaborators, not only among politicians but also among writers and artists, was quite high (Burrin, 1993, 202–204; Gildea, 2002, 42–69, 403–411; Jackson, 2003; Ousby, 1997, 141–150, see especially chapters 8, 9, 12, 13). It is no accident that in these times many people remember Gui de Maupassant's famous story "Boule de suif," in which the writer described the collaboration of the French middle class with the same Germans, but this time after the defeat in the Franco-Prussian war in 1870–71.

As several studies show, the French administration collaborated with the Germans more closely than ordinary people, even if with a great deal of friction. It was local officials, so-called notables, who functioned as intermediaries between the Germans and the local population. Although the notables tried to protect the French communities from requisitioning the grain, they and the Vichy administration fully accepted the German policy toward Jews and actively participated in their deportation (Ousby, 1997, 98–99).

However, as soon as the fortune of war began leaving Nazi Germany, the collaboration started to decline, and, according to a widespread perception of these times, it was possible to see "a meta-morphosis of the forty million Petainists into forty million DeGaullist," an assertion vehemently denied by many French authors (Burrin, 1993, 177). Even more interesting is that the same notables, for the sake of continuity of order and preventing Communists from grabbing power, were accepted by De Gaulle's administration until the new elections after the war.

CONCLUSION

Considering social order as almost automatically maintained in society, the mainstream in sociology suggests that this occurs mostly through the processes of socialization and the influence of family, the community, public opinion and peer groups. It ignores the role of formal control or downgrades it as either ineffective or even damaging to society. The mainstream praises informal control as the most efficient way to maintain order. It is thought to be based on persuasion and internalized moral values, as opposed to coercion and the fear of sanctions used by the institutions of formal control. In fact, all informal groups use fear to force their members to follow their rules of behavior. Of special interest is the hostility of many sociologists to the state. In denouncing the state as the only source of evil, they suggest the necessity of diminishing the role of the state in maintaining order. I belong to a group of social scientists who preach a balanced view of the state. Not forgetting the tragic experiences of totalitarian states, I think it is necessary to have a strong civil society that is able to check the tendency of bureaucracy to expand its power in society. At the same time, I believe that without the state and the judicial system, social order cannot be maintained. Only the state, with the help of the judiciary, can enforce values and turn them into laws and rules. The role of the state in creating order in society can be seen in the fact that the population usually endows the state and its leaders with legitimacy, that is, with the right to use its power and coercion for maintaining order.

Concluding Remarks

The major goal of this book was to show that the maintenance of social order is an enormous task for any society. The dominant belief that in democratic societies it is possible to establish order on the basis of social values alone is a simplification. There is no doubt that in many cases people's internalized values prompt them to behave in an orderly manner. Otherwise, people would feel morally uncomfortable. However, moral compunctions are not strong enough to maintain order in society.

There are four groups of flaws in the dominant culturological explanations of order in society. First of all, many sociologists simplify the impact of these values on order. What researchers take as internalized values in fact are the rules that people want to follow for fear of being punished. Many authors who deal with values as the basis of order disregard the low correlation between values and behavior. The next obstacle for the high influence of values on behavior, which is also neglected in the literature, is the strong conflict among values, as well as the fact that many values are considered by several people as obliging "others," but not them. This phenomenon is known as "values for me and values for others." The advocates of the cultural basis of order also tend to ignore the fact that some values, such as status values, have an ambivalent impact on social order.

The second group of flaws in the dominant view is related to the disregard of the values that play only a destructive role in society. Indeed, many people internalize not only positive values, but negative ones as well. Drunkenness, drug addiction, violence, promiscuity, rudeness in behavior, xenophobia, the hatred of minorities, corruption and anti-intellectualism are only a small part of a long list of values that play key roles in the value systems of a major part of the population in any society. In some segments of society, such as the corporate and criminal sectors, the negative values that challenge order are espoused by a considerable number of people. With the spread of negative values in society, it is evident that they influence the minds of young people when they prepare themselves for adult life. In many cases the socialization of new generations prepares them with negative attitudes toward order.

The third group of weaknesses of the culturalogical concept can be ascribed to the belief that the same positive values are shared by the majority of the population in a society. Meanwhile, most societies are rather heterogeneous in the attitudes of the population toward the major values that influence social order. This is not only true about all the empires that existed in the past, but also about such relatively stable countries as Norway or Sweden.

The fourth group of weaknesses of the culturological concept of order can be attributed to the exaggeration of the stability of values. Indeed, for values to play the role ascribed to them by Parsons they must be steady and impervious to the current political or economic processes. Without denying the inertia of several values and beliefs, I agree with those scholars who assume that social values are quite flexible, as well as culture in general.

The exaggeration of the role of culture (and the role of values in the first place) in the formation of social order in the contemporary sociological literature is accompanied by the downgrading of the importance of fear in maintaining order. The disregard of the positive role of the fear is correlated with the underestimation of the impact of social fears on the quality of life, such as the fear of crime or the fear of unemployment (negative fears). The disregard of the role of fear in society is also combined in the sociological literature with a refusal to recognize the importance of Hobbes as a social thinker who made a strong contribution to the analysis of social order. Among other things, he underscored the role of the state and the fear of sanctions to prevent anarchy in society.

Meanwhile, the mainstream in sociology, looking for the institutions that are responsible for order, focus only on family, community, public opinion and peer groups, which supposedly use only informal control and persuasion as the main instruments of order. In fact, all informal groups widely use the fear of sanctions to force their members to follow the rules of behavior expected from them. The crucial role in the maintenance of order in any society belongs to law and the state that enforces it.

NOTES

CHAPTER I   SOCIAL ORDER IN THE CONTEMPORARY SOCIOLOGICAL LITERATURE: THE EVOLUTION OF A CONCEPT

1. See Parsons, 1975; for more about the differences between the Hobbesian and Parsonian views, see Wrong, 1994, 29, 99–108.
2. See, for instance, Babbie, 1983; Fichter, 1971; Light and Keller, 1982; Turner, 1985.
3. See an elaboration of this view of the role of agents in crime in Hirschi, 2002.
4. Here is a typical excerpt from this book: "The social meaning of crime and deviance does not simply arise out of the laws, norms, and values that demonize, stigmatize, taint, or otherwise label certain actions, words, or deeds vis-à-vis others. Troublesome individuals are not simply a product of a codification process that reflects, for example, the parameters of tolerance of the majority of the population in a democracy. Rather, 'trouble' is constantly made and remade through the everyday metaphors that render some acts more heinous than others and some behaviors more worthy of social control than others" (Ferrell and Websdale, 1999, 355).
5. See, for instance, Babbie, 1983; Fichter, 1971; Light and Keller, 1982; Macionis, 2001. Among general books on political science, see Donovan et al., 1993.
6. For more about La Pen's success in the first round of the presidential election in France on April 21, 2002, see *New York Times*, April 23, 2002.
7. For more about this figure, see Riding, 2002.
8. See, for instance, Emerson's *From Empire to Nation* (1960) in which the author describes the process of decolonization, almost completely ignoring the chaos that accompanied this process in many countries.
9. Joseph Stiglitz (2002) was one of the few economists who focused on this issue in his analysis of the works of American economists on the failures of post–Soviet economic reforms.
10. See Pie, 1966. For more about the concept of "state capacity," see Skocpol, 1985; Engelbert, 2000.
11. Indeed, for "democracy to be consolidated" there are five conditions: "free and lively civil society," "autonomous and valued political society,"

"a rule of law to ensure legal guarantees for citizens," "freedoms usable by a democratic government state bureaucracy" and "institutionalized economic society" (Linz and Stepan, 1996, 7).

12. See Lins, 2002; see also the movie based on this novel (director Fernando Meirelles, 2003).

Chapter 2   The Major Theories about the Nature and Origin of Values and Order

1. For the diversity in the definition of values see Hechter, 1993, 3–4.

2. Fazio (1989) defines an attitude as an association in memory between an attitude object and an evaluation. For this reason, in some ways, the terms values and attitudes are interchangeable. After Katz (1960), attitudes and values in their cognitive function "engender the meaning upon the world" whereas in its utilitarian function they help people to maximize reward and minimize punishment.

3. Quite often norms are used for the same purpose as values, particularly when the norms are defined as instruments that "aid in accomplishing the goals of the group" (Allison, 1992). Other authors, such as Cialdini and Trost (1998, 153), even suggest the possibility to integrate societal value and functional perspectives on norm development; see also Fine, 2001, 139–140.

4. See Hechter and Opp (2001b). It is interesting that while here Hechter operates in this volume as the author and an editor only with the concept of norms (values are mentioned casually only two times in the 400–page volume). A few years earlier, he totally ignored the concept of norms (see Hechter, 1993).

5. See Horne, 2001, 4; see also the definition of values and norms in Allison, 1992; Cialdini and Trost, 1998.

6. This term is simply absent in Ellickson, 1991.

7. See an excellent analysis of these two trends in American social science in Hechter et al. (2003, 329).

8. The different definitions of culture are discussed in Eisenstadt, 1992, 65–67; Giddens, 1989, 31.

9. Rokeach, 1973, 1979; Williams, 1979.

10. As an exception, see David Bayley, who regarded the fear of sanctions as a main point in his theoretical approach to crime (1995, 14–15).

11. Augustine's suggestion in the fourth and fifth centuries to love first of all God as the single perfect entity in the universe, as the bearer of immutable Truth and Wisdom, as the source of "the moral law," and also, as a derivative, the laws of justice that are designed to create order and peace. This was very important to Augustine, who lived in a world of turmoil in the last period of the decaying Roman Empire. For Augustine, God's "Moral law" replaced the Roman Empire as the

single source of order, as it was for the Stoics close to the time of Augustine (Arrington, 1998).

12. In their textbook, Federico and Schwartz insist that "the rules" finally acquire a ethical dimension and children will soon "feel guilty" when they deviate from rules (1983, 200).

13. See Ackoff, 1999, 8. The author insists that each part of the system "is necessary . . . for carrying out" a "defining function" of the given system (6).

14. Among recent publications, see Hefter, 2000, 156–157; see also Light and Keller, 1982, 64.

15. See Hall, 1987; Strauss, 1991.

16. Clay, 1997a,b; 1998; Coase and Orlean, 1994; Barak, 2002; Bernstein, 1992; Ellickson, 1986; Macaulay, 1963.

17. It is interesting that Rousseau, the apologist of "general will," nevertheless gravitated to the idea that it is not common people but the elitist people who can play the role of lawgivers. He agrees with Plato that most people are stupid. Thus, the general will, though always morally sound, is sometimes mistaken. Hence, Rousseau suggests that the people need a lawgiver, a great mind such as Solon, Lycurgus or Calvin, to draw up a constitution and system of laws. He even suggests that such lawgivers need to claim divine inspiration in order to persuade the dim.

CHAPTER 3   THE LIMITED ROLE OF POSITIVE INTERNALIZED VALUES

1. See the critique of the approach of neoclassical economists to values in Kay, 2004; see also Davies, 2003.

2. This was the opinion of the prominent Russian Menshevik and historian Boris Nikolaevsky, who talked even about "mass defeatism" during the war (Kalinin, 1998; Nikolaevsky, 1948a,b, 209–234; see also Volkogonov, 1998b).

3. For more on the discrimination of immigrants, see Traverso, 1964, 9–75.

4. Samuel Huntington (2004) paid great attention to various social consequences of the national identity (22–24).

5. Among the few publications on envy, see Salovey and Rothman, 1991, 12; Schoek, 1969; Smith et al., 1999.

6. See a special study about the role of envy in Shakespeare's works in Girard, 2004.

7. See also a funny discussion on why professors rarely throw parties to celebrate the departure of their colleagues for a better job in Salovey and Rothman, 1991, 12.

8. A well-known discussion of envy, as well as other cardinal sins, can be found in Thomas Aquinas's thirteenth-century work *Summa Theologica* (1978).

9. Some recent micro studies dealt with this well–known issue of how people try to conceal their pure envy with the claim of injustice (see Smith, 1991; Smith et al., 1999).

CHAPTER 4   AGGRESSIVE NEGATIVE VALUES

1. For more on the use of anti-Americanism in the domestic policies of various countries, see Shlapentokh and Woods, 2004; Shlapentokh et al., 2005.
2. Take, for instance, the occupation of stripper (see a detailed description of the life of strippers in Las Vegas in Kershaw, 2004).
3. See the program "Antisocial society in England," BBC, May 25, 2003.
4. Since the early 1980s, the literature on rent-seeking activity has expanded (among the major works, see Baumol, 2002; Buchanan et al., 1980; Krueger, 1994, 86–89; Mitchell and Munger, 1991). About the various definitions of corruption, which, however, converge on the bribing of officials, see Heidenheimer and Johnson, 2002, 3–14.
5. For the recent debates on the influence of big money on democracy, see Domhoff, 2002; Rye, 2002; Smith, 1999; Walton, 1998. As an example of the "aggregate approach" to lobbyists and interests groups, see Baumgartner and Leech, 1996; Hojnacki and Kimball, 1998.
6. "Corruption," said Chubais, "depends very little on the authorities. It depends on the people" (see Chubais, 2002; see also a typical article by Gudkov, 2000).
7. For more on the connections between criminals and governmental agencies in the United States, see Liddick, 1999, 199–205.
8. There was not a single word about negative socialization in the big section on socialization in Babbie, 1983, 141–170, or in Turner, 1985, 122–123. As an exception, it is possible to cite Light and Keller, who wrote about children in the social environment of poverty with its high level of crimes and were socialized into criminal style of life; see also Doob, 1994, 169–170.
9. An exception could be found in a new edition of Sutherland (1978) with the coauthor Donald Cressey.
10. See Simons, 2003; on the alienation of Turks in Denmark, see Bernsteign, 2004 (according to a survey, 98% of the Turks who live in this country marry a wife or husband from Turkey).
11. On the connection between trust and expectations see Claus Offe (1991, 47).
12. Levada-zentr, Press vypusk, November 13 and 16, 2000.
13. The answer to this question was received in only 13 of 43 countries (Inglehart et al., 2001, 288).
14. See "Trust in government," *Gallup Organization*, September 13–15, 2004.

CHAPTER 5   NATIONAL COMMON VALUES:
PARTIALLY A MYTH

1. Using the description of the world before the collapse of Communism, i.e., consisting of three groups—Western, socialist and developing countries—a Russian author argues that post-Soviet Russian society consists of four worlds: the first containing the richest and the most powerful people, who are already ahead (in terms of their standard of living and aspirations) of their Western counterparts; the second, a relatively small middle class that dreams of joining the first world; the third includes the poor working class and retired folks; and the fourth world consists of de-classed lumpen people, who are chronically unemployed, homeless or criminals (Solovei, 2002).
2. On the debates on the origin of England, see Bogdanor, 2003.
3. For more on the debates over the origin of nationalism, see Nairn, 2003.
4. See also the same view of David Brooks, who in his various publications develops the idea that Americans with the same social status and various demographic characteristics share the same ideology (Brooks, 2004a).
5. As one of the leading Sovietologists, Stephen White noted that the prospect for creating complete unity among the Soviet people before 1985 might not be wholly unrealistic (White, 1993, 151).

CHAPTER 6   CHANGES AND STABILITY OF
SOCIAL VALUES AND NORMS

1. See the recent analysis of Parsons's evolution theory in Sanderson, 2001, 17–20.
2. Using Ruth Kornhauser's observation, these authors operate with an overboard concept of culture with which it is impossible to test any theory that considers culture as a cause of any social development. She proposes the idea of restricting the realm of culture to only the ultimate ends and the meanings of existence (see Kornhauser, 1978).
3. It is remarkable that the world vision of Andrei Tsygankov (2004), a young Russian scholar, stretched cultural determinism to its extreme, almost to a caricature. Tsygankov believes that ideas generate other ideas with minimal interference from the material world. In his "ideational" analysis (21) of Russia's numerous ideologies, Tsygankov tends to ignore the complexities of social reality and their influence on the ideological struggle in Russia, as well as in other post-Soviet countries. He devotes only a few sentences to the social and economic developments in the country (84–85). Of course, there is no room in this book for a discussion of poverty, corrupt privatization or the criminalization of Russian society after 1991.
4. See the critical review of this book in Ortner, 2003.
5. His books aroused debates in the scholarly community and media (Diamond, 1997, 2005).

6. For more on such a controversial issue as the place of intellectuals, see Bottomore, 1993, 52–71; Shlapentokh, 1990.

7. See an analysis of Elias's book in Garland, 1990, 216–218.

8. In 1998, after being asked about the cause of the Soviet collapse, only 20% of the Russian people pointed out the "inefficacy of the socialist system" (in 1995, the figure was 23%); 63% blamed the Soviet leaders (VTSIOM, 1998, 14). The November 1998 survey conducted by the Fund of Public Opinion (1998) found that 48% of the Russians rejected capitalism as a good system for Russia and only 30% were in favor of it.

9. In the late 1960s, 28% of the people in the Penza region and 22% in the Voronezh region declared themselves "believers." Among the respondents under the age of 30, the number of believers was only 5%; among those older than 60, the number was 40%. In rural areas, the number of believers was two to three times higher than in the cities (Pivovarov, 1974, 155; Yablokov, 1979, 139–140).

10. After the fall of the Soviet Union, Edward Shevarnadze, who had worked as the minister of the Georgian KGB and the first party secretary, became the president of the independent Georgian Republic. In this new capacity, he was baptized in the Orthodox Church in 1992.

11. Among the intelligentsia in the Penza region, 4% were "believers"; the numbers for clerical workers, workers and collective farmers were 4%, 8% and 28% respectively (Yablokov, 1979, 140).

12. Vladimir Shubkin along with David Konstaninovsky studied the prestige of various occupations in the Novosibirsk region from the early 1960s up to the end of the 1990s (see Shubkin, 1970; see also Konstantinovsky, 1999).

13. According to the liberal Moscow newspaper *Moskovskie Novosti*, between 1985 and 1991, 79% of the mothers asked by the foundation "The Right of Mothers" reported that their son joined the army as a draftee "with great aspiration," or "with the feeling of duty" (see *Moskovskie Novosti*, November 11, 1994).

14. The survey was conducted by the Independent Institute of Social and National Issues (*Moskovskii Komsomolets*, February 2, 1998).

15. The movement "Soldiers' Mothers" is a clear sign of the public senti-ment. The movement is against the participation of their children in war, and particularly dislikes the hazing practices in the military.

16. About the role of the American elites in the promotion of new values, see Judis, 2000, 253, 255.

17. See Clendinen, 2003 and Clendinen and Nagourney, 1999; see also the TV movie "Angels in America," which describes attitudes toward homosexuals in America in the mid-1980s.

18. See on-line source: http://www.aicgs.org/c/kommersc.shtml.

Chapter 7 Fear as a Neglected Variable

1. There are several classifications of fear. Rush Dozier, for instance, identifies three kinds: the primitive fear system, the rational fear system, and consciousness, which he believes developed primarily as a means for relatively defenseless hominids to handle dangerous situations (Dozier, 1998).

2. According to our survey, in 1998–1999, up to two-thirds of the people in the countries included in the project attributed the emergence of fear to their personal experience (Ukrainians, 65%; Russians, 63%; Lithuanians, 48%; Bulgarians, 33%), and roughly one-third ascribed the origin of their fears to the media (Lithuanians, 39%; Bulgarians, 36%; Russians, 27%; and Ukrainians, 22%). Interpersonal communication (talks among friends, relatives and colleagues) claimed the role of the third source of fear (in Bulgaria it was mentioned by 31%; in Lithuania, 11%; Ukraine, 8%; and in Russia by 5%) (Shlapentokh and Shiraev, 2002).

3. For more on the place of fear in the history of philosophy, see Matveeva and Shlapentokh, 2000, 10–29.

4. Alexis de Tocqueville talked about people who were "frightened by the limitless independence" (1969, 436, 444, 520, 643–645).

5. For more on the link between culture and fear, see Tuan, 1979.

6. For more about a national study that included a survey of 36,000 people in 42 locations accomplished by the French Ministry of Health between 1999 and 2003, see Carey, 2005a; Petitnicoals, 2004.

7. For more on this sort of fear, particularly the fears of war, see Rachman, 1990.

8. For more on Hobbes's materialism, see Strauss, 1965, 12–13 and Thomas, 1965, 189–190.

9. Hobbes, 1996, 82–83; see Rousseau, 1988a,b, 238.

10. For reflections on Goethe's famous dictum, see on-line source: http://www.steria.co.uk/index.asp?ItemId=1883.

11. On Parsons's attitudes toward utilitarianism, see Mayhew, 1982, 9, 14, 17, 31.

12. For more on the discussion of the character of Hobbes's individualism, see Ryan, 1988, 81–106.

13. See Wrong, 1994, 34; for a comparison of Hobbes and Locke in favor of Locke, see Parsons, 1982, 96–101; for an argument in favor of Hobbes, see Shlapentokh, 2003.

14. See, for instance, an article by John Barnesly (1972), a British sociologist.

15. See the on-line source: http://people–press.org/reports/pdf/196.pdf.

16. See, for instance, Michael Lovaglia and Jeffrey Houser's article "Emotional reaction and status in groups" (1996), or Erica Summers's article, "The micro potential for social change: emotion, consciousness and social movement formation" (2002).

17. See, for instance, the conspicuous absence of this term in Robert Ellickson's famous book *Order without Law* (1991), even if the book claims to describe the function of contemporary society.

18. It is true also about Albert Reiss, who wrote one of the first postwar empirical works on crime in America (1967).

19. For more on this tendency in the social science literature, see Lewis and Salem, 1986.

20. Cialdini and his coauthors have named them "injunctive norms," which promise social rewards and punishments (see Cialdini et al., 1991).

21. See, for instance, Hayek, 1976, 36–37.

22. See a critique of this view in Sutton, 2001, 6, 56.

23. The debates on the origin of the crime decline in New York are extremely fierce. The authors of the books and articles on this issue vehemently deny the validity of each other's theories (see Francies, 2005; Harcourt, 2001; Karmen, 2000; Kelling et al., 1996).

24. See Michener et al., 2004, 63–64. However, it is impossible to find a mention of punishment in many texts on socialization.

CHAPTER 8   THE LEADING ROLE OF FORMAL CONTROL AS THE BASIS OF ORDER

1. As Allen Liska notes, the tendency to reduce the study of social control to the study of acts of deviance that disrupt an otherwise integrated social system started in the 1940s–1950s (Liska, 1992, 2).

2. Federico and Schwartz, as an exception, point to the role of fear as an instrument of control in informal groups (2002).

3. See Lewis and Salem, 1986, 19. It is also amusing how Confucianism, so harshly used in contemporary Communist China to justify the repressive control of ordinary people, is used by American sociologists—the enemies of formal control and the state—to assert, contrary to conventional wisdom, that the main point in this ancient Chinese philosophy is not so much obedience to superiors, but the focus on civility and harmony in social relations, which does not make it necessary to intervene from above, i.e., from the state in the first place (Barry, 1998, 3–10, 14).

4. One of the most recent examples was Christiania, a district in downtown Copenhagen. Lizette Alvarez, the author of the article "Free spirit in their fortress," describes how the problems that emerge in the life of the community are solved inhouse. Residents debate the issues until they reach consensus, whether on sanitation or schooling. However, even in this case, if violence breaks out, the threat of baseball bats does the job (*The New Times*, July 1, 2003). In this case, the community lives under the umbrella of formal authorities to which the residents will resort in extreme cases. The commune existed for

more than 20 years. However, by 2003, the prospects for its survival were not good.

5. It is remarkable that many American intellectuals tried to suggest that *1984* is not an image of the Soviet totalitarian state, but a description of the American state (see, for instance, Sheldon, 1991, 513–514).

6. As an example of such an absurd critique, see Higgs, 2003.

7. For the history of this idea, see Sidgwick, 1891, 41.

8. Joel Migdal noted that in the 1950s and 1960s, the state was rarely mentioned by social scientists who study state–society relations (Migdal, 1988, 43).

9. For a similar definition, see Brownlie, 1979, 73–76.

10. Among them is Tatiana Zaslavskaia, a prominent Russian sociologist who made a distinction between two types of actions in labor relations: legal and illegal (Zaslavskaia, 2002, 205–256; see Elias, 1998, 22).

11. See the discussion of the role of law in Weber's sociology in Sutton, 2001, 99–132.

12. For more on American values, see Heslin, 1975 and Williams, 1970.

13. See, for instance, Harris, 1986, 145–149.

14. Habermas, 1973, 36, 46–50, 73. It is curious that, Habermas, citing Weber profusely, did not pay attention to how Weber treats "legitimacy" with a very narrow meaning (96–97).

15. For the differences between Adorno and Arendt, on one side, and Orwell on the other, see Shlapentokh, 2004b.

16. See, for instance, Outhwaite, 1994, 328–329.

17. See the Fund of Public Opinion, 1998.

18. Yuri Levada, a leading Russian analyst, insisted that Putin's high rating occurred because he was "the president of hope." Levada's theory was refuted by the data of his own public opinion center, which showed that his rating was combined with a high level of pessimism in the country.

19. Burrin, 1993, 199–200; see a description of "cohabitation" in the diary of a German officer in Junger, 1995.

BIBLIOGRAPHY

Abramowitz, Alan and Jeffrey A. Segal (1992). *Senate Elections*. Ann Arbor: University of Michigan Press.

Abramson, Paul and Ronald Inglehart (1998). *Value Changes in Global Perspective*. Ann Arbor: University of Michigan Press.

Acharya, Amitav (2004). *Age of Fear: Power versus Principle in the War on Terror*. Singapore: Marshall Cavendish Academic.

Ackoff, Russel (1999). *Re-Creating the Corporation*. New York: Oxford University Press.

Acocella, Joan (2005). Becoming the emperor. *The New Yorker*. February 21.

Adorno, T.W., E. Frenkel-Brunswik, D. Levinson and D. Sanford (1950). *The Authoritarian Personality*. New York: Harper.

Agger, Ben (1991). Critical theory, post structuralism and postmodernism. *Annual Review of Sociology*, 17: 105–131.

Albrecht, H.J. (1993). Ethnic minorities: crime and criminal justice in Europe. In F. Heidensohn, and M. Farrell, eds. *Crime in Europe*. London: Routledge.

Alexander, Jeffrey and Neil Smelser (1999a). Introduction: the ideological discourse of cultural discontent. In Jeffrey Alexander and Neil Smelser, eds. *Diversity and Its Discontents*. Princeton: Princeton University Press.

Alexander, Jeffrey and Neil Smelser, eds. (1999b). *Diversity and Its Discontents*. Princeton: Princeton University Press.

Allard, E. (1972). *A Frame of Reference for Selecting Social Indicators*. Helsinki: Comentationes Scientarum Socialium.

Allison, Paul D. 1992. Cultural evolution of beneficent norms. *Social Forces*, 71: 279–301.

Almond, Gabriel and Bingham Powell (1966). *Comparative Politics: A Developmental Approach*. Boston: Little, Brown.

Alvarez, Julia (1997). *¡Yo*. Chapel Hill: Algonquin Book.

AMA (1974). *Quality of Life: The Middle Years*. Acton, Mass.: Publishing Sciences Group.

Amalrik, Andre (1980). *Will the Soviet Union Survive until 1984?* Harmondsworth, Middlesex and New York, N.Y.: Penguin Books.

Andersen, Margaret and Howard Taylor (2002). *Sociology, Understanding a Diverse Society*. Belmont: Wadsworth.

Anderson, Benedict R. (1983). *Imagined Communities: Reflections on the Origin and Spread of Nationalism*. London: Verso.

Andrew, Christopher M. and Vasili Mitrokhin (1999). *The Sword and the Shield: The Mitrokhin Archive and the Secret History of the KGB*. New York: Basic Books.

Andrews, Frank, ed. (1986). *Research on the Quality of Life*. Ann Arbor: University of Michigan.

Aquinas, Saint Thomas (1978). *Summa Theologica* (Nature and Grace: Selections from the Summa Theologica of Thomas Aquinas). Translated and edited by A.M. Fairweather. Philadelphia: Westminster Press.

Arbatov, Georgii (1992). *The System: An Insider's Life in Soviet Politics*. New York: Times Books.

Archer, D. and R. Gartner (1984). *Violence and Crime in Cross-National Perspective*. New Haven: Yale University Press.

Archer, John 1994. *Male Violence*. London and New York: Routledge.

Arendt, Hanna (1976). *The Origin of Totalitarianism*. New York: Harcourt.

Armstrong, John (1982). *Nations before Nationalism*. Chapel Hill: University of North Carolina Press.

Arnold, Andrea (1990). *Fear of Food*. New York: The Free Enterprise Press.

Arrington, Robert L. (1998). *Western Ethics: An Historical Introduction*. Malden: Blackwell Publishers.

Arrow, Kenneth (1974). *The Limits of Organization*. New York: Norton.

Arts, Will, Jacques Hagenaars and Loek Halman (2003). Cultural diversity of European unity. Leiden-Boston: Brill.

Babbie, Earl (1983). *Sociology Introduction*. Belmont: Wadsworth.

Bailey, Robert (1958). *Sociology Faces Pessimism*. The Hague: Martinus Nijhof.

Bailey, Ronald, ed. (2002). *Global Warming and other Eco-Myths: How the Environmental Movement Uses False Science to Scare Us to Death*. Roseville, Calif.: Forum.

Baley, Paul (1996). *Post-War Japan: 1945 to Present*. Cambridge: Blackwell.

Bandura, A. (1969). Social learning theory of identificatory processes. In D.A. Goslin, ed. *Handbook of Socialization Theory and Research*, pp. 213–262. Chicago: Rand-McNally.

Banfield, Edward (1965). *The Moral Basis of Backward Society*. New York: Free Press.

Barak, Richman (2002). Community enforcement of informal contracts: Jewish diamond merchants in New York. *John M. Olin Center for Law, Economics & Business*, Discussion Paper No. 384.

Barbalet, J.M. (1998). *Emotion, Social Theory, and Social Structure. A Macrosociological Approach*. Cambridge: Cambridge University Press.

Barber, Benjamin R. (2003). *Fear's Empire: War, Terrorism, and Democracy*. New York: W.W. Norton & Co.

Barkun, Michael (1968). *Law without Sanctions: Order in Primitive Society and the World Community*. New Haven: Yale University Press.

Barnes, Julian (2004). *A History of the World in $10^{1/2}$ Chapters*. New York: Knopf.

Barry, Theodore De (1998). *Asian Values and Human Rights*. Cambridge: Harvard University Press.

Barson, Michael and Steven Heller (2001). *Red Scare: The Commie Menace.* San Francisco: Chronicle Books.

Bate, Roger (2000). *Life's Adventure: Virtual Risk in a Real World.* Oxford, England and Boston: Butterworth-Heinemann.

Bates, Robert (1981). *Market and States in Tropical Africa.* Berkeley: University of California Press.

Baum, Andrew and Yakov Epstein, eds. (1978). *Human Response to Crowding.* Hillsdale: L. Erlbaum.

Bauman, Zygmunt (1989). *Modernity and the Holocaust.* Ithaca, N.Y.: Cornell University Press.

Baumgartner, Frank R. and Beth L. Leech (1996). The multiple ambiguities of "counteractive lobbying." *American Journal of Political Science,* 40: 521–542.

Baumol, William J. (2002). *The Free-Market Innovation Machine: Analyzing the Growth Miracle of Capitalism.* Princeton: Princeton University Press.

Bayley, David H. (1969). *Minorities and the Police: Confrontation in America.* New York: Free Press.

Bayley, David H. (1995). *The Best Defense.* Washington, D.C.: Police Executive Research Forum.

Becker, Gavin de (2002). *Fear Less. Real Truth about Risk, Safety, and Security in a Time of Terrorism.* Boston: Little, Brown.

Bell, Daniel (1960). *The End of Ideology: On the Exhaustion of Political Ideas in the Fifties.* Glencoe, Ill.: Free Press.

Bell, Daniel (1996). *The Cultural Contradictions of Capitalism.* New York: Basic Books.

Bellah, Robert N. et al. (1991). *The Good Society.* New York: Knopf (distributed by Random House).

Bellah, Robert N., Richard Madsen, William M. Sullivan, Ann Swidler and Steven M. Tipton (1986). *Habits of the Heart: Individualism and Commitment in American Life.* New York: Harper & Row.

Bennett, William J. (1995). Moral corruption in America. *Commentary* (November).

Berger, Peter L. and Thomas Luckmann (1966). *The Social Construction of Reality: A Treatise in the Sociology of Knowledge.* Garden City, N.Y.: Doubleday.

Berkowitz, A.D. (2004). An overview of the social norm approach. In L. Lederman, ed. *Change in the Culture of College Drinking.* Cresskill, N.J.: Hampton Press.

Berkowitz, Peter (1998). Fear and thinking. *The New Republic.* July 13.

Berlin, Isaiah (1969). *Four Essays on Liberty.* London and New York: Oxford University Press.

Berlin, Isaiah (2002a). *Freedom and Its Betrayal: Six Enemies of Human Liberty.* Princeton, N.J.: Princeton University Press.

Berlin, Isaiah (2002b). *Liberty: Incorporating Four Essays on Liberty.* Oxford: Oxford University Press.

Berlin, Isaiah and Bernard Williams (1994). Pluralism and liberalism: a reply. *Political Studies*, 42(2): 306–309.

Bernanos, Georges (1948). *Le chemin de la croix-des Ames*. Paris: Gallimard.

Bernstein, Lee (1999). Unlucky Luciano. In Nancy Schultz, ed. *Fear Itself. Enemies Real and Imagined in American Culture*. West Lafayette: Purdue University Press.

Bernstein, Lisa (1992). Opting out of the legal system: extralegal contractual relations in the diamond industry. *Journal of Legal Studies*, 21: 115–157.

Bernstein, Richard (2004). Weddings vow can lock out Danes out of their homeland. *New York Times*. September 10.

Betts, Julian and Magnus Loftsrom (2000). The educational attainment of immigrants. In George Borjas, ed. *Issues in the Economics of Immigration*. Chicago: The Chicago University Press.

Biderman, Albert D. et al. (1967). *Report on a Pilot Study in the District of Columbia on Victimization and Attitudes toward Law Enforcement*. Washington, D.C.: U.S. Government Printing Office.

Black, Donald (1983). Crime as social control. *American Sociological Review*, 48: 34–45.

Bliakhman, L., A. Zdravomyslov and O. Shkaratan (1965). *Dvizhenie rabochei sily napromyshlennykh predpriiatiiakh*. Moscow: Ekonomika.

Bloch, Marc (1961). *Feudal Society*. Translated from French by L.A. Manyon. Foreword by M.M. Postan. Chicago: University of Chicago Press.

Bloch, Marc and Léopold Benjamin (1939). *La société féodale; la formation des liens de dépendance; avec 4 planches hors texte, par Marc Bloch*. Paris: A. Michel.

Blumer, Herbert (1969). *Symbolic Interactionism*. Engelwood Cliff: Prentice Hall.

Bogdanor, Vernon (2003). Ostriches captured by writers. *TLS*. June 6.

Bohm, Robert and Keith Haley (1999). *Introduction to Criminal Justice*. New York: Glencoe.

Boies, John L. (1989). Money, business, and the state. *American Sociological Review*, 54: 821–883.

Borjas, George J. (1999). *Heaven's Door: Immigration Policy and the American Economy*. Princeton, N.J.: Princeton University Press.

Borshchagovsky, A. (1988). V chetyre aochi prishli iz GPU. *Komosomolskaia Pravda*. March 1 and September 25.

Bottomore, Tom (1993). *Elites and Society*. New York: Routledge.

Boulding, Kenneth Ewart (1962). Conflict and defense: a general theory. New York: Harper.

Bourdieu, Pierre (1993). *The Field of Cultural Production*. New York: Columbia University Press.

Bouvier, Leon (1992). *Peaceful Invasions: Immigration and Changing America*. New York: Free Press.

Brim, Orville and Jerome Kagan, eds. (1980). *Constancy and Change in Human Development*. Cambridge: Harvard University Press.

Brimelow, Peter (1995). Conservatism and immigration. *Commentary* (November).

Brooks, David (2004a). Circling the wagons. *New York Times.* June 5.

Brooks, David (2004b). Age of political segregation. *New York Times.* June 26.

Brooks, David (2004c). *On paradise Drive. How We Live Now (and always have) in the Future Tense.* New York: Simon and Schuster.

Brooks, David (2005a). The education gap. *New York Times.* September 25.

Brooks, David (2005b). All cultures are not equal. *New York Times.* August 11.

Brooks, David (2005c). The bursting point. *New York Times.* September 4.

Brooks, Richard Rexford Wayne (1999). *Fear and Fairness in the City: Criminal Enforcement and Procedural Fairness in High-Crime Communities.* Ithaca, N.Y.: Legal Information Institute, Cornell University.

Brown, Kate (2004). *A Biography of No Place: From Ethnic Borderland to Soviet Heartland.* Cambridge: Harvard University Press.

Brownlie, Ian (1979). *The Principles of Public International Law.* Oxford: Clarendon Press.

Brubaker, Roger and David Laitin (1968). Ethnic and nationalist violence. *American Review of Sociology,* 24: 423–452.

Bruce Russett, Harvey Starr and Richard Stoll (1989). *Choices in World Politics: Sovereignty and Interdependence.* New York: W.H. Freeman.

Buchanan, James, Robert Tollison and Gordin Tullock, eds. (1980). *Toward a Theory of the Rent Seeking Society.* College Station: Texas A&M University Press.

Bureau of Justice Statistics (1998–2002). *Crime and Victims Statistics.* Washington, D.C.: U.S. Department of Justice.

Burnett, John (2003). Tyrant in shadows. *New York Times.* June 26.

Burns, John (2003). In Baghdad, reflections on the past and hopes for the future. *New York Times.* April 27.

Burns, John (2004). The general departs, with a scandal to ponder. *New York Times.* July 22.

Burrin, Phillipe (1993). *France under Germany.* New York: The Free Press.

Butterfield, Fox (2002). Father steals best: crimes in the American family. *New York Times.* July 21.

Calabresi, Guido and Douglas Melamud (1972). Property rules, liability rules, and inalienability. *Harvard Law Review,* 85.

Callahan, David (2004). *The Cheating Culture. Why More Americans Are Doing Wrong.* New York: Harcourt.

Campbell, A. (1981). *The Sense of Well Being in America: Recent Patterns and Trends.* New York: McGraw-Hill Book Company.

Campbell, A., P. Converse and W. Rogers (1976). *The Quality of American Life: Perceptions, Evaluations, and Satisfactions.* New York: Russell Sage Foundation.

Cantril, Albert H. (1971). *Hopes and Fears of the American People.* New York: Universe Books.

Carey, Benedict (2005a). Most will be mentally ill, at some point, study says. *New York Times*. June 7.

Carey, Benedict (2005b). Storm will have a long-term emotional effect on some, experts said. *New York Times*. September 4.

Carnoy, Martin (1984). *The State and Political Theory*. Princeton: Princeton University Press.

Cascardi, Anthony (1992). *The Subject of Modernity*. New York: Cambridge University Press.

Case, Karl and Ray Fair (1996). *Principles of Macroeconomics*. 4th edition. Upper Saddle River: Prentice.

Caspi, Avshalom and Daryl Bem (1990). Personal continuity and change across the life course. In L. Pervin, ed. *Handbook of Personality. Theory and Research*. New York: Guilford.

Caspi, Avshalom and Moffit, T.E. (1992). The continuity in maladaptive: from description to understanding in the study of behavior antisocial behavior. In Dante Cicchetti and Donald Cohen, eds. *Manual of Development of Psychopathology*. New York: Wiley.

Changli, I., ed. (1978). *Sotsialisticheskoie Sorevnovaniie*. Moscow: Nauka.

Chapin, Steven (1995). Here and everywhere: sociology of scientific knowledge. *Annual Review of Sociology*, 21: 289–321.

Chege, Michael (2003). Why Africa fails. *TLS*. January 3.

Chubais, Anatolii (2002). Interview with *Moskovskie Novosti*. July 29.

Cialdini R.B. and M.R. Trost (1998). Social influence: social norms, conformity, and compliance. In D.T. Gilbert and S.T. Fiske, eds. *The Handbook of Social Psychology*, pp. 151–192. 4th edition. Boston: McGraw-Hill.

Clay, Karen (1997a). Trade without law: private-order institutions in Mexican California. *Journal of Law, Economics, and Organization*, 13(1).

Clay, Karen (1997b). Trade, institutions, and credit: contract enforcement on the California Coast, 1830–1846. *Explorations in Economic History*, 34(4).

Clay, Karen (1998). Trade, institutions, and law: the experience of Mexican California. In Sally M. Miller, A.J.H. Latham and Dennis O. Flynn, eds. *California and the Pacific Rim: Past, Present, Future*. New York: Routledge, 1998.

Clendinen, Dudley (2003). AIDS: Not Gone, Not Forgotten. *New York Times*, December 16.

Clendinen, Dudley and Adam Nagourney (1999). *Out for Good: The Struggle to Build a Gay Rights Movement in America*. New York: Simon & Schuster.

Clinton, Bill (2004). *My Life*. New York: Knopf.

Coase, Stiglietz and Andre Orlean, eds. (1994). *Analyse economicque des conventions*. Paris: Presse Universitaire de France.

Coghill, Jeffrey J. (1970). *The Red Scare and Radical Labor, 1919–1920*. Report of an independent study.

Cohen, Albert (1955). *Delinquent Boys: The Culture of Gang*. Glencoe: Free Press.

Cohen, Stanley (1985). *Vision of Social Control.* Cambridge: Polity Press.

Cohen, Stanley and Andrew Scull (1983). Introduction: social control in history and in sociology. In Stanley Cohen and Andrew Scull, eds. *Social Control and the State.* New York: St. Martin.

Coleman, James (1990). *Foundation of Social Theory.* Cambridge: Belknap Press.

Colley, Linda (1992). *Britons: Forging the Nation, 1707–1837.* New Haven, Conn.: Yale University Press.

Collingwood, R.G. (1942). *New Leviathan.* Oxford: The Clarendon Press.

Condran, John G. (1979). Changes in white attitudes toward blacks: 1963–1977. *The Public Opinion Quarterly,* 43: 463–476.

Converse, Phillip (1964). The nature of belief systems in mass publics. In David Apter, ed. *Ideology and Discontent.* New York, N.Y.: Free Press.

Cooter, Robert (1996). Decentralized law for a complex economy. *University of Pennsylvania Law Review,* 5: 1643–1696.

Crain, C. (1985). *Theories of Development.* Englewood Cliffs, N.J.: Prentice Hall.

Croce, Paul Jerome (1993). Erosion of mass culture. *Society,* 30(July/August): 16.

Crouch, Ben (1993). Is incarceration really worse? *Justice Quarterly,* 10: 67–88.

D'Emilio, John (2003). *Lost Prophet, The Life and Time of Bayard Rustin.* New York: Free Press.

Dahl, R. (1989). *Democracy and Its Critics.* New Haven: Yale University Press.

Daley, Suzanne (2002). Anti-Le Pen protests draw a million into streets in France. *New York Times.* May 2.

Darwin, Charles (1965). *The Expression of Emotions in Man and Animals.* Chicago: Chicago University Press.

Davies, Howard (2003). Heroic assumptions. *TLS.* September 26.

Davies, Peter (2001). *France and the Second World War. Occupation, Collaboration and Resistance.* London: Routledge.

Davies, Piter Ho (2000). *Equal Love.* Boston and New York: Houghton Mifflin.

Davis, Nanette J. and Clarice Stasz (1990). *Social Control of Deviance: A Critical Perspective.* New York: Random House.

De Botton, Alain (2004). *Status Anxiety.* New York: Pantheon Books.

DeBlois, C.S. and M.A. Stewart (1980). Aggressiveness and antisocial behavior: research communication in psychology. *Psychiatry and Behavior,* 5: 303–311.

Defrasne, J. (1982). *L histoire de la collaboration.* Paris: Presses Universitaires de France.

Demerath, Nicholas and Anthony Wallace (1957). Human adaptation to disaster. *Human Organization,* 16: 1–2.

DePalma, Anthony (2005). Spending 15 years on the bottom rung. *New York Times.* May 26.

Diamond, Jared (1997). *Guns, Germs and Steel: The Fates of Human Societies.* New York: Norton.

Diamond, Jared (2005). *Collapse: How Societies Choose to Fail or Succeed*. New York: Viking.

Dickie, John (2004). *Cosa Nostra: A History of the Sicilian Mafia*. London: Hodder & Stoughton.

Dillon, Sam and Sara Rimer (2005). President of Harvard tells women's panel he's sorry. *New York Times*. January 22.

DiMaggio, Paul (1997). Culture and cognition. *American Review of Sociology*, 23: 263–287.

DiMaggio, Paul, John Evans and Bethany Bryson (1996). Have Americans' social attitudes become more polarized? *American Journal of Sociology*, 102: 690–755.

Ditton, Jason and Stephen Farrall, ed. (2000). *The Fear of Crime*. Burlington, Vt.: Ashgate/Dartmouth.

Dixon, Thomas (2004). Why I am angry. The return to ancient links between reason and emotion. *The Times Literary Supplement*. October 1.

Dobrynin, Anatolii (1995). *In Confidence: Moscow Ambassador to America's Six Cold War Presidents*. New York: Random House.

Doka, Kenneth J. (1997). *AIDS, Fear, and Society: Challenging the Dreaded Disease*. Washington, D.C.: Taylor & Francis.

Dolgova, Azaliia Ivanovna (2003). *Prestupnost, ee organizovannost I kriminalnoe obshchestvo*. Moskva: Rossiĭskaia kriminologicheskaia assotsiatsiia.

Domhoff, William (1996). *State Autonomy or Class Dominance?* New York: Aldine de Gruyter.

Domhoff, William (1998). *Who Rules America? Power and Politics in the Year 2000*. Mountain View, Calif.: Mayfield Pub. Co.

Domhoff, William (2002). *Who Rules America? Power and Politics*. Boston: McGraw-Hill.

Donovan, John, Richard Morgan, Christian Potholm and Marcia Weigle (1993). *People, Power and Politics*. Boston: Littlefield.

Doob, Christopher (1994). *Sociology: An Introduction*. Fort Worth: Harcourt.

Dozier, Rush W. (1998). *Fear Itself: The Origin and Nature of the Powerful Emotion that Shapes Our Lives and Our World*. New York: St. Martin's Press.

D'Sousa, Dinesh (1992). The big chill. In Paul Berman, ed. *The Controversy about Political Correctness of College Campuses*. New York: Dell.

Dunn, John (1996). *The History of Political Theory and other Essays*. Cambridge: Cambridge University Press.

Durkheim, Émile (1960). *The Division of Labor in Society*. Translated from French by George Simpson. Glencoe, Ill.: Free Press.

Durkheim, Émile (1964). *The Rules of Sociological Method*. Translated by Sarah A. Solovay and John H. Mueller and edited by George E.G. Catlin. New York: Free Press.

Durkheim, Émile (1965). *The Elementary Forms of Religious Life*. Glencoe, Ill.: Free Press.

Durkheim, Émile (1997). *Suicide*. Translated by John A. Spaulding and George Simpson. New York: Free Press.

Duus, P. (1976). *The Rise of Modern Japan*. Boston: Houghton Mifflin.

Dwyer, Jim and Christopher Drew (2005). *New York Times*. September 29.

Dynes, Russell (1966). Disaster as a social science field. *National Review of Social Sciences*, 13: 75–84.

Dynes, Russell (1970). *Organized Behavior in Disaster*. Lexington, Mass.: D.C. Heath.

Eagly, Alice and Shelly Chaiken (1998). Attitudes structure and functions. In Daniel T. Gilbert, Susan T. Fiske and Gardner Lindzey, eds. *The Handbook of Social Psychology* (Vol. 1). Boston: McGraw-Hill.

Eckstein, Harry and Ted Gurr (1975). *Patterns of Authorities*. New York: John Wiley.

Eggertsson, Thrainn (1991). *Economic Behavior and Institutions*. Cambridge Surveys of Economic Literature, Cambridge University Press.

Eggertsson, Thrainn (2001). Norms in economics. In Michael Hechter and Karl-Dieter Opp, eds. *Social Norms*. New York: Russel.

Eicher, Jeffrey, Wendy Stuhldreher and Thomas Stuhldreher (2001). Attitudes toward income taxes: regional versus national. *Tax Notes*, No. 8.

Einstein, Albert and Sigmund Freud (1964). Why wars. In *Standard Edition of the Complete Psychological Works of Sigmund Freud*. London: Hogart Press.

Eisenstadt, S. (1992). The order-maintaining and order-transforming dimension of culture. In Richard Münch and Neil J. Smelser, eds. *Theory of Culture*. Berkeley: University of California Press.

Elias, Norbert (1978). *The Civilized Process*. Oxford: Basil Blackwell.

Elias, Norbert (1998). *On Civilization, Power, and Knowledge. Selected Writings*. Chicago: University of Chicago Press.

Ellickson, Robert C. (1986). Of coase and cattle. *Stanford Law Review*. February.

Ellickson, Robert C. (1991). *Order without Law: How Neighbors Settle Disputes*. Cambridge, Mass.: Harvard University Press.

Emerson, Rupert (1960). *From Empire to Nation: The Rise to Self-Assertion of Asian and African Peoples*. Cambridge: Harvard University Press.

Emil, Mitev, Veroniak Ivanova and Vladimir Shubkin (1998). Katastroficheskoie Soznanie v Bulgarii i Rossis (the catastrophic mind in Russia and Bulgaria). *Sotsiologiuchekie isseldovania*, No. 10.

Engelbert, Pierre (2000). *State Legitimacy and Development in Africa*. Boulder: Lynne Rienner Publisher.

Ennis, Philip H. (1967). *Criminal Victimization in the United States: A Report of a National Survey*. Washington, D.C.: U.S. Government Printing Office.

Escobar, Edward (1999). *Race, Police, and the Making of Political Identity*. Berkeley: University of California Press.

Evans, John (1997). Worldview or social groups as the source of moral values attitudes: implications for the cultural war thesis. *Sociological Forum*, 12(3): 371–404.

Evans, Peter B., Dietrich Rueschemeyer and Theda Skocpol, eds. (1985). *Bringing the State Back In*. Cambridge and New York: Cambridge University Press.

Eyre, Linda and Richard Eyre (1993). *Teaching Our Children Values*. New York: Simon & Schuster.

Farraro, Thomas (2001). *Social Action Systems: Foundation and Symbols in Sociological Theory*. Westport: Praeger.

Fazio, R. (1989). On the power and functionality of attitudes: the role of attitude accessibility. In A. Pratkanis, S. Breckler and A. Greenwald, eds. *Attitudes Structure and Function*. Hillsdale: Erlbaum.

Federico, Ronald and Janet Schwartz (1983). *Sociology*. 3rd edition. Boston, Mass.: Addison Wesley.

Fedoseyev, P.N., ed. (1974). *Scientific Communism and Its Falsification*. Translated from Russian by David Skvirsky. Moscow: Progress Publishers.

Fehr, B. and Russel, J. (1991). The concept of love viewed from a protype perspective. *Journal of Personality and Social Psychology*, 60: 424–438.

Ferguson, Niall (2001). *The Cash Nexus: Money and Power in the Modern World*. New York: Basic Books.

Ferguson, Niall (2003). Why America outpaces Europe. *New York Times*. August 11.

Ferguson, Niall (2004). *Colossus: The Price of America's Empire*. New York: The Penguin Press.

Fernandez-Armesto, Felipe (1995). *Millennium: A History of Our Last Thousand Years*. New York: Bantam.

Ferrell, Jeff and Neil Websdale (1999). *Making Trouble: Cultural Constructions of Crime, Deviance, and Control*. New York: Aldine de Gruyter.

Fichter, Joseph (1971). *Sociology*. Chicago: University of Chicago Press.

Field, Frank (2003). *Neighbours from Hell: The Politics of Behaviour*. London: Politico.

Fine, Gary (2001). Enacting norms: mushrooming and the culture of expectations and explanations. In Michael Hechter and Karl-Dieter Opp, eds. *Social Norms*. New York: Russel.

Finer, Samuel (1975). State and nation building in Europe. In Charles Tilly, ed. *The Formation of National States in Western Europe*. Princeton: Princeton University Press.

Fishbein, M. and Aizen, I. (1974). Attitudes toward object as predictors of single and multiple criteria. *The Psychological Review*, 81: 59–74.

Fisher, Claude (1999). Uncommon values, diversity and conflict in city life. In Jeffrey Alexander and Neil Smelser, eds. *Diversity and Its Discontents*. Princeton: Princeton University Press.

Fiske, Alan, Shinobu Kitayama, Hazel Markus and Richard Nisbett (1998). The cultural matrix of social, ethnic and psychology. In Daniel T. Gilbert, Susan T. Fiske and Gardner Lindzey, eds. *The Handbook of Social Psychology*. Boston: McGraw-Hill.

Fitzpatrick, Sheila, ed. (1978). *Cultural Revolution in Russia, 1928–1931*. Bloomington: Indiana University Press.

Fitzpatrick, Sheila (1979). *Education and Social Mobility in the Soviet Union, 1921–1934*. Cambridge and New York: Cambridge University Press.

Fitzpatrick, Sheila (1999). *Everyday Stalinism*. New York: Oxford University Press.

Foucault, Michel (1976). Histoire de la sexualité. Paris: Gallimard.

Foucault, Michel (1995). *Discipline and Punishment*. New York: Vintage Books.

Fradier, Georges (1976). *About the Quality of Life*. UNESCO.

Francies, David (2005). *What Reduced Crimes in New York City*. NBAR website, June 25.

Frank, Andre (1969). *Capitalism and Underdevelopment in Latin America*. New York: Monthly Review Press.

Freud, Sigmund (1930). *Civilization and Its Discontents*. London: L. & Virginia Woolf at the Hogarth Press.

Friedman, Thomas (2003). Bored with Baghdad—already. *New York Times*. May 18.

Friedman, Thomas (2005). Rooting out the Jihadist cancer. *New York Times*. July 8.

Fritz, Charles (1961). Disaster. In Robert Merton and Robert Nisbet, eds. *Social Problems*. New York: Harcourt Brace and World.

Fromm, Eric (1961). Foreword. In *George Orwell 1984*. New York: Signet Classic, 1961.

Fromm, Erich (1967). *Escape from Freedom*. New York: Avon Books.

Fukuyama, Francis (1995). *Trust: The Social Virtues and the Creation of Prosperity*. New York: Free Press.

Fukuyama, Francis (1999). *The Great Disruption: Human Nature and the Reconstitution of Social Order*. New York: Free Press.

Fukuyama, Francis (2000). Social capital. In Lawrence Harrison and Samuel P. Huntington, eds. *Culture Matters*. New York: Basic Books.

Fund of Public Opinion (1998). *Bulletin*. November 27.

Fund of Public Opinion (2001). *Bulletin*. December 6.

Fund of Public Opinion (2003). *Bulletin*. October 9.

Fund of Public Opinion (2004). *Bulletin*. January 15.

Fund of Public Opinion (2004a). *Bulletin*. April 1.

Fund of Public Opinion (2004b). *Bulletin*. April 22.

Fund of Public Opinion (2004c). *Bulletin*. October 14.

Gabrilovich, Evgeni (1989). *Sovietskaia Kultura*. June 17.

Galbraith, John Kenneth (1967). *The New Industrial State*. Boston: Houghton Mifflin.

Gallup (2003a). *Gallup Polls News Service*. August 22.

Gallup (2003b). *Gallup Polls News Service*. June 11.

Gallup (2004a). *Gallup Polls News Service*. February 3.

Gallup (2004b). *Gallup Polls News Service*. December 9.

Gallup (2004c). *Gallup Polls News Service*. August 31.

Gallup (2005a). *Gallup Polls News Service*. April 5.

Gallup (2005b). *Gallup Polls News Service*. January 7.

Gallup (2005c). *Gallup Polls News Service*. April 5.

Gallup (2005d). *Gallup Polls News Service.* May 23–26.

Galston, William (1999). Values pluralism and liberal political theory. *American Political Science Review*, 4(December).

Gans, Herbet (1988). *Middle American Individualism: The Future of Liberal Democracy.* New York: Free Press.

Garfinkel, Harold (1967). *Studies in Ethnomethodology.* Englewood Cliffs, N.J.: Prentice-Hall.

Garland, David (1990). *Punishment and Modern Society: A Study in Social Theory.* Chicago: University of Chicago Press.

Garland, David (2001). *The Culture of Control: Crime and Social Order in Contemporary Society.* Chicago: University of Chicago Press.

Garofalo, James and John Laub (1979). The fear of crime: broadening our perspectives. *Victimology*, 3: 242–253.

Gauthier, David P. (1969). The logic of Leviathan: the moral and political theory of Thomas Hobbes. Oxford: Clarendon Press.

Geertz, Clifford (1973). *The Interpretation of Cultures: Selected Essays.* New York: Basic Books.

Gelbspan, Ross (2004). *Boiling Point: How Politicians, Big Oil and Coal, Journalists, and Activists Are Fueling the Climate Crisis—and What We Can Do to Avert Disaster.* New York: Basic Books.

Gergen, Kenneth (1973). *Realities and Relationships. Sounding in Social Constructions.* Cambridge: Harvard University Press.

Gerrard, Michael (1994). *Whose Backyard, Whose Risk. Fear and Fairness in Toxic and Nuclear Waste Siting.* Cambridge: MIT Press.

Gibbons, Don C. (1992). *Society, Crime, and Criminal Behavior.* Englewood Cliffs, N.J.: Prentice Hall.

Gibbs, Jack (1989). *Control Sociology's Central Notion.* Urbana: University of Illinois Press.

Giddens, Anthony (1972). *Emile Durkheim: Selected Writings.* Cambridge: Cambridge University Press.

Giddens, Anthony, ed. (1986). *Durkheim on Politics and the State.* Stanford: Stanford University Press.

Giddens, Anthony (1989). *Sociology.* Cambridge: Polity Press.

Gilbert, Daniel T., Susan T. Fiske and Gardner Lindzey, eds. (1998). *The Handbook of Social Psychology.* Boston: McGraw-Hill.

Gildea, Robert (2002). *Marianne in Chains.* New York: Henri Holt.

Girard, Rene (2004). *A Theater of Envy. William Shakespear.* South Bend: St. Augustine Press.

Glaser, Daniel (1956). Criminality theories and behavioral images. *American Journal of Sociology*, 61(5): 433–444.

Glassner, Barry (1999). *The Culture of Fear: Why Americans Are Afraid of the Wrong Things.* New York: Basic Books.

Gleason, Abbot (1995). *Totalitarianism. The Inner History of the Cold War.* New York: Oxford University Press.

Glueck, Sheldon and Eleanor Glueck (1950). *Unraveling Juvenile Delinquency.* New York: Commonwealth Fund.

Goffman, Erving (1959). *Presentation of Self in Everyday Life*. Garden City: Double Day.

Goode, Erich and Nachman Ben-Yehuda (1994). *Moral Panics*. Oxford: Blackwell.

Gordon, Berthran (1980). *Collaboration in France during the Second World War*. Ithaca: Cornell University Press.

Gordon, Berthran (2004). The "Vichy syndrome." Problem of history. *French Historical Studies*, 19(2): 495–518.

Gordon, Margaret T. et al. (1979). Crime in the newspapers and fear in the neighborhoods: some unintended consequences. Reactions to crime papers. *Journal of Research in Crime and Delinquency*, 5: 101–116.

Gordon, Milton (1964). *Assimilation in American life: The Role of Race, Religion, and National Origins*. New York: Oxford University Press.

Gottfredson, Michael and Travis Hirschi (1990). *A General Theory of Crime*. Stanford: Stanford University Press.

Gray, John (1995). *Enlightenment Wake: Politics and Culture at the Close of Modern Age*. London: Routledge.

Grechin, A. (1983). Opyt sotsiologicheskogo issledovania pravosoznania. *Sotsiologicheskie Issledovania*, 2.

Greeley, Andrew M. and Paul B. Sheatsley (1971). Attitudes toward racial integration. *Scientific American*, 225(December): 13–19.

Greeley, Andrew M. and Paul B. Sheatsley (1974). Attitudes toward racial integration. In Lee Rainwater, ed. *Social Problems and Public Policy: Inequality and Justice*. Chicago: Aldine Hacker, Helen Mayer.

Green, Donald P., Bradley Palmquist and Eric Schickler (2002). *Partisan Hearts and Minds: Political Parties and the Social Identities of Voters*. New Haven: Yale University Press.

Greenberg, Stanley B. (2004). *The Two Americas: Our Current Political Deadlock and How to Break It*. New York: Thomas Dunne Books.

Greenfeld, Liah (1992). *Nationalism: Five Roads to Modernity*. Cambridge, Mass.: Harvard University Press.

Greenfeld, Liah (2001). *Spirit of Capitalism. Nationalism and Economic Growth*. Cambridge: Harvard University Press.

Greenhouse, Steven (2004). Crossing the border in the middle class. *New York Times*. June 3.

Grosso, Michael (1995). *The Millennium Myth: Love and Death at the End of Time*. Wheaton, Ill.: Quest Book.

Gudkov, Lev (2000). O negativnoj identifikatsii. *Monitoring obshchestvennogo mnenia*, No. 5.

Habermas, Jurgen (1973). *Legitimization Crisis*. Boston: Beacon Press.

Hagan, J. (1989). *Structural Criminology*. New Brunswick, N.J.: Rutgers University Press.

Hagan, John and Alberto Palloni (1999). Sociological criminology and the mythology of Hispanic immigration and crime. *Social Problems*, 46: 617–632.

Hall, John (1995). In search of civil society. In John Hall, ed. *Civil Society. Theory. History*. Cambridge: Polity Press.

Hall, John and Charles Lindholm (1999). *Is America Breaking Apart?* Princeton: Princeton University Press.

Hall, Peter (1987). Interactionism and the study of social organization. *Sociological Quarterly*, 28: 1–22.

Hampton, Jean (1986). *Hobbes and the Social Contract Tradition*. Cambridge and New York: Cambridge University Press.

Handlin, Oscar (1990). *The Uprooted*. Boston: Little, Brown.

Hane, Mikiso (1996). *Eastern Phoenix. Japan since 1945*. Boulder: Westview Press.

Harcourt, Bernard E. (2001). *Illusion of Order: The False Promise of Broken Windows Policing*. Cambridge: Harvard University Press.

Hardie, W. (1980). *Aristotle's Ethical Theory*. Oxford: Clarendon Press.

Hardin, Garrett (1968). The tragedy of the commons. *Science*, 162: 1243–1248.

Hardin, Russell (2002). *Trust and Trustworthiness*. New York: Russell Sage Foundation.

Harer, Miles (1993). *Recidivism among Federal Prisons Releases in 1987: A Preliminary Report*. Federal Bureau of Prison, December 9.

Harries, Merion and Susie Harris (1997). *Last Days of Innocence: America at War, 1917–1918*. New York: Random House.

Harrington, Michael (1969). *The Other America: Poverty in the United States* (with a new introduction). New York: Macmillan.

Harris, Nigel (1986). *The End of the Third World: Newly Industrialized Countries and the End of Ideology*. New York: Penguin Books.

Harrison, Ross (2003). *Hobbes, Locke, and Confusion's Masterpiece: An Examination of Seventeenth-Century Political Philosophy*. Cambridge, U.K. and New York: Cambridge University Press.

Hart, Oliver, 2001. Norms and the theory of the firm. *NBER Working Papers 8286*. National Bureau of Economic Research, Inc.

Hayek, Friedrich (1973). *Rules and Order*. Chicago: University of Chicago Press.

Hayek, Friedrich (1976). *The Mirage of Social Justice*. Chicago: University of Chicago Press.

Hayek, Friedrich (1979). *The Political Order of Free People*. Vol. 3. Chicago: University of Chicago Press.

Hebberecht, P. (1997). Minorities, crime and criminal justice in Belgium. In I.H. Marshall, ed. *Minorities, Migrants and Crime*. Thousand Oaks, Calif.: Sage.

Hechter, Michael (1993). Values research in the social and behavioral sciences. In Michael Hechter, Lynn Nadel and Richard Michod, eds. *The Origin of Values*. New York: Aldine de Gryuter.

Hechter, Michael (2000). *Containing Nationalism*. Oxford and New York: Oxford University Press.

Hechter, Michael and Karl-Dieter Opp (2001a). What have we learned about the emergence of social norms. In Michael Hechter and Karl-Dieter Opp, eds. *Social Norms*. New York: Russel.

Hechter, Michael and Karl-Dieter Opp. (2001b). Introduction. In Michael Hechter and Karl-Dieter Opp, eds. *Social Norms*. New York: Russel.

Hechter, Michael, Debra Friedman and Satoshi Kanazava (2003). The attainment of social order in heterogeneous society. In Michael Hechter and Christian Horne, eds. *Theories of Social Order. A Reader*. Stanford: Stanford University Press.

Hefter, Michael (2000). *Containing Nationalism*. Oxford: Oxford University Press.

Heidenheimer, Arnold and Michael Johnson, eds. (2002). *Political Corruption. Concepts and Contents*. New Brunswick: Transaction.

Henderson, Harry (2004). *Global Terrorism*. New York: Facts On File.

Henslin, James, ed. (1989). *Deviance in American Life*. New Brunswick: Transaction.

Henslin, James (2004). *Sociology: A Down-to-Earth Approach*. Boston: Allyn and Bacon.

Herbst, Jeffrey (2003). States and Power in Africa. Comparative Lessons in Authority and Control. Princeton: Princeton University Press.

Hess, Beth, Elizabeth Markson and Peter Stein (1993). *Sociology*. 4th edition. New York: Macmillan.

Higgs, Robert (2003). *Against Leviathan*. Oakland: The Independent Institute.

Higham, John (1999). Cultural response to immigration. In Jeffrey Alexander and Neil Smelser, eds. *Diversity and Its Discontents*. Princeton: Princeton University Press.

Hindelang, Michael J., Michael R. Gottfredson and James Giarofalo (1978). *Victims of Personal Crime: An Empirical Foundation for a Theory of Personal Victimization*. Cambridge, Mass.: Ballinger Publishing Co.

Hindess, Barry (1996). *Discourses of Power. From Hobbes to Foucault*. London: Blackwell.

Hirschi, Travis (2002). *Causes of Delinquency*. New Brunswick, N.J.: Transaction Publishers.

Hobbes, Thomas (1991). De Cive. In Bernard Gert, ed. *Man and Citizen*. Indianapolis, Ind.: Hackett.

Hobbes, Thomas (1996). *Leviathan*. Edited with an introduction by J.C.A. Gaskin. Oxford: Oxford University Press.

Hodgkinson, Peter E. and Michael Stewart (1991). *Coping with Catastrophe: A Handbook of Disaster Management*. London and New York: Routledge.

Hofstadter, Richard (1989). *The American Political Tradition and the Men Who Made It*. With a foreword by Christopher Lasch. New York: Vintage Books.

Hohn, Maria (2002). *GIs and Froleins: The German–American Encounter in 1950s West Germany*. North Carolina: University of North Caroline Press.

Hojnacki, Marie and David Kimball (1998). Organized interests and the decision of whom to lobby in congress. *American Political Science Review*, 92(4): 775–790.

Hopkins, Raymond (1972). Security authority: the view from the top. *World Politics*, 24: 275–276.

Horne, Christine (2001). Sociological perspectives on the emergence of social norms. In Michael Hechter and Karl-Dieter Opp, eds. *Social Norms*. New York: Russel.

Horowitz, Donald L. (1985). *Ethnic Groups in Conflict*. Berkeley: University of California Press.

Horowitz, Irving (1989). Disenthralling sociology. In James Henslin, ed. *Deviance in American Life*. New Brunswick: Transaction.

Hunt, Matthew (2000). Status, religion, and the "belief in a just world": comparing African Americans, Latinos, and Whites. *Social Science Quarterly*, 81: 325–343.

Huntington, Samuel P. (1968). *Political Order in Changing Societies*. New Haven: Yale University Press.

Huntington, Samuel P. (2004). *Who Are We? The Challenges to America's National Identity*. New York: Simon & Schuster.

Hyman, H. and C. Wright (1979). *Education's Lasting Influence on Values*. Chicago: University of Chicago Press.

Hyman, Herbert H. and Paul B. Sheatsley (1964). Attitudes toward desegregation. *Scientific American*, 211: 16–23.

Iadov, Vladimir (1997). Strakhi v Rossii (Fears in Russia). *Sotsiologicheskii Journal*, No. 3.

The Inaugural Addresses of the Presidents of the United States (1985). Atlantic City, N.J.: American Inheritance Press.

Inglehart, Ronald (1977). *The Silent Revolution*. Princeton, N.J.: Princeton University Press.

Inglehart, Ronald (1991). Trust, well being and democracy. In Marc Warren, ed. *Democracy and Trust*. Cambridge: Cambridge University Press.

Inglehart, Ronald (1997). *Modernization and Post Modernization. Cultural, Economic and Political Change in 43 Societies*. Princeton: Princeton University Press.

Inglehart, Ronald, Miguel Basañez and Alejandro Moreno (1998). *Human Values and Beliefs: A Cross-Cultural Sourcebook: Political, Religious, Sexual, and Economic Norms in 43 Societies; Findings from the 1990–1993 World Value Survey*. Ann Arbor: University of Michigan Press.

Inglehart, Ronald, Miguel Basanez and Alejandro Moreno, eds. (2001). *Human Values and Beliefs: A Cross-Cultural Source Book*. Ann Arbor: University of Michigan Press.

Inglehart, Ronald et al. (2004). *Human Beliefs and Values: A Cross-Cultural Sourcebook Based on the 1999–2002 Values Surveys*. México: Siglo XXI, 2004.

Irwin, John (1985). *The Jail*. Berkeley: University of California Press.

Ishida, T. and E. Krauss, eds. (1989). *Democracy in Japan*. Pittsburgh: University of Pittsburgh Press.

Iutkevich, Sergei (1988). My s uvlecheniem nachal s'emki. *Iskusstov kino*, No. 2.

Ivanova, Veronika (2003). Ierarkhia strakov. *fom.ru*. January 16.

Jackman, Mary R. (1978). General and applied tolerance: does education increase commitment to racial integration? *American Journal of Political Science*, 22(2): 302–323.

Jackman, Robert W. (1993). *Power Without Force: The Political Capacity of Nation-States*. Ann Arbor: University of Michigan Press.

Jackman, M. and M.J. Muha (1984). Education and intergroup attitudes. *American Sociological Review*, 49: 751–769.

Jackman, Robert W. and Ross A. Miller (1996). A Renaissance of Political Culture? *American Journal of Political Science*, 40(3): 632–660.

Jackson, Julian (2003). *France. The Dark Years, 1940–1944*. New York: Oxford University Press.

Janis, Irving and Leon Mann (1977). Emergency decision making: a theoretical analysis of responses to disaster warnings. *Journal of Human Stress*, 3(2): 35–48.

Janovitz, Morris (1975). Sociological theory and social control. *American Journal of Sociology*, 81: 82–108.

Jefferson, Thomas (1967). *The Writings of Thomas Jefferson*. Collected and edited by Paul Leicester Ford. New York: G.P. Putnam's Sons.

Jencks, Christopher (2002). Who should get in. *The New York Review of Books*, 20(December).

Jenny, Nicholas (2002). New York State crime rates decline. *New York State Statistical Briefs*, Vol. 1, No. 2. The Rockefeller Institute of Government.

Jessop, B. (1982). *Capitalist State*. London: Martin Robertson.

Johnson, Allan (1995). *The Blackwell Dictionary of Sociology*. Oxford: Blackwell.

Judis, John (2000). *The Paradox of American Democracy. Elites, Special Interests and the Betrayal of Public Trust*. New York: Pantheon Books.

Judt, Tony (2004). Dreams of empire. *The New York Review of Books*. November 4.

Junger, Ernst. (1995). *Premier journal parisien: journal II, 1941–1943*. Paris: Christian Bourgeois Editeur.

Kagan, Robert (2003). *Of Paradise and Power: America and Europe in the New World Order*. New York: Alfred A. Knopf.

Kagarlitsky, Boris (2002). "Political capitalism" and corruption in Russia. *Links*, No. 21(May–August).

Kahler, Erich (1967). *Man the Measure*. Cleveland: World Publishing Company.

Kalinin, Nikolai (1998). Nasilno patriotom ne stanesh. *Izvestia*, July 7.

Kane, James M. (1992). *The Crooked Ladder. Gangsters, Ethnicity and American Dream*. New Brunswick: Transaction.

Kant, Immanuel (1959). *Foundations of the Metaphysics of Morals*. Trans. Lewis White Beck. Indianapolis, Ind.: Bobbs-Merrill.

Kant, Immanuel (1970). *Kant's Political Writings*. Edited with an introduction by Hans Reiss. Trans. H.B. Nisbet. Cambridge, Eng.: University Press.

Kaplan, Robert D. (1993). *Balkan Ghosts: A Journey through History*. New York: St. Martin's Press.

Kaplan, Robert D. (1996). *The Ends of the Earth: A Journey at the Dawn of the 21st Century*. New York: Random House.

Kaplan, Robert D. (1997). *The Ends of the Earth: From Togo to Turkmenistan, From Iran to Cambodia—A Journey to the Frontiers of Anarchy*. New York: Vintage Books.

Kaplan, Robert D. (2000). *The Coming Anarchy: Shattering the Dreams of the Post Cold War*. New York: Random House.

Kaplan, Robert D. (2005). Next war against nature. *New York Times*. October 12.

Kara-Murza, Sergei (2000). Otkliuchenia smysla. *Zavtra*. June 13.

Karmen, Andrew (2000). *New York Murder Mystery: The True Story Behind the Crime Crash of the 1990s*. New York: New York University Press.

Katz, D. (1960). The functional approach to the study of attitudes. *Public Opinion Quarterly*, 24: 163–204.

Kavka, Gregory S. (1986). *Hobbesian Moral and Political Theory*. Princeton, N.J.: Princeton University Press.

Kawai, K. (1960). *Japan's American Interlude*. Chicago: University of Chicago Press.

Kay, J.A. (2004). *The Truth about Markets: Why Some Nations Are Rich but Most Remain Poor*. New York, N.Y.: Harper Business.

Kelling, George L., Catherine M. Coles and James Q. Wilson (1996). *Fixing Broken Windows: Restoring Order and Reducing Crime in Our Communities*. New York: Free Press.

Kemper, Theodore (1978). *A Social Interactional Theory of Emotions*. New York: Wiley.

Keohane, Robert (1986). Realism, neorealism and the study of world politics. In Keohane, R., ed. *Neorealism and Its Critics*. New York: Columbia University Press.

Keohane, Robert O., ed. (1986). *Neorealism and Its Critics*. New York: University of Columbia Press.

Keohane, Robert O. (2002). *Power and Governance in a Partially Globalized World*. London and New York: Routledge.

Kershaw, Sarah (2004). Life is alive! Nude! Girl! *New York Times*. June 2.

Kerslake, Susan (1984). *The Book of Fears*. Charlottetown, P.E.I.: Ragweed Press.

Keynes, John Maynard (1936). *The General Theory of Employment, Interest and Money*. New York: Harcourt, Brace.

Kharchev, A. and M. Mazkovskii (1979). *Sovremennaia semia i ee problemy*. Moscow: Mysl.

Khariton, Yulii and Yurii Smirnov (1994). Otkuda vzialos' I bylo li nam neobkhodimo iadernoe oruzhie. *Izvestia*. July 21.

Khilnani, Sunil (1997). *The Idea of India*. London: H. Hamilton.

Khilnani, Sunil (2002). *The Survival of Culture: Permanent Values in a Virtual Age*. Edited with an introduction by Hilton Kramer and Roger Kimball. Chicago: Ivan R. Dee, 2002.

Kiesler, A. and S. Kiesler (1969). *Conformity*. Reading, Mass.: Addison-Wesley.

Kimball, Roger (2002). *Lives of the Mind: The Use and Abuse of Intelligence from Hegel to Wodehouse*. Chicago: Ivan R. Dee.

Kincaid, Jamaica (1994). *Lucy.* London: Picador.

Kinder (1983). Diversity and complexity in American public opinion. In Ada Finifter, ed. *Political Science: The State of the Discipline.* Washington, D.C.: American Political Science Association.

King, Erika (1990). *Crowd Theory as a Psychology of the Leader and the Led.* Lewiston: E. Mellen Press.

King, Robert (1986). *The State in Modern Society.* Chatham: Chatham House Publisher.

Kinzer, Steohen and Jim Rutenberg (2004). Grim images seem to deepen nations polarization on Iraq. *New York Times.* May 14.

Klimov, I. (2004). Vreamia tragedii. Vtemia voprosov. The Fund of Public Opinion (www.fom.ru). September 9.

Knafla, Louis and Susan Binnie (1994). Introduction. In Louis Knafla and Susan Binnie, eds. *Law, Society and State: Essays in Modern Legal History.* Toronto: University of Toronto Press.

Kohn, Melvin L. (1977). *Class and Conformity.* Chicago: University of Chicago Press.

Kolhberg, Lawrence (1969). Stage and sequence: the cognitive developmental approach to socialization. In David Gosalin, ed. *Handbook of Socialization and Research*, pp. 347–348. Chicago: Rand McNally.

Kollock, P. (1998). Social dilemmas: the anatomy of cooperation. *Annual Review of Sociology*, 24: 183–214.

Konstantinovsky, David (1999). Musorshchiku platiat kak pzofessoru. *Argumenty i Fakty*, 51.

Kornhauser, Ruth (1978). *Social Sources of Delinquency: Appraisal of Analytical Models.* Chicago: Chicago University Press.

Kornilov V. (1988). Polza vpechtlenii. *Literaturnaia Gazeta.* July 13.

Kostikov, Viacheslav (1999). Rekviem dlia rodiny. *Nezavisimaia Gazeta.* February 2.

Krasner, Stephen (1978). United States commercial and monetary policy. In Peter Katzenstein, ed. *Between Power and Plenty: Foreign Economic Policy of Advanced Industrial States.* Madison: University of Wisconsin Press.

Kreps, Gary (1978). The organization of disaster response: some fundamental theoretical issues. In E.L. Quarantelli, ed. *Disasters: Theory and Research.* London: Sage.

Kreps, Gary (1983). The organization of disaster response: core concepts and processes. *International Journal of Mass Emergencies and Disasters*, 1: 439–467.

Kristol, Irving (1975). *The America's Continuing Revolution: An Act of Conservation.* Washington: American Enterprise Institute for Public Policy Research.

Krueger, Anne (1994). Economists' changing perceptions of government. In Bornstein, ed. *Comparative Economic Systems, Models and Cases.* Burr Ridge, Ill.: Irwin.

Kuhn, Thomas S. (1970). The structure of scientific revolutions. Chicago: University of Chicago Press.

Kumar, Krishan (2003). *The Making of English National Identity*. Cambridge and New York: Cambridge University Press.

Kuper, Leo (1969). Plural societies: perspectives and problems. In Leo Kuper and M.G. Smith, eds. *Pluralism in Africa*. Berkeley: University of California Press.

Kymlicka, Will (1988). Liberals and communitarians. *Canadian Journal of Philosophy*, No. 18.

Lahiri, Jhumpa (1999). *Interpreters of Maladies*. New York: Harper Collins.

Lamm, Richard and Gary Imhoff (1985). *The Immigration Time Bomb: The Fragmenting America*. New York: Truman Talley.

Lamy, Philip and Devon Kinne (1999). Urology and the millennial myth. In Nancy Schultz, ed. *Fear Itself. Enemies Real and Imagined in American Culture*. West Lafayette: Purdue University Press.

Lane, Jody (2002). Fear of gang crime. *Journal of Research in Crime and Delinquency*, 39(4): 437–471.

Lane, Roger (1989). On the social meaning of homicide trends in America. In Ted Gurr, ed. *Violence in America*, Vol. 1. Newbury Park: Sage.

Langer, Gary (2004). A question of values. *New York Times*. November 6.

Lauer, Robert (1982). *Social Problems and the Quality of Life*. Dubuque: Brown.

Laushway, Lynda (2000). *Freedom from Fear*. Salt Spring Island, B.C.: SWOVA.

Le, Gerhard, Patrick Nolan and Jean Lenski (1995). *Human Society: An Introduction to Macrosociology*. 7th edition. New York: McGraw-Hill.

Lee, Mathew (2003). *Crime on the Border: Immigration and Homicide in Urban Communities*. New York: LFB Scholarly Publishing LLC.

Lego, Suzanne (1994). *Fear and AIDS/HIV: Empathy and Communication*. Albany, N.Y.: Delmar Publishers.

Leibniz, Gottfried Wilhelm, Freiherr von (1988). *Prose Works*. Cambridge and New York: Cambridge University Press.

Lemert, Edwin (1972). *Human Deviance, Social Problems, and Social Control*. Englewood Cliffs: Prentice-Hall.

Lessig, Lawrence (1998). The new Chicago school. *Journal of Legal Studies*, 27: 661–691.

Levada, IU. (1990). *Est' mnenie!: itogi sotsiologicheskogo oprosa*. Moscow: Izd-vo "Progress."

Levada, Yurii, ed. (1993). *Sovietskii Prostoi Chelovek*. Moscow: Interzentr.

Levada, Yurii (2004). Chelovek sovietkii:chetvertaia volna. *Vestnik Obshchestvennogo Mnenia*, No. 4.

Levada-zentr (2004a). *Press vypusk*. March 19.

Levada-zentr (2004b). *Press vypusk*. October 14.

Levada-zentr (2004c). *Press vypusk*. October 28.

Levada-zentr (2005). *Press vypusk*, May 1.

Levine, Andrew (2002). *Engaging Political Philosophy: From Hobbes to Rawls*. Malden, Mass.: Blackwell.

Lewis, Charles (2000). *The Buying of the President*. New York: Avon Books.

Lewis, D.A. and G. Salem (1986). *Fear of Crime: Incivility and the Production of a Social Problem*. New Brunswick: Transaction Books.

Liddick, Donald (1999). *The Empirical, Theoretical and Historical Overview of Organized Crimes*. Lewiston: The Edwin Mellen Press.

Light, Donald and Suzanne Keller (1982). *Sociology*. New York: Knopf.

Lins, Paulo (2002). *Cidade de Deus: romance*. Sao Paulo: Companhia das Letras.

Linz, Juan J. and Alfred Stepan (1996). *Problems of Democratic Transition and Consolidation: Southern Europe, South America, and Post-Communist Europe*. Baltimore, Md.: Johns Hopkins University Press.

Lipset, Seymour (1960). *Political Man: The Social Bases of Politics*. Garden City, N.Y.: Doubleday.

Lipset, Seymour (1973). *The First New Nation: The United States in Historical and Comparative Perspective*. New York: Norton.

Lipset, Seymour (1981). *Political Man*. 2nd edition. Baltimore: Johns Hopkins University Press.

Lipset, Seymour (1996). *American Exceptionalism: A Double-Edged Sword*. New York: Norton.

Lipski, David (2004). *Absolutely American. Four Years at West Point*. Boston: Houghton Mifflin.

Liska, Allen (1982). Fear as a social fact. *Social Forces*, 60(3): 760–770.

Liska, Allen (1992). Introduction to the study of social control. In Allen Liska, ed. *Social Threat and Social Control*. New York: University of New York Press.

Locke, John (1959). *An Essay Concerning Human Understanding*. Alexander Campbell Fraser, ed. New York: Dover Publications.

Locke, John (1966). *Of Civil Government. Second Treatise*. Chicago: Gateway Edition.

Locke, John (1988). *Two Treatises of Government*. Cambridge: Cambridge University Press.

Lockwood, David (1992). *Solidarity and Schism*. Oxford: Clarendon Press.

Loeber, R. and Stouthamer-Loeber, M. (1986). Family factors as correlates and predictors of juvenile conduct problems and delinquency. In Nichael Tonry and Norval Morris, eds. *Crime and Justice*, Vol. 7. Chicago: The Chicago University Press.

Lofland, Lyn (1973). *A World of Strangers*. New York: Basic Books.

Loftstedt, Ragnar and Lynn Frewer, eds. (1998). *Risk & Modern society*. London: Earthscan.

Logan, John R., Richard D. Alba and Thomas McNulty (1994). Ethnic economies in metropolitan regions: Miami and beyond. *Social Forces*, 72: 691–724.

Lovaglia, Michael and Jeffrey Houser (1996). Emotional reaction and status in groups. *American Sociological Review*, 61(5): 867–883.

Lowenstein, Roger (2004). *Origins of the Crash: The Great Bubble and Its Undoing*. New York: Penguin Press.

Lucas, Anthony (1995). Thunder on the hill. *The New York Books Review*. May 1996.

Lukes, S. (1974). *Power: A Radical View*. London: Macmillan.

Luneev, Victor (1997). *Prestupnost' XX veka*. Moscow: Nauka.

Luo, Michael and Clifford Levy (2005). As Medicaid balloons, watch dog shrinks. *New York Times*. July 19.

Lyall, Sarah (2004). Britain cracks down on nasties like "neighbor from hell." *New York Times*. April 2.

Lyall, Sarah (2005). At wit's end, a town dithers over its millionaire pest. *New York Times*. September 30.

Lykken, David T. (1995). *The Antisocial Personalities*. Hillsdale, N.J.: Lawrence Erlbaum Associates.

Macaulay, Stewart (1963). Noncontractual relations in business. *American Sociological Review*, 28(1): 55–70.

Macionis, John (2001). *Sociology*. 8th edition. Upper Saddle River: Prentice Hall.

Macionis, John (2004). *Society: The Basics*. Upper Saddle River: Prentice Hall.

Maher, Kristen (2003). Workers and strangers. The household service and the landscape of suburban fear. *Urban Affair Reviews*, 38(6): 751–786.

Malia, Martin E. (1999). *Russia under Western Eyes*. Cambridge: Harvard University Press.

Malia, Martin E. (1994). *The Soviet Tragedy: A History of Socialism in Russia, 1917–1991*. New York: Free Press.

Malutin, Mikhail and Alexander Dugin (2004). Nado li zhdat "narodnogo soprotivlenia." *Literaturnaia Gazeta*. December 14.

Mandelshtam, Nadezhda (1990). *Vtoraia kniga*. Moskva: Moskovskii raboc.

Mankiv, Gregory (2001). *Principles of Macroeconomics*. New York: Harcourt.

Mann, Michael (1970). The social cohesion of liberal democracy. *American Sociological Review*, 35: 423–439.

Mann, Michael (1986). *The Sources of Social Power*. Cambridge and New York: Cambridge University Press.

Marcus, Brian (1999). Freemasonry and the illumination as archetypes of fear in America. In Nancy Schultz, ed. *Fear Itself. Enemies Real and Imagined in American Culture*. West Lafayette: Purdue University Press.

Marcuse, Herbert (1955). *Eros and Civilization*. New York: Vintage.

Marcuse, Herbert (1964). *One Dimensional Man*. Boston: Beacon.

Markel, Howard (2004). *When Genes Travel*. New York: Pantheon Books.

Marmot, M.G. (2004). *The Status Syndrome: How Social Standing Affects Our Health and Longevity*. New York, N.Y.: Times Books/Henry Holt.

Marshall, Gordon, ed. (1994). *The Concise Oxford Dictionary of Sociology*. Oxford: Oxford University Press.

Martin, J. (1992). *Cultures in Organizations: Three Perspectives*. New York: Oxford University Press.

Martinez, Ramiro, Jr. (2002). *Latino Homicide: Immigration, Violence, and Community*. New York: Routledge.

Martinez, Ramiro, Jr. and Matthew T. Lee (1998). Immigration and the ethnic distribution of homicide. *Homicide Studies*, 2: 291–304.

Martire, Gregory and Ruth Clark (1982). *Anti-Semitism in the United States: A Study of Prejudice in the 1980s*. New York: Praeger.

Matveeva, Susanna and Vladimir Shlapentokh (2000). *Strakhi v Rossii.* Novosibirsk: Sibirskii Khronograf.

May, Ernest (2004). Astride the world. *The Times Literary Supplement.* July 16.

McAdams, Richard (1997). The origin, development, and the regulation of norms. *The Michigan Law Review*, 96: 338–343.

McChesney, Fred S. (1991). Rent extraction and interest-group organization in a Coasean model of regulation. *Journal of Legal Studies*, 73.

McClelland, J.S. (1989). *The Crowd and the Mob: From Homer to Canetti.* Boston: Unwin Hyman.

McClosky and Brill (1983). *Dimension of Tolerance.* New York: Russel Sage.

McCormick, Charles H. (1997). *Seeing Reds: Federal Surveillance of Radicals in the Pittsburgh Mill District, 1917–1921.* Pittsburgh, Pa.: University of Pittsburgh Press.

McEwan, Ian (1999). *Enduring Love.* Toronto: Vintage Canada.

McIntire, Alasdair (1987). *Whose Justice? Whose Rationality.* South Bend: University of Notre Dame Press.

McMahon, Judith, Frank McMahon and Tony Romano (1995). *Psychology and You.* St. Paul, Minn.: West Publishing.

McPhail, Clark (1991). *The Myth of the Maddening Crowd.* New York: A. de Gruyter.

Mead, George (1934). *The Mind, Self and Society.* Chicago: University of Chicago Press.

Meier, Robert (1982). Perspectives on the control of social control. *Annual Reviews of Sociology*, No. 8.

Mellosi, Dario (1990). *The State of Social Control: A Sociological Study of Concepts of State and Social Control in the Making of Democracy.* New York: St. Martin's Press.

Melville, Herman (1948). *Billy Budd.* Cambridge, Mass.: Harvard University Press.

Merelman, Richard M. (1980). Democratic politics and the culture of American education. *American Political Science Review*, 74: 317–332.

Merton, Robert King (1949). *Social Theory and Social Structure: Toward the Codification of Theory and Research.* Glencoe, Ill.: Free Press.

Messner, Steven and Richard Rosenfeld (1997). *Crimes and the American Dream.* Belmont: Wadsworth.

Michalos, Alex C. (2003). *Essays on the Quality of Life.* Boston: Kluwer Academic Publishers.

Michener, Andrew, John DeLamater and Daniel Myers (2004). *Social Psychology.* Belmont: Wadsworth.

Michener, James A. (1970). *The Quality of Life.* Philadelphia and New York: J.B. Lippincott company.

Mileti, Dennis, Thomas Drabek and J. Eugene Haas (1975). *Human Systems and Extreme Environments.* Boulder: Institute for Behavioral Science.

Miliband, R. (1969). *State in Capitalist Society.* London: Weidenfeld and Nicolson.

Millman, Joel (1997). *Other Americans*. New York: Viking.

Mitchell, William and Michael Munger (1991). Economic models of interests groups: an introductory survey. *American Journal of Political Science*, 35: 525.

Montville, J.V., ed. (1990). *Conflict and Peacemaking in Multi Ethnic Societies*. Lexington: Heath.

Mooney, L. and Roger Bates, eds. (1999). *Environmental Health: The Third World Problem, First World Preoccupations*. Oxford: Butterworth, Heinemann.

Mavriac, Claude (1990). Bergere o Tour Eiffel. Paris: B. Grasset.

Mozgovaia, A. (1994). *Sotsialnyie Problemy Ekologii*, Vol. 7. Moscow: Institute of Sociology.

Munch, Richard and Neil J. Smelser (1993). *Theory of Culture*. California: University of California Press.

Murdock, George Peter (1954). *Outline of World Cultures*. New Haven: Human Relations Area Files.

Migdal, Joel (1988). *Strong Societies and Weak States*. Princeton: Princeton University Press.

Migdal, Joel (2001). *State and Society. Studying How the State and Societies Transform and Constitute one Another*. Cambridge: Cambridge University Press.

Nagourney, Adam (2002). Clinton said party failed midterm test over security issue. *New York Times*. December 4.

Nairn, Tom (2003). It's not economy, stupid. *TLS*. May 9.

National Commission on Law Observance and Enforcement (1931). *Report on Crime and Foreign Born*, No. 10. Washington, D.C.: U.S. Government Printing Office.

Némirovsky, Irène (2004). *Suite française: roman*. Paris: Denoël.

Nemtsov, A. (2001). *Alkogolnaia smertnost v Rossii. 1980–90 gody*. Moscow: Nalex.

Nemtsov, A. (2003). Alkogolnaia smertnost v regionakh Rossia. *Naselenie i Obshchestvo*, No. 78.

Neocleous, Mark (2000). *The Fabrication of Social Order. A Critical Theory of Police Power*. London: Pluto.

New York Times (2002). France's Disgruntled Voters. April 23.

New York Times (2004a). A Nation Seeks Its Moral Compass. May 23.

New York Times (2004b). How Americans voted: the political portrait. November 7.

New York Times (2005a). Census report details lives of U.S. Arabs. March 9.

New York Times (2005b). Who's minding Medicaid. July 20.

New York Times (2005c). Chicago official to get more oversight. September 27.

Newman, Gerald (1997). *The Rise of English Nationalism: A Cultural History, 1740–1830*. New York: St. Martin's Press.

Nicholls, David (1974). *Three Varieties of Pluralism*. New York: St. Martin's Press.

Niebuhr, Reinhold (1932). *Moral Man and Immoral Society.* New York: C. Scribner's.

Niebuhr, Reinhold (1944). *The Children of Light and the Children of Darkness. An Indication of Democracy and a Critique of Its Traditional Defense.* New York: C. Scribner's.

Nietzsche, Friedrich Wilhelm (1955). *Beyond Good and Evil.* South Bend, Ind.: Gateway Editions.

Nikolaevsky, B. (1948a). O novoi i staroi emigratsii. *Sotsialisticheskii Vestnik,* January 28.

Nikolaevsky, B. (1948b). Porazhenchestvo 1941–1945 godov i general Vlasov. *Novyi Zhurnal,* 18.

Nisbett, Richard (2003). *The Geography of Thought. How Asians and Westerners Think Differently and Why.* New York: The Free Press.

Nisbett, Robert, Kaiping Peng, Incheol Choi and Ara Norenzayan (2001). Culture and the systems of thought: holistic versus analytic cognition. *Psychological Review,* 108(2): 291–310.

Nobel Lectures, Economics 1991–1995 (1997). Singapore: World Scientific Publishing.

Nottingham, Stephen (2003). *Eat Your Genes.* London: Zed Books.

Novak, Michael (1977). *Further Reflections on Ethnicity.* Middletown: Jednota Press.

Nunn, Clyde Z., Harry J. Crockett and J. Allen Williams (1978). *Tolerance for Nonconformity.* San Francisco: Jossey-Bass.

O'Kane, James M. (1992). *The Crooked Ladder: Gangsters, Ethnicity, and the American Dream.* New Brunswick, N.J.: Transaction Publishers.

Oakeshott, Michael Joseph (1975). *Hobbes on Civil Association.* Berkeley: University of California Press.

Oates, Joyce Carol (1998). The aesthetics of fear. *Salmagundi,* 120(Fall): 176–185.

Offe, Claus (1991). How we can trust our fellow citizens? In Marc Warren, ed. *Democracy and Trust.* Cambridge: Cambridge University Press.

Oleinik, Anton N. (2003). *Organized Crime, Prison, and Post-Soviet Societies.* Aldershot, Hants and Burlington, Vt.: Ashgate.

Olesha, Yuri (1975). *Envy.* Trans. T.S. Berczynski. Ann Arbor, Mich.: Ardis.

Olson, Mancur (1963). Rapid economic growth as a destabilizing force. *Journal of Economic History,* 23: 529–552.

Olson, Mancur (1965). Durkheim's two concepts of anomie. *Sociological Quarterly,* 6: 37–44.

Olzak, S. (1992). *The Dynamics of Ethnic Competition and Conflict.* Stanford: Stanford University Press.

Ortner, Sherry (2003). East brain, west brain. *The New York Times Book Review.* April 20.

Ortony, Andrew, Gerald Glore and Allan Collins (1990). *The Cognitive Structure of Emotions.* Cambridge: Cambridge University Press.

Orwell, George (1949). *1984.* New York: New American Library.

Ousby, Ian (1997). *Occupation. The Ordeal of France, 1940–1944.* New York: St. Martin's Press.

Outhwaite, William (1994). Legitimacy. In Ernest Gellner, Robert Nisbet and Allaine Touraine, eds. *The Blackwell Dictionary of Twentieth Century Thought.* Oxford: Blackwell.

Outhwaite, William, Tom Bottomore, Ernest Gellner, Robert Nisbet and Alain Touraine, eds. (1994). *The Blackwell Dictionary of Twentieth Century Social Thought.* Oxford: Blackwell.

Pantazis, Christina (2000). Fear of crime, vulnerability and poverty. *The British Journal of Criminology,* 40(3): 414–436.

Paris, David (1991). Moral education and "the tie that binds" in liberal political theory. *American Political Science Review,* 85(3): 875.

Park, R. and E. Burgess (1924). *Introduction to Science of Sociology.* Chicago: University of Chicago Press.

Parsons, Talcott (1982). *On Institutions and Social Evolution.* Chicago: University of Chicago Press.

Parsons, Talcott (1951). *The Social System.* Glencoe, Ill.: Free Press.

Parsons, Talcott (1960). *Structure and Process in Modern Societies.* Glencoe, Ill.: Free Press.

Parsons, Talcott (1964). Evolutionary universals in society. *American Sociological Review,* 29: 339–357.

Parsons, Talcott (1969). *Politics and Social Structure.* New York: Free Press.

Parsons, Talcott (1975). *On Institutions and Social Evolution.* Chicago: University of Chicago Press.

Parsons, Talcott (1977). *Social Systems and the Evolution of Action Theory.* New York: Free Press.

Parsons, Talcott (1982). *On Institutions and Social Evolution.* Chicago: University of Chicago Press.

Parsons, Talcott and Edward Shills (1951). *Toward a General Theory of Action.* Cambridge: Harvard University Press.

Partnoy, Frank (2003). *Infectious Greed: How Deceit and Risk Corrupted the Financial Markets.* New York: Times Books.

Passin, H. (1992). The occupation—some reflections. In C. Gluck and S. Graubard, eds. *Showa: The Japan of Hirohito.* New York: Norton.

Patterson, Gerald (1982). *Coercive Family Process.* Eugene: Castalia.

Patterson, Orlando (1991). Freedom. New York, N.Y.: Basic Books.

Patterson, Orlando (2005). The speech misheard round the world. *New York Times.* January 22.

Pearson, David E. (1993). Post-Mass Culture. *Society,* 30(July/August): 22.

Perkins, D.N. (1986). *Knowledge as Design.* Hillsdale, N.J.: Lawrence Erlbaum Associates.

Perkins, H.E., ed. (2004). *The Social Norms Approach to Preventing College Age Substance Abuse.* San Francisco: Jossey Bass.

Perry, Ronald (1985). *Comprehensive Emergency Management: Evacuating Threatened Populations.* Greenwich, Conn.: JAI Press.

Petitnicoals, Catherine (2004). La sante mentale des Francais en chiffre. *La Figaro*. October 25.

Petrova, A. (2003). Zennostnyie orinetatsii Rossian I politicheskie partii. Fund of Public Opinion. *Bulletin*. August 23.

Petty, Richard and Duane Wegener (1998). Attitude changes: multiple roles for persuasion variables. In Daniel T. Gilbert, Susan T. Fiske, and Gardner Lindzey, eds. *The Handbook of Social Psychology*, Vol. 1. Boston: McGraw-Hill.

Pew Research Center (1990). *Political Landscape 2004*, Vol. 57. Washington, D.C.: Pew Research Center.

Pew Research Center (1996). *State of the Union Poll*. Washington, D.C.: Pew Research Center, November 22–December 1.

Pew Research Center (2003). News Release. September 4 and August 5.

Piasheva, Larisa (1989). Kontury radikal'noi sotsial'noi reformy. In Fridrikh Borodkin et al., eds. *Postizhenie*. Moscow: Progress.

Piasheva, Larisa (1990a). V korzinke i koshelke. *Literaturnaia Gazeta*. September 5.

Piasheva, Larisa (1990b). Umom poniat' Rossiu. *Ogonek*, 44(October).

Piasheva, Larisa (1991). Son o trekh ukazakh. *Literaturnaia Gazeta*. March 13.

Pie, Lucian (1966). *Aspects of Political Development*. Boston: Little, Brown.

Pipes, Richard (1993). *Russia under the Bolshevik Regime*. New York: A.A. Knopf.

Pivovarov, Vladimir (1974). *Na Etapakh 11Sotsiologicheskogo Issledovania*. Groznyi: Checheno-Ingushskoie Izdatelstvo.

Polanyi, Karl (1944). *The Good Society*. New York: Rinehart.

Polterovich, Victor (1998). Faktory corruptzii. *Ekonomiko—matemathicheskie metody*, 34(3).

Portes, Alejandro (1997). Immigration theory for a new century: some problems and opportunities. *International Migration Review*, 31: 799–825.

Portes, Alejandro and Robert Bach (1985). *Latin Journey: Cuban and Mexican Immigrant in the USA*. Berkeley: University of California Press.

Portes, Alejandro and Alex Stepick (1993). *City on the Edge: The Transformation of Miami*. Berkeley: University of California Press.

Portes, Alejandro and Ruben G. Rumbaut (1996). *Immigrant America. A Portrait*. Berkeley: University of California Press.

Portes, Alejandro and Ruben G. Rumbaut (2001). *Legacies: The Story of the Immigrant Second Generation*. Berkeley: University of California Press and New York: Russell Sage Foundation.

Poulantzas, N. (1978). *State, Power, Socialism*. London: New Left Book.

Powell, Douglas and William Leiss (1997). *Mad Cows and Mother's Milk. The Perils of Poor Risk Communication*. Montreal: McGill-Queen's University Press.

Powers, Richard Gid (1995). *Not without Honor: The History of American Anti-Communism*. New York: Free Press.

Pridemore, William Alex (2005). *Ruling Russia: Law, Crime, and Justice in a Changing Society*. Rowman & Littlefield Publishers.

Prince, Samuel (1920). *Catastrophe and Social Change, based upon a Sociological Study of the Halifax Disaster.* New York: University of Columbia Press.

Pritchard, Justin (2004). Immigrants outlive U.S.-born residents. *Associated Press.* May 26.

Prothro, James W. and Charles M. Grigg (1960). Fundamental principles of democracy: bases of agreement and disagreement. *Journal of Politics,* 22(2): 276–294.

Pry, Peter Vincent (1999). *War Scare: Russia and America on the Nuclear Brink.* Westport, Conn.: Praeger.

Putin, Vladimir (2005). Presidential address (www.president.kremlin.ru).

Putnam, Robert D. (2000). *Bowling Alone: The Collapse and Revival of American Community.* New York: Simon & Schuster.

Quarantelli, E.L. (1954). The nature and conditions of panic. *American Journal of Sociology,* 60: 267–275.

Quinley, H. and C.Y. Glock (1979). *Anti-Semitism in America.* New York: Free Press.

Quinney, Richard (1979). *Criminology: Analysis and Critique of Crime in America.* Boston: Little, Brown.

Rachman, S. (1990). *Fear and Courage.* New York: Freeman.

Rachman, S. and Jack Maser, eds. (1988). *Panic: Psychological Perspectives.* Hillsdale: Lawrence Erlbaum.

Radzikhopvsky, Leonind (2005). *Ezhdnevny Journal.* June 27.

Rauch, Leo (1981). *The Political Animal: Studies in Political Philosophy from Machiavelli to Marx.* Amherst, Mass.: University of Massachusetts Press.

Rawls, John (1987). The idea of an overlapping consensus. *Oxford Journal of Legal Studies,* 7(1): 1–25.

Reiss, Albert J., Jr. (1967). *Studies in Crime and Law Enforcement in Major Metropolitan Areas. Field Survey III, Vol. I of the Presidential Commission on Law Enforcement. The Administration of Justice.* Washington, D.C.: U.S. Government Printing Office.

Reppetto, Thomas A. (2004). *American Mafia: A History of Its Rise to Power.* New York: H. Holt.

Rich, Frank (2005). Bring back Warren Harding. *New York Times.* September 25.

Rich, Motoko (2005). Life in the shelters: isolated and perilous. *New York Times.* September 18.

Riding, Alan (2002). Domino effect? New gain for far right in Europe. *New York Times.* April 23.

Ridley, M. (1997). *Disease.* London: Viking.

Riezler, Kurt (1944). The social psychology of fear. *The American Journals of Sociology,* 6(6): 489.

Rimer, Sara (2005). At Harvard, the bigger concern of the faculty is president's management style. *New York Times.* January 26.

Ringen, Stein (2002). Helvetious and friends. *The Times Literary Supplement.* November 15.

Rivera, Tomas (1993). Salamadras. In Nicolas Kanellos, ed. *Short Fiction by Hispanic Writers of the United States.* Houston: Arte Publico Press.

Robb, Peter (2004). *A Death in Brazil: A Book of Omissions.* New York: H. Holt.

Robertson, Ian (1981). *Sociology.* New York: Worth.

Robertson, Ian (1987). *Sociology.* 3rd edition. New York: Worth.

Robin, Corey (1999). Why do opposites attract. Fear and freedom in the modern political imagination. In Nancy Schultz, ed. *Fear Itself. Enemies Real and Imagined in American Culture.* West Lafayette: University of Purdue Press.

Robin, Corey (2004). *Fear: The History of a Political Idea.* New York: Oxford University Press.

Rogow, Arnold A. (1986). *Thomas Hobbes: Radical in the Service of Reaction.* New York: W.W. Norton.

Rohde, David (2002). American fears: changes and continuity. In Vladimir Shlapentokh and Eric Shiraev, eds. *Fears in Post-Communist Societies.* New York: Palgrave.

Rokeach, Milton (1973). *The Nature of Human Values.* New York: Free Press.

ROMIR (2003). *Monitoring.* July.

Rose, Jerry (1982). *Outbreaks. The Sociology of Collective Behavior.* New York: Free Press.

Rosenblum, Gerald (1973). *Immigrant Workers: Their Impact on American Radicalism.* New York: Basic Books.

Rothschild, Emma (2004). Real, pretended or imaginary. *The New York Review of Books,* 51(5): March 25.

Rousseau, Jean-Jacques (1992). *Discourse on the Origin of Inequality.* Indianapolis: Hackett Publishing Co.

Rudnitsky K. (1988). Krushenie teatra. *Ogoniok,* 22.

Russel, Bertrand (1930). *The End of Happiness.* New York: Leverlight.

Russell, Katheryn K. (1998). *The Color of Crime: Racial Hoaxes, White Fear, Black Protectionism, Police Harassment, and other Macroaggressions.* New York: New York University Press.

Russett, Bruce and Harvey Starr (1989). *World Politics: The Menu for Choice.* New York: W.H. Freeman.

Russian TV (2005). *Channel One.* Program "Vremai." July 13.

Rutland, Peter (2002). The muse of history. *History and Theory,* Winter.

Ryan, Alan (2003). The way to reason. *New York Review of Books.* December 4.

Ryan, Kathleen and Daniel Oestreich (1998). *Driving Fears out of the Workplace.* 2nd edition. San Francisco: Jossey Bass.

Dye, Thomas R. (2001). *Who Is Running America? The Bush Restoration.* 7th edition. Englewood Cliffs, N.J.: Prentice Hall.

Sachs, Susan and Edmund Andrews (2003). Iraq's slide into lawlessness squanders good will for U.S. *New York Times.* May 18.

Salovey, Peter and Alexander Rothman (1991). Envy and jealousy: self and society. In Peter Salovey, ed. *The Psychology of Jealousy and Envy.* New York: Guilford Press.

Sampson, Robert and John Laub (1994). *Crime in the Making. Pathway and Turning Points through Life*. Cambridge: Harvard University Press.

Sanderson, Stephen (2001). *The Evolution of Human Social Life*. Boston: Pearson.

Sarget, Lyman, ed. (1995). *Extremism in America*. New York: New York University Press.

Scalapino, R. (1989). *The Politics of Developments: Perspectives on Twentieth Century Asia*. Cambridge, Mass.: Harvard University Press.

Schlesinger, Arthur M., Jr. (1988). *The Vital Center: The Politics of Freedom*. New York: DaCapo Press.

Schlesinger, Arthur M., Jr. (1991). *The Disuniting of America*. New York: Norton.

Schlesinger, Arthur M., Jr. (2005). Forgetting Reinhold Niebuhr. *The New York Book Review*. September 18: 12–13.

Schlosser, Eric (2003). *Reefer Madness. Sex, Drugs and Cheap Labor in the American Black Market*. Boston: Houghton Mifflin.

Schmidt, Carl Theodore. (1938). *The Plough and the Sword*. New York: Columbia University Press.

Schmitt, Eric (2004). Rumsfled's aid and general clash at Iraq abuse hearings. *New York Times*. May 13.

Schoek, Helmut (1969). *Envy. A Theory of Social Behavior*. London: Secker and Warburg.

Schultz, Nancy, ed. (1999). *Fear Itself. Enemies Real and Imagined in American Culture*. West Lafayette: Purdue University Press.

Schumacher, Rose et al. (1989). *World Quality of Life Indicators*. Santa Barbara: ABC-CLIO.

Schwartz, Benjamin (1995). The diversity myth. *Atlantic Monthly*. May.

Schwartz, Thomas (1991). *America's Germany. John McCloy and the Federal Republic of Germany*. Cambridge: Harvard University Press.

Sedov, Leonind (2001). Sostoanie obshchestvennogo mnenia rossian v marte 2001 goda. *Levada-zentr, Press vypusk*, June 4.

Sedov, Leonind (2002). Obshchestvennoie mnenie rossian o sobytiakh ianvaria 2002. *Levada-zentr, Press vypusk 2*, February 12.

Seliunin, Vasilii (1990). Rynok: khimery i realnost. In Andrei Protashchik, ed. *Zherez ternii*. Moscow: Progress.

Selvern, Susan J. (1968). *Red Scare in New York State, 1919–1920*. Senior honors thesis, Brandeis University.

Selznick, Gertrude J. and Stephen Steinberg (1969). *The Tenacity of Prejudice: Anti-Semitism in Contemporary America*. New York: Harper & Row.

Sen, Amartya Kumar (2002). *Rationality and Freedom*. Cambridge, Mass.: Belknap Press of Harvard University Press.

Sennett, Richard (2004). *Respect: The Formation of Character in a World of Inequality*. New York: The Penguin Press.

Shalamov, Kolymskie (1982). *Rasskazy*. Paris: Iymka-Press.

Shalamov, Varlam Tikhonovich (1981). *Kolymskie rasskazy* (English Graphite). Translated from Russian by John Glad. New York: Norton.

Shama, Simon (2003). *The History of Britain. The Fate of Empire, 1776–2000.* New York: Miramax.

Shaw, Clifford and Henry McKay (1969). *Juvenile Delinquency and Urban Areas.* Chicago: University of Chicago Press.

Sheldon, Michael (1991). *Orwell. The Authorized Biography.* New York: Harper.

Shelef, Leon (1975). From restitutive law to repressive law. *Archives Europeanne de sociologie,* 16: 16–45.

Shepard, John (1990). *Sociology.* 4th edition. St. Paul: West Publishing Company.

Shestoperova, Yulia (2005). Pobeda vsukhuiu. *Moskovskii Komsomolets.* May 6.

Shipler, D. (1983). *Russia: Broken Idol, Solemn Dreams.* New York: Times Books.

Shipler, D. (2004). *The Working Poor: Invisible in America.* New York: A. Knopf (distributed by Random House).

Shiraev, E. and Levy, D. (2004). *Cross-Cultural Psychology.* 2nd edition. Boston: Allyn and Bacon.

Shklar, Judith N. (1984). *Ordinary Vices.* Cambridge, Mass.: Belknap Press of Harvard University Press.

Shklar, Judith (1987). *Montesquieu.* New York: Oxford University Press.

Shklar, Judith (1988). Rousseau and inequality. In *Rousseau's Political Writings.* Cambridge: Cambridge University Press.

Shklar, Judith (1991). *American Citizenship: The Quest for Inclusion.* Cambridge: Harvard University Press.

Shklar, Judith (1998). *Political Thought and Political Thinkers.* Chicago: University of Chicago Press.

Shlapentokh, Vladimir (1982). The study of values as a social phenomenon: the Soviet case. *Social Forces,* 61(2): 403–417.

Shlapentokh, Vladimir (1984). Moscow's war: propaganda and Soviet public opinion. *Problems of Communism.* September–October.

Shlapentokh, Vladimir (1986). *Soviet Public Opinion and Ideology: The Interaction between Mythology and Pragmatism,* New York: Praeger.

Shlapentokh, Vladimir (1989). *The Public and Private Life of the Soviet People.* New York: Oxford University Press.

Shlapentokh, Vladimir (1990). *Soviet Intellectuals and Political Power.* Princeton: Princeton University Press.

Shlapentokh, Vladimir (1995). *Russia: Privatization and Illegalization of Social and Political Life.* Cambridge, U.K.: Conflict Studies Research Center, Royal Military Academy, Sandhurst.

Shlapentokh, Vladimir (1996). Contemporary Russia: the best parallel to it— feudal Europe. *Europe-Asia,* Spring.

Shlapentokh, Vladimir (1997). Catastrophism on the eve of 2000: apocalyptic ideology between Russia's past and future. *Demokratizatsia,* 5(Winter).

Shlapentokh, Vladimir (1998). Four Russias. *The Tocqueville Review,* XIX(1).

Shlapentokh, Vladimir (2001). *A Normal Totalitarian Society. How Soviet Union Functioned and How It Collapsed.* Armonk, N.Y.: M.E. Sharpe.

Shlapentokh, Vladimir (2003). Hobbes and Locke at odds in Putin's Russia. *Europa-Asia*, 7: 981–1007.

Shlapentokh, Vladimir (2004a). *An Autobiographical Narration of the Role of Fear and Friendship in the Soviet Union*. Lewiston, N.Y.: Edwin Mellon Press.

Shlapentokh, Vladimir (2004b). George Orwell: Russia's Tocqueville. In Thomas Cushman and John Rodden, eds. *George Orwell into the Twentieth Century*. Boulder: Paradigm Publishers.

Shlapentokh, Vladimir (2004c). Wealth versus political power: the Russian case. *Communist and Post-Communist Studies*, 37: 135–160.

Shlapentokh, Vladimir (2005). Two pictures of Putin's Russia: both wrong. *World Policy Journal*, Spring.

Shlapentokh, Vladimir and Eric Shiraev (2002). *Fears in Post-Communist Societies*. New York: Palgrave.

Shlapentokh, Vladimir and Joshua Woods (2004). The threat of international terrorism and the image of the United States abroad. *Brown Journal of World Affairs*, 10(2): Winter/Spring.

Shlapentokh, Vladimir, Vladimir Shubkin and Vladimir Yadov, eds. (1999a). *Katastrofichseskoie Soznanie v sovremennom mire (The Catastrophic Mind in the Contemporary World)*. Moscow: Rossiiskaia assotsiatsia Nauchnykh Fondov.

Shlapentokh, Vladimir, Christopher Vanderpool and Boris Doktorov, eds. (1999b). *The New Elite in Post-Communist Eastern Europe*. College Station: Texas A&M University Press.

Shlapentokh, Vladimir, Joshua Woods and Eric Shiraev, eds. (2005). *America: Sovereign Defender or Cowboy Nation?* Aldershot, Hants and Burlington, Vt.: Ashgate.

Show, Clifford (1929). *Delinquency Area*. Chicago: University of Chicago Press.

Show, Clifford (1931). *Social Factor in Juvenile Delinquency*. Chicago: University of Chicago Press.

Shubkin, V. (1970). *Sotsiologicheskiie opyty*. Moscow: Mysl.

Shulgin, Vasilii Vitalevich (1991). *Tri stolitsy*. Moskva: Sovremennik.

Sidgwick, Henry (1891). *The Elements of Politics*. London: Macmillan.

Siegel, Marc (2005). *False Alarm: The Truth about the Epidemic of Fear*. Hoboken, N.J.: John Wiley & Sons.

Siegelbaum, Lewis (1997). Building Stalinism, 1929–1941. In Gregory Freeze, ed. *Russia: A History*. Oxford: Oxford University Press.

Simon, Herbert (1957). *Models of Man: Social and Rational; Mathematical Essays on Rational Human Behavior in Society Setting*. New York: Wiley.

Simons, Marlise (2003). An outspoken Arab in Europe: demon or hero. *New York Times*. March 1.

Singh, Gopal K. and Barry A. Miller (2004). Health, life expectancy, and mortality patterns among immigrant populations in the United States. *Canadian Journal of Public Health*, May–June.

Sirgy, M. Joseph, Don Rahtz and A. Coskun Samli, eds. (2003). *Advances in Quality of Life Theory and Research*. London: Kluwer Academic Publishers.

Skinner, Quentin (1972a). Conquest and consent: Thomas Hobbes and the engagement controversy. In G.E. Aylmer, ed. *The Interregnum: The Quest for Settlement*, pp. 79–98. London: Macmillan.

Skinner, Quentin (1972b). The context of Hobbes' theory of political obligation. In M. Cranston and R.S. Peters, eds. *Hobbes and Rousseau*, pp. 109–142. New York: Doubleday.

Skinner, Quentin (1972c). Social meaning and the explanation of social action. In P. Laslell et al., ed. *Philosophy. Politics and Society*, pp. 136–157. 4th series. Oxford: Blackwell.

Skinner, Quentin (1978). *The Foundations of Modern Political Thought*. Cambridge: Cambridge University Press.

Skinner, Quentin (2002). *Visions of Politics*. Cambridge: Cambridge University Press.

Skocpol, Theda (1985). Strategy of analysis in current research. In Peter B. Evans, Dietrich Rueschemeyer and Theda Skocpol, eds. *Bringing the State back In*. Cambridge and New York: Cambridge University Press.

Skocpol, Theda (1995). *Social Policy in the United States: Future Possibilities in Historical Perspective*. Princeton, N.J.: Princeton University Press.

Slemrod, Joel (1988). Fear of nuclear war and inter-country differences in the rate of saving. *NBER working paper series*, No. 2801.

Slomp, Gabriella (2000). *Thomas Hobbes and the Political Philosophy of Glory*. New York: St. Martin's Press.

Slovic, Paul (2004). *The Perception of Risk*. London: Earthscan.

Smelser, Neil (1994). *Sociology*. Oxford: Blackwell.

Smelser, Neil, ed. (1998). *Handbook of Sociology*. Newbury Park: Sage.

Smith, Adam (1982). *The Theory of Moral Sentiments*. Oxford: Oxford University Press.

Smith, Anthony D. (2001). *Nationalism: Theory, Ideology, History*. Cambridge: Polity Press and Malden, Mass.: Blackwell.

Smith, Mark (1999). Public opinion, election, and representation within market economy. *American Journal of Political Science*, 43(3): 8420.

Smith, R. (1991). Envy and the sense of injustice. In Salovey, ed. *The Psychology of Envy and Jealousy*. New York: Guilford Press.

Smith, R.H., W.G. Parrott, E. Diener, R.H. Hoyle and S.H. Kim (1999). Dispositional envy. *Personality and Social Psychology Bulletin*, 25: 1007–1020.

Smith, Tony (1986). Requiem or new agenda for the Third World studies. *World Politics*, 31: 532–561.

Solivetti, Luigi M. (2005). Who is afraid of migration and crime. *The Howard Journal of Criminal Justice*, 44(July): 322–325.

Solomon, Robert (2003). *Not Passion's Slave: Emotions and Choice*. Oxford and New York: Oxford University Press.

Solomon, Robert, ed. (2004). *Thinking about Feeling: Contemporary Philosophers on Emotions.* New York: Oxford University Press.

Solovei, Valerii (2002). Voina mirov po russki. *Vek.* July 5.

Solzhenitsyn, Aleksandr Isaevich (1975). *The Gulag Archipelago, 1918–1956.* Translated from Russian by Thomas P. Whitney. New York: Harper & Row.

Somerville, Johann (1992). *Thomas Hobbes. Political Ideas in Historical Context.* London: McMillan.

Sorell, Tom, ed. (1996). *The Cambridge Companion to Hobbes.* Cambridge and New York: Cambridge University Press.

Sorensen, Aage (1996). The structural basis of social inequality. *American Journal of Sociology,* 101(5): 1333–1365.

Sorokin, Pitirim Aleksandrovich (1968). *Man and Society in Calamity: The Effects of War, Revolution, Famine, Pestilence upon Human Mind, Behavior, Social Organization, and Cultural Life.* New York: Greenwood Press.

Spinoza, Benedictus de (1949). *Ethics* (preceded by On the improvement of the understanding by Benedict de Spinoza). Edited with an introduction by James Gutmann. New York: Hafner Publishing Co.

Stalin, Joseph (1952). *Voprosy Leninizma.* 11th edition. Moscow: Gospolitizdat.

Stark, Rodney (2001). *Sociology.* Wadsworth: Belmont.

Stiglitz, Joseph (2002). *Globalization and Its Discontents.* London: Allen Lane.

Stiglitz, Joseph (2003). *The Roaring Nineties: A New History of the World's Most Prosperous Decade.* New York: W.W. Norton & Co.

Stinchcombe, Arthur (1997). On the virtues of old institutionalism. *American Review of Sociology,* 23: 1–18.

Stone, L. (1987). *The Past and the Present Revisited.* London: Routledge & Kegan Paul.

Stouffer, Samuel Andrew (1955). Communism, conformity, and civil liberties; a cross-section of the nation speaks its mind. Garden City, N.Y.: Doubleday.

Strauss, Anselm (1991). *Creating Sociological Awareness.* New Brunswick: Transaction.

Strozier, Charles (1994). *Apocalypse: On the Psychology of Fundamentalism in America.* Boston: Beacon Press.

Sulton, Anne T., ed. (1994). *African-American Perspectives on Crime Causation, Criminal Justice Administration and Crime Prevention.* Englewood, Colo.: Sulton Books.

Summers, Erica (2002). The micro potential for social change: emotion, consciousness and social movement formation. *Sociological Theory,* 20(1), March.

Sunstein, Cass R. (1993). *Democracy and the Problem of Free Speech.* New York: The Free Press, Toronto: Maxwell Macmillan and New York: Maxwell Macmillan International.

Sunstein, Cass R. (2003). *Risk and Reason.* Cambridge: Cambridge University Press.

Sutherland, Edwin (1939). *Principles of Criminology*. Philadelphia: Uppincott.

Sutherland, Edwin and Donald Cressey (1947). *Criminology*. Philadelphia: J.P. Lippincott.

Sutherland, Edwin and Donald Cressey (1978) *Principles of Criminology*. Philadelphia: Uppincott.

Sutton, John (2001). *Law/Society*. Thousand Oaks: Pine Forge.

Swanson, Guy (1970). Toward corporate actions: a reconstruction of elementary collective processes. In Tamotsu Shibutani, ed. *Human Nature and Collective Behavior: Papers in Honor of Herbert Blumer*. Englewood Cliffs: Prentice-Hall.

Takemae, Eiji (2002). *Inside GHQ. The Allied Occupation of Japan and Its Legacy*. New York: Humanities Press.

Tannenhouse, Sam (1999). The red scare. *The New York Review of Books*. January 14.

Tarasov, K. and Iu. Kotunov (1984). *Vsestoennie razvitie lichnosti v usloviakh zrelogo kapita; lisma*. Moscow: Mysl.

Taylor, Charles (1992). *Multiculturalism and the Politics of Recognition*. Princeton, N.J.: Princeton University Press.

Taylor, Charles (1995). Liberal politics and the public sphere. In Amitai Etzioni, ed. *New Communitarian Thinking: Persons, Virtues, Institutions, and Communities*. Charlottesville: University of Virginia Press.

Taylor, I. et al., eds. (1975). *Critical Criminology*. Boston: Routledge.

Taylor, L., P. Walton and J. Young (1973). *The New Criminology: For a Theory of Social Deviance*. New York: Harper and Row.

Taylor, Shelley, Leticia Peplau, and David Sears, eds. (2003). *Social Psychology*. Upper Saddle River: Pearson Educational International.

Thomas, William and Florian Znaniecki (1920). *The Polish Peasant in Europe and America*, Vol. 14. Boston: Gorham Press.

Thomas, William, Robert Park and Herbert Miller (1966). Assimilation: the old world traits transplanted. In Mori Janovitz, ed. *On Social Organization and Personality*. Chicago: University of Chicago Press.

Thompson, Damian (1996). *The End of Time. Faith and Fear in the Shadow of the Millennium*. Hannover: University of New England Press.

Thornton, Helen (2005). *State of Nature or Eden? Thomas Hobbes and His Contemporaries on the Natural Condition of Human Beings*. Rochester, N.Y.: University of Rochester Press.

Thucydides (1982). *The Peloponnesian War*. The Crawley translation revised, with an introduction by T.E. Wick. New York: Modern Library.

Tienda, Marta (1999). Immigration, opportunities, and social cohesion. In Jeffrey Alexander and Neil Smelser, eds. *Diversity and Its Discontents*. Princeton: Princeton University Press.

Tierney, John (2003). A Baghdad traffic circle is a microcosm for chaos. *New York Times*. September 12.

Tocqueville, Alexis de (1969). *Democracy in America*. New York: Anchor Books.

Tournier, P. (1997). Nationality, crime and criminal justice in France. In M. Tonry, ed. *Ethnicity, Crime and Immigration: Comparative and Cross-National Perspectives.* Chicago and London: University of Chicago Press.

Traub, James (2005). Lawrence Summers, provocateur. *New York Times.* January 23.

Traugott, Marc, ed. (1994). *Emile Durkheim on Institutional Analysis.* Chicago: University of Chicago Press.

Traverso, Edmund (1964). *Immigration. A Study of American Values.* Boston: Heath.

Trevino, Javier (2001). Introduction. In Javier Trevino, ed. *Talcott Parsons Today. His Theory and Legacy in Contemporary Sociology.* Boulder: Rowman.

Triandis, Harry Charalambos (1994). *Culture and Social Behavior.* New York: McGraw-Hill.

Tsygankov, Andrei (2004). *Whose World Order? Russia's Perception of American Ideas after the Cold War.* Notre Dame, Ind.: University of Notre Dame Press.

Tuan, Yi-fu (1979). *Landscapes of Fear.* New York: Pantheon Books.

Tuck, Richard (2002). *Hobbes: A Very Short Introduction.* Oxford and New York: Oxford University Press.

Tullock, Gordon (1985). Adam Smith and the prisoner's dilemma. *Journal of Political Economy*, 100: 1073–1081.

Tully, J. (1995). *Strange Multiplicity.* Cambridge: Cambridge University Press.

Tunnel, Kenneth (1990). Choosing crimes: close your eyes and take your chances. *Justice Quarterly*, 7(4): 673–690.

Turner, Henry Ashby (1992). *Germany from Partition to Reunification.* New Haven: Yale University Press.

Turner, Jonathan (1985). *Sociology. The Science of Human Organization.* Chicago: Nelson-Hall.

U.S. Bureau of Census (2002). *Statistical Abstracts of the United States*, No. 56.

Ullmann-Margalit, Edna (1977). *The Emergence of Norms.* Oxford, U.K.: Clarendon Press.

United States Department of Justice. (1983). *Recidivism of Prisoners Released in 1983.* Bureau of Justice Statistics, Special report, April.

United States Department of the Army (1975). *The American Soldier.* Washington, D.C.: Office of Military History.

Velikhov, Evgenii (1999). Sovetskaia A-bomba: I ad, I pervaia liubov'. *Izvestia.* August 28.

Villaume, Poul (1996). *Cement of Fear: The Cold War and NATO until 1961.* Boulder: Westview Press.

Viscusi, Kip, ed. (2003). *The Risk of Terrorism.* Boston: Kluwer.

Viscusi, W. (1992). *Fatal Trade-Offs.* Oxford: Oxford University Press.

Vodzinskaia, V. (1967). K Voprosu o sotsial'noi obuslovlesnosti vybora pro-fessil. *Chelovek i obshchestvo 2.* Leningrad.

Vogel, E. (1979). *Japan as Number One.* Cambridge, Mass.: Harvard University Press.

Vold, George (1958). *Theoretical Criminology*. New York: Oxford University Press.

Volkogonov, Dmitry (1998b). *The Rise and Fall of the Soviet Empire: Political Leaders from Lenin to Gorbachev*. London: Harper Collins.

Voss, Thomas (2001). Game theoretical perspective on the emergence of social norms. In Michael Hechter and Karl-Dieter Opp, eds. *Social Norms*. New York: Russel.

VTSIOM (1998). *Bulletin*. No. 6.

VTSIOM-A (2002a). *Bulletin*. August 9.

VTSIOM-A (2002b). *Bulletin*. December 2.

VTSIOM-A (2003a). *Bulletin*. December 12.

VTSIOM-A (2003b). *Bulletin*. December 17.

VTSIOM-A (2004). *Bulletin*. November.

Walklate, Sandra (2004). *Gender, Crime, and Criminal Justice*. Cullompton, Devon and Portland, Or.: Willan Pub.

Wallerstein, Immanuel (1974). *The Modern World System*. New York: Academic Press.

Walsh, James (1998). *How Risk Affects Your Everyday Life*. Lansdowne, Pa.: Silver Lake Publishing.

Walton, Clarence (1998). *Archons and Acolytes. The New Power Elite*. Lanham: Rowan and Littlefield.

Walzer, Michael (1989). What does it mean to be American? *Social Research*, 57(1).

Walzer, Michael (1994). *Thick and Thin: Moral Argument at Home and Abroad*. Notre Dame: University of Notre Dame Press.

Walzer, Michael (2002). Can there been a decent left? *Dissent*, Spring.

Ward, R. (1968). The American occupation of Japan: political retrospect. In G. Goodman, ed. *The American Occupation of Japan. A Retrospective View*. Lawrence: Center for East Asian Studies, University of Kansas.

Ward, R. and Sakamoto Yoshikau, eds. (1987). *Democratizing Japan: The Allied Occupation*. Honolulu: University of Hawaii Press.

Wark, Mckenzie (1999). Latent destiny. In Yahya R. Ramalipour, ed. *Images of the U.S. around the World*. New York: State University of New York Press.

Warner, Jessica (2000). *Gin and Debaucheries in the Age of Reason*. New York: Four Walls Eight Windows.

Weber, Max (1947). The theory of social and economic organization. New York: Oxford University Press.

Weber, Max (1978). *Economy and Society*. Berkeley: University of California Press.

Weber, Max (1985). Churches and sects in North America. *Sociological Theory*, 3: 7–13.

Welch, Michael (2002). Moral panic over youth violence. *Youth & Society*, 34(1): 3–30.

White, John Kenneth (2003). *The Values Divide: American Politics and Culture in Transition*. New York: Chatham House Publishers/Seven Bridges Press.

White, Stephen (1993). *After Gorbachev*. Cambridge and New York: Cambridge University Press.

Whybrow, Peter (2005). *American Mania: Where More Is not Enough*. New York: Norton.

Wilgoren, Jodi (2005). Racketeering and fraud trial begins for Illinois ex-governor. *New York Times*. September 20.

Williams, Robin (1968). The concept of values. In D.L. Sills, ed. *International Encyclopedia of the Social Sciences*, Vol. 16. New York: Macmillan and Free Press.

Williams, Robin (1979). Change and stability in values and value systems: a sociological perspective. In Milton Rokeach, ed. *Understanding Human Values: Individual and Societal*. New York: Free Press.

Williams, Robin (1994). The sociology of ethnic conflicts: comparative international perspective. *Annual Review of Sociology*, 20: 49–79.

Wilson, James Q. and Richard J. Hernstein (1985). *Crime and Human Nature*. New York: Simon and Schuster.

Winter, Greg (2004). Colleges tell students the oversees party is over. *New York Times*. August 23.

Wittchen, H. (1986). Epidemiology of panic attacks and panic disorders. In I. Hand and H. Wittchen, eds. *Panic and Phobias*. Berlin: Springer.

Wolfe, Alan (1989). *Whose Keeper? Social Science and Moral Obligation*. Berkeley: University of California Press.

Wolfe, Alan (1998). *One Nation, after All*. New York: Viking.

Wolfe, Tom (1987). *The Bonfire of the Vanities*. New York: Farrar, Straus and Giroux.

Wolfe, Tom (1998). *A Man in Full*. New York: Farrar, Straus and Giroux.

Wolfe, Tom (2004). *I am Charlotte Simmons*. New York: Farrar, Straus and Giroux.

Wolin, Sheldon S. (1970). Hobbes and the epic tradition of political theory. Los Angeles: William Andrews Clark Memorial Library.

Wright, James and Peter Rossi (1981). *Social Science and Natural Hazards*. Cambridge, Mass.: Abt Books.

Wrong, Dennis (1961). The oversocialized conception of man in modern sociology. *American Sociological Review*, 26(2): 183–193.

Wrong, Dennis (1994). *The Problem of Order. What Unites and Divides Society*. New York: The Free Press.

Wuthnow, Robert (1999). The culture of discontent. In Jeffrey Alexander and Neil Smelser, eds. *Diversity and Its Discontents*. Princeton: Princeton University Press.

Yablokov, Igor (1979). *Sotsiologia Religii*. Moscow: Mysl.

Young, Iris Marion (1990). *Justice and the Politics of Difference*. Princeton: Princeton University Press.

Young, James (1999). The cold war comes top erie. In Nancy Schultz, ed. *Fear Itself. Enemies Real and Imagined in American Culture*. West Lafayette: Purdue University Press.

Zajonz, Robert (1998). Emotions. In Daniel T. Gilbert, Susan T. Fiske and Gardner Lindzey, eds. *The Handbook of Social Psychology*, Vol. 1. Boston: McGraw-Hill.

Zakaria, Fareed (2003). The previous superpower. *NYT Book Review*. July 27.

Zaslavskaia, Tatiana (2002). *Sozietalnaia transformatsia rossiiskogo obshchestva.* Moscow: Delo.

Zelizer, Viviana (1999). Multiple market: multiple culture. In Jeffrey Alexander and Neil Smelser, eds. *Diversity and Its Discontents*. Princeton: Princeton University Press.

Zerubavel, E. (1991). *The Fine Line: Making Distinctions in Everyday Life*. New York: Free Press.

Zerubavel, E. (1992). *Terra incognita. The Mental Discovery of America*. New Brunswick: The Rutgers University Press.

Zhiromskaia, Valentina (1998). Tainy perepisis naselenia 1937 goda. *Nezavisimaia Gazeta*. July 18.

Zollberg, Aristide (1966). *Creating Political Order: Party States in West Africa*. Chicago: Rand McNally.

Zorkaia, Natalia (2003). *Obshchestvennoie Mnenie, 2003*. Moscow: Vtsiom-A.

NAME INDEX

Abramson, Paul, 12, 109, 111, 120
Ackoff, Russel, 27, 179
Adorno, Theodore, 25, 160, 168
Alexander, Jeffrey, 51, 149
Aquinas, Thomas, 61, 77, 127,
    144, 179
Arendt, Hanna, 160, 168, 185
Aristotle, 30, 44, 57, 127
Arrow, Kenneth, 34
Ataturk, Kamal, 109
Augustine, 9, 127, 178, 179

Banfield, Edward, 114, 148
Bauman, Zygmunt, 165
Baumol, William, 180
Bayley, David, 148, 178
Becker, Gary, 140
Bell, Daniel, 163
Bellah, Robert, 11, 27, 90, 104,
    108, 120, 148, 163, 165
Bellamy, Edward, 143
Bentham, Jeremy, 30, 132, 161
Berger, Peter, 32, 43–4, 107
Berlin, Isaiah, 13, 103, 146
Bloch, Marc, 30, 125, 160
Blumer, Herbert, 31–2, 35
Boll, Heinrich, 118
Boulding, Kenneth, 134
Bourdieu, Pierre, 25, 113
Brooks, David, 58, 99, 100, 135,
    139, 181
Buchanan, James, 180
Burgess, E., 10, 153

Calvin, John, 179
Campanella, Tommaso, 143

Cantrill, Albert, 137
Carnegie, Andrew, 66
Chubais, Anatolii, 75, 180
Claudel, Paul, 173
Clinton, Bill, 144
Coase, Ronald, 161, 179
Collingwood, R. G., 65
Coleman, James, 22, 30–1, 35,
    154, 161

Dahl, Robert, 111
Dante, Alighieri, 61
Darwin, Charles, 41, 126, 131
De Botton, Alian, 59
De Gaulle, Charles, 174
Defoe, Daniel, 31
Dewey, John, 125
Domhoff, William, 74, 157, 180
Draiser, Theodor, 75
Durkheim, Emile, 10, 14, 24, 27,
    35, 37, 40, 110, 135

Einstein, Albert, 130
Elias, Norbert, 113–14, 182, 185
Ellickson, Robert, 22, 33–4, 36–7,
    111, 155, 161, 178–9, 184
Engels, Friedrich, 113

Fellini, Federico, 147
Ferguson, Neil, 42–3, 74, 114
Festinger, Leon, 54
Fiske, Alan, 28, 33, 106
Foucault, Michel, 12, 23–4, 140,
    158–9
Freud, Sigmund, 31, 41, 65, 77,
    126, 130, 144, 153

Friedan, Betty, 120
Fromm, Eric, 3, 126, 160, 168
Fukuyama, Francis, 11, 30, 34–5, 82, 108

Gabrilovich, Evgenii, 1–2
Gans, Herbert, 42
Garfinkel, Harold, 35
Garland, David, 14–15, 17, 24, 70, 107, 146, 157, 159, 182
Geertz, Clifford, 28
Gellner, Ernest, 94
Giddens, Anthony, 10, 17, 88, 178
Glassner, Barry, 142
Goethe, Johann Wolfgang von, 130
Goffman, Erving, 27, 32, 46
Golding, William, 31
Gorbachev, Mikhail, 116, 118
Gottfedson, Michael, 78
Greene, Graham, 118

Habermas, Jurgen, 25, 27, 113, 167, 185
Hailey, Arthur, 42
Harrington, Michael, 91
Hayek, Friedrich, 22, 30, 149, 161, 184
Hechter, Michael, 22, 30, 33–4, 88, 91, 114, 148, 154–5, 178
Heidegger, Martin, 126
Heine, Heinrich, 126
Hemingway, Ernest, 118
Henslin, James, 14, 16, 59, 136, 140, 156, 158
Hirschi, Travis, 78–9, 177
Hitler Adolf, 3, 168
Hobbes, Thomas, 5–6, 9–11, 23–5, 28, 35, 41, 58, 113, 126–35, 142–4, 148, 151, 156, 161, 167–8, 171, 176–7, 183
Horkheimer, Max, 25
Hofstadter, Richard, 89
Homer, 61, 126
Horney, Karen, 126
Horowitz, Irving, 16

Huntington, Samuel, 12–13, 29, 42–3, 46–7, 50, 80, 87, 91–3, 95, 98, 108, 114, 166, 179

Inglehart, Donald, 11–12, 23, 26, 53, 56, 81–3, 95, 102, 108–9, 111, 115, 120–1, 137, 142, 180

Jackman, Mary, 57
Jackman, Robert, 157, 164, 166–7
Judt, Tony, 147

Kant, Immanuel, 30, 127, 131
Kaplan, Robert, 19, 163
Keller, Suzanne, 177, 179, 180
Kemper, Theodore, 138
Keohane, Robert, 134,
Keynes, John Maynard, 162
Kierkegaard, Soren, 126
Kinder, Ronald, 56–7
King, Robert, 157
Kiesler, Charles and Sara, 54, 204
Kipling, Rudyard, 73
Kohlberg, Lawrence, 42, 44
Kohn, Melvin, 42
Kristol, Irving, 89
Kropotkin, Peter, 143
Kuhn, Thomas, 7

La Pen, Jean-Marie, 17, 177
Levada, Yurii, 116, 127–8, 170, 185
Lipset, Seymour, 11, 57, 89
Liska, Allen, 137, 139, 184
Locke, John, 25, 30, 34, 128, 130–2, 160, 168, 183
Lockwood, David, 10, 24, 37, 88
Luckmann, Thomas, 32, 43–4, 107
Lukacz, Georg, 25

Machiavelli, Niccolo, 41, 129
Malia, Martin, 138, 170
Mandel'shtam, Nadezhda, 1
Mannheim, Karl, 113
Mankiv, Gregory, 141
Mann, Michael, 90, 135, 167
Mao, 3, 4, 111

Marcuse, Herbert, 25
Marx, Carl, 1, 24–5, 27, 39, 41, 75,
    91, 94, 107, 111, 113, 117,
    128, 131–2, 134, 140, 157–9,
    162–3
Mead, George, 35, 153–4
Melville, Herman, 61
Merton, Robert, 14–15, 65, 132,
    156
Messner, Steven, 14, 77, 80, 91,
    154
Migdal, Joel, 19, 28, 164, 167, 185
Montaigne, Michel, 127, 136
Montesquieu, Charles, 55, 127
Moriac, Claude, 173
Mosca, Gaetano, 113
Murdock, George, 88

Nash, John, 33
Niebuhr, Reinhold, 65–6
Nietzsche, Friedrich, 14, 33, 129

Oakeshott, Michael, 58, 132
Oates, Joyce Carol, 126
Olesha, Yuri, 61
Olson, Mancur, 18
Opp, Dieter, 30, 33–4, 114, 148, 178
Orwell, George, 2–3, 5–6, 73, 134,
    138, 143, 158–9, 168, 185

Park, Robert, 10, 153
Parsons, Talcott, 5, 10–1, 21–38,
    44, 65, 77, 87, 94, 105–7, 110,
    111, 124, 128, 132, 135,
    150–1, 153, 156, 161, 168,
    176–7, 181, 183
Petain, Philippe, 172–4
Piaget, Jean, 1, 43
Pipes, Richard, 170
Polanyi, Karl, 162
Poulantzas, Nicos, 213
Prince, Samuel, 137
Pushkin Alexander, 61
Pye, Lucian, 18

Quarantelli, Enrico, 135

Rawls, John, 30, 103–4
Reiss, Albert, 137, 184
Remarque, Erich Maria, 118
Robin, Corey, 33, 127, 146, 159
Roosevelt, Franklin, 136, 160
Rosenfeld, Richard, 14, 77, 80, 91
Rousseau, Jean Jacques, 30, 59,
    129, 167, 179, 183
Russel, Bertrand, 61
Rustin, Bayard, 120

Salinger, J.D., 118
Sartre, Jean-Paul, 33, 126
Schlesinger, Arthur, 66, 91, 160
Schmitt, Carl, 131
Skocpol, Theda, 109, 177, 195, 219
Sen, Amartya Kumar, 54
Shalamov, Varlem Tikhonovich, 59
Shiraev, Eric, 69–70, 139, 183
Shklar, Judith, 43, 59, 127, 146, 160
Show, Clifford, 77
Shubkin, Vladimir, 182
Shulgin, Vasilii, 170
Sinclair, Upton, 75
Slovic, Paul, 136, 219
Smelser, 19, 25, 51, 136, 166, 187
Smith, Adam, 126
Solo, Robert, 28
Solon, 179
Solzhenitsyn, Aleksandr, 59
Sorokin, Pitirim, 106, 137
Spencer, Herbert, 27, 34, 135, 161
Spinoza, Baruch, 127
Stalin, Joseph, 2–3, 101, 111, 115,
    117, 131, 162
Stark, Rodney, 154–5, 157, 159
Stiglitz, Joseph, 75, 177
Stinchcombe, Arthur, 148
Stouffer, Samuel, 52, 57
Strauss, Levy, 24, 179, 183
Sutherland, Edwin, 77–8, 180

Thackeray, William, 60
Tocqueville, 89, 113, 127, 183
Tonnies, Ferdinand, 35
Triandis, Garry, 12, 21

Vercors, 172

Walzer, Michael, 90, 92, 163
Weber, Max, 24, 27, 35, 89, 130,
    135, 148, 164, 167, 169,
    185
White, Stephen, 181
Williams, Robin, 52, 60, 65, 103,
    178, 185
Wolfe, Alan, 99, 165
Wolfe, Tom, 42, 47, 61, 72, 75

Wrong, Denis, 12, 25, 28, 41–2,
    58–9, 77, 88, 131–3, 144, 165,
    177, 183,

Yeltsin, Boris, 111, 115, 170–1
Yoursenar, Marguerite, 94

Zajonz, Robert, 125
Zaslavskaia, Tatiana, 185
Zerubavel, Eviatar, 90
Znaniecki, Florian, 10, 79

Subject Index

Anti-Semitism, 1, 68, 122
Anomie, 10

Bolsheviks, 5, 115–16, 170

Chicago School, 10
China, 3–4, 51, 82, 92, 97, 111, 184
Coercion, 44, 79, 103, 113, 130,
    147–8, 155–7, 163, 174
Colombia, 19, 96, 97
Communism, 17, 181
Conformity, 29, 45, 54
Constructivism in sociology, 33
Corruption, 7, 10–12, 14, 16–20,
    58, 67, 69, 75–6, 84–5, 166,
    170–1, 173, 175, 180
Cult of leader, 3, 122, 170
Cultural capital, 25, 113
Cultural model of order, 26

Dependence theory, 19

Elites, 7, 14, 18, 34, 36, 38, 60, 82,
    84, 90, 109–15, 117, 119–20,
    124, 137, 159, 164–7, 169, 182
Empires, 18, 88, 93–5, 104,
    114–15, 118, 164, 176–8
Envy, 2, 60–3, 126, 179–80

Fear
    acceptable level of, 147
    adaptation to, 125
    aesthetics of, 126
    amongst its oppressed, powerless
        subjects, 159
    and love of Big Brother, 3
    and studies of Soviet society, 138
    as a regulator of behavior, 21
    as a signal, 125
    as an instrument of control, 184
    as societal issue, 136
    change and, 128
    classic writers and, 126
    classifications of, 183
    culture of, 183
    definition of, 22, 125
    demoralizing effect of, 2–3
    discrimination of minorities and,
        6, 139–40
    economics of, 140
    emotion and, 22, 125
    existential philosophy and, 126
    fear of, 127, 136
    fear-love complex, 3–4, 136
    formal control and, 155, 174
    freedom from, 160
    hierarchical organizations and, 147
    human physiology and, 127
    human psychology and, 126
    impact on behavior and human
        relations, 4, 5
    in America, 2, 5
    in contemporary fiction, 127
    in contemporary sociology,
        dictionaries and textbooks, 6–7,
        9, 125, 135–7, 139–41, 151
    in democratic society, 5
    in developing countries, 138
    in different societies, 8
    in economics, 140
    in Middle Ages, 128
    in post-Soviet Russia, 127

Fear—*continued*
  in Soviet society, 1, 2, 4,
      44, 101
  in the workplace, 147
  in totalitarian society, 4, 138, 159
  internalized values and, 167
  mongers, 136
  of anarchy, 160
  of animals, 126
  of any social group, 146
  of bankruptcy, 6, 139
  of crime, 6, 14, 127, 138–41
  of epidemics, 136
  of foreign intervention and war,
      4, 135, 183
  of freedom, 165
  of illness, 136
  of peer-review, 156
  of poisonous food, 136
  of police, 139
  of pollution and toxic waste, 136
  of poverty, 127, 160
  of repressions, 101
  of sanctions and punishment, 3,
      6, 23, 36, 38, 44, 45, 52, 62,
      65, 67, 84–6, 88–9, 103,
      110, 125, 147–8, 150–7,
      165, 175–6, 178
  of state power, political police, the
      KGB, 4–5, 44–5, 129, 151
  of terrorism, 135
  of the future, 125
  of unemployment, 6, 139, 160
  of violating rules and laws, 26, 47,
      165, 176
  order and, 7, 9, 103, 128, 149,
      176
  Orwell and, 138
  personal experiences of survey
      respondents and, 183
  philosophy, 127, 183
  positive and negative, 151, 156,
      160, 176
  propaganda and, 126
  quality of life and, 9,138,139,176
  rationalization and, 2, 41

  real, rational and fictitious, 5,
      126, 183
  risk and, 136
  self-regulated communities and,
      156
  social and existential, l, 2, 127–8,
      131, 138, 151
  social psychology's disregard of,
      137–8, 151
  socialization and, 150
  studies of, 136–138
  trust and, 147
  values and, 7, 22, 149
Formal control, 7, 73, 143, 153–9,
      161–74, 184
France, 17, 43, 51, 80, 94, 121,
      128, 169, 172–3, 177
Frankfurt School, 25
Freedom, 13–14, 33, 39, 44, 68, 74,
      99, 102–3, 106, 107, 117, 120,
      129–31, 157, 160, 165, 178
French Revolution, 66

Gallup data, 40–1, 66, 68, 84, 165,
      180
Game theory, 33, 103, 133–4
Germany, 3, 17, 43–4, 80, 96, 98,
      111, 115, 121–2, 124, 172–3
Glasnost, 3

Handbook of Social Psychology, 61,
      106, 138
Handbook of Sociology, 136
Hobbes, underestimation of, 128,
      135, 176
Homosexuality, 120–1, 139, 182
Hurricane Katrina, 10, 72, 126

Ideology, 32, 51, 126, 169
  as an instrument of the state, 23
  class, 89
  dominant and official, 2–3, 26, 109
  elite, 111, 112
  Gorbachev's new, 118
  in America, 26, 42, 46, 89,
      90, 181

liberal, 74
Nazi, 168
of criminal organizations, 76–7
oligarchic or corporative, 74–5, 85
Order, 173
positive and negative, 44, 66
postmodern, 162
Soviet, 66, 101, 117–18, 170
utilitarian, 34
Immigration and immigrants, 5, 8,
    17, 24, 46–52, 62, 79 80–1, 90,
    93, 99, 110, 139–40, 150, 179
India, 69, 82, 92, 95, 97–8, 115
Informal control, 7, 36, 153–6,
    174, 176
Intellectuals, 4, 51, 76, 101, 112, 113,
    117, 134, 159–60, 182, 185
Iraq, 10, 73, 89
Italy, 74, 98, 114

Japan, 51, 96, 97, 98, 99, 102, 115,
    121, 122, 123, 124, 155

KGB, the, 1, 2, 5, 44–5, 118,
    171, 182

Legitimacy, 157, 167–71, 174, 185
Libertarianism, 17, 148, 160–1
Love, 1–3, 6, 59, 65, 71, 74, 117,
    126, 128, 136, 138, 142, 144,
    169, 178–9, 181

Mafia, 76, 84, 130, 148
Marxism, 1, 41, 111, 117
McCarthyism, 4, 159
Mexico, 19, 48, 82, 96–8, 138
Middle Ages, 9, 109, 125, 128,
    159–60

National Socialism, 131
New norms theory, 34–6, 38
New York City, 72, 149
Norway, 10, 96, 98, 99, 104, 176

October Revolution, 115, 118
Opportunity costs, 109

Order or social order, 9
law and, 9, 100, 164, 165
continuous variables and levels of,
    10
under monarchies, 9
in Norway, 10
in Soviet society, 2
in Iraq, 10
in social science, 10
as a condition for economic
    development, 10
Chicago School and, 10
Parsons and, 10–11, 26–8, 77, 110
in the United States, 5, 88, 92,
    100, 165
society and, 6
maintenance of, 6–7, 77, 82, 104,
    109, 112, 134, 143, 149,
    151, 167, 168
Big Brother and, 6
Orwell and, 6
underestimation of in social
    science, 7
in contemporary social science, 9,
    157, 167
quality of life and, 9
and urbanization, 10
in Foucault's works, 12, 158
as a precondition for progress, 12
in Huntington's works, 12
in Wrong's works, 12
as an obstacle to progress, 12
and downgrading of the role of
    crimes, 13
attitudes toward, 15
and democracy and freedom, 18,
    82, 102, 130, 142
post-colonial countries, 18–20
as an essential condition for social
    life, 20
state and law as the basis of,
    24–5
and self-control, 26
and socialization, 26
and self regulation, 26
and social capital, 30

Order or social order—*continued*
  in symbolic interactionism, 31
  in postmodernism, 33
  and rules, 61
  and antisocial personality disorder, 69–70
  and rent-seeking activity, 75
  and organized crime and mafia, 76, 148
  and religion, 77
  and fear of sanction, 84, 103, 143, 149, 151
  and church, 94
  level of, 94
  the holistic and segmented vision of society and order, 112
  as value, 120
  and Goethe, 130
  and Locke, 131
  and altruism, 143
  and Weber, 148, 164
  and formal control, 153
  and the masses, 157
  and Hayek, 161
  and legitimacy, 167, 169
  in the Soviet Union, 170
  in occupied France, 171–4
  and elites, 112–13, 158, 179
  and fear, 128–9, 143
  Hobbes and, 11, 129–30, 132–3, 135
  in post-Soviet Russia, 18, 170–1
  and immigrants, 46–7, 51–2
  and oligarchs and corporations, 74–5
  state and, 5–6, 23, 24, 10, 87–8, 143, 148, 156–7, 160–2
  and empire, 93–4
  fear and, 7, 9
  Durkheim and, 10, 37, 40
  and the wellbeing (quality of life) of society, 13, 20
  values, culture and, 6–7, 9, 21, 29, 39, 40–1, 52–4, 58, 60, 66, 71, 85, 87–8, 103–5, 112, 132, 143–4, 148

  from below and from above, 22, 24, 29–31, 33, 35
  in social science in the 1990s, 17–18
  religion and divine origin of, 9–10
  in Inlegart's works, 11–2, 111
  as an instrument of conservatives, 12–13
Organized crime, 10, 17, 20, 76, 85

Pew Research Center, 97, 137
Postmodernism, 32, 33, 38, 153
Post-Communist countries, 18, 89, 96, 101
Post-Soviet Russia, 5–6, 8, 10, 18, 37, 44, 67–9, 74, 76, 81–4, 89, 92, 96–9, 100–1, 103, 111, 115, 119, 124, 127, 145, 170–1, 177, 181–3, 199
Prisoner's Dilemma, 133
Public institutions, 82–4

Rational choice theory, 30, 33, 34, 38–9, 129
Religion, 12, 24, 31, 40, 43, 49, 51–2, 60–1, 66, 77, 86, 89, 94, 98, 109–10, 114–16, 116, 124, 154
  Catholic, 35, 51, 82, 148
  Islamic, 82
  Protestant, 12, 42–3, 46, 51, 82, 91–3, 114
  Ten Commandments, 23, 53
Relativization of deviant behavior, 13–16
Rent seeking activity, 16, 74–5, 180

Self-control, 5, 15, 26, 52, 70, 79
Social norms, 22–3, 31, 33–5, 42, 69–70, 78, 81, 148
Socialization, 8, 13–14, 22, 26, 37, 39, 40, 44, 46, 50, 62, 77–81, 86, 150, 155, 174–5, 180, 184
Society as integrative or holistic, 27, 112

Sociology and sociologists, 2, 5–9,
  11–12, 14–7, 21, 23–9, 33, 38,
  41–2, 53–7, 60, 75, 77–8,
  85–6, 103–4, 107, 110, 116,
  118–19, 124–5, 128–9, 132–3,
  135–41, 150–1, 153–4, 157,
  160, 165–6, 174–7, 183–5
Somali, 10, 37, 164
Soviet Union, 2–4, 5, 8, 14, 41,
  55–6, 84, 93, 100, 103, 111,
  116, 118, 159–60,169, 170, 182
State, the, and power, 1, 5–6, 10–11,
  18–19, 23–4, 28–30, 36, 38–9,
  52, 60, 67, 69, 76, 79, 87, 92,
  94, 101–3, 110, 113–15, 118,
  129–34, 143–6, 148, 150–1,
  153–68, 170–1, 174, 176, 184–5
Status, 9, 14, 42, 51, 58, 59, 60, 63,
  86, 100, 116, 175, 181, 183
Stoics, 125, 179
Sweden, 10, 78, 81, 96, 104, 176
System, 27
Symbolic interactionism, 31–3, 38

Terrorism, 18, 20, 99, 135, 163
Tolerance, 46, 56–8, 69, 75, 85,
  143, 149–50, 177
Totalitarian society, totalitarian state,
  1, 3–5, 14, 41, 94, 101, 103,
  118, 129, 138, 143, 156,
  159–60, 161, 166, 168–9, 174,
  185
Trust and mistrust, 34, 57, 76,
  81–6, 108, 129, 144, 147, 163,
  171, 180

United States, the, 4–5, 8, 11, 42,
  45–50, 68–9, 74–9, 82–4, 88,
  90, 92, 95–8, 100, 102, 108,
  115, 119, 121, 126, 128, 145,
  153, 158–60, 180

Values
  Anglo-Protestant, 46
  autonomy of, 103
  change in, 114, 124, 137, 150
  competing, 90
  consensus on, 120
  coordination of human behavior
    and, 22–3
  desirable, 42
  deviant behavior and, 54
  dominant, 56
  envy and, 60
  fear and, 22
  fragmentation of, 92
  freedom as, 165
  good compensation for job as, 98
  happiness as supreme, 29
  in America, 42, 98, 114, 165
  in criminal organizations, 76
  in developed countries, 137
  in Russia, 101, 118, 121, 170
  negative elements of, 65
  negative, 85
  of criminal structures, 76, 85
  order and, 12, 18
  post-materialist, 12
  private property, 101
  religion and, 98
  respect as, 58
  Soviet, 118
  state as supreme or central, 118,
    170
  status, 58–60
  the systems of, 108, 114, 118,
    175
  tolerance and, 57
  trust as, 108
  universal, 9, 117–18
  verbal statement of, 42

Wars
  Soviet war against Germany, 44
  World War I, 8
  World War II, 45–6, 124, 172
World Value Survey, 12, 42, 56–7,
  81–2, 84, 95, 97–8, 102, 104,
  120
World War I, 8

Xenophobia, 60, 68, 85, 175